eBay

Income:

How ANYONE of Any Age, Location, and/or Background Can Build a Highly Profitable Online Business with eBay

Cheryl L. Russell

8-23-6

eBay Income: How ANYONE of Any Age, Location, and/or Background Can Build a Highly Profitable Online Business with eBay

Copyright © 2006 by Atlantic Publishing Group, Inc.

1210 SW 23rd Place • Ocala, Florida 34474 • 800-814-1132 • 352-622-5836–Fax

Web site: www.atlantic-pub.com • E-mail: sales@atlantic-pub.com

SAN Number: 268-1250

ISBN-13: 978-0-910627-58-0   ISBN-10: 0-910627-58-4

Library of Congress Cataloging-in-Publication Data

Russell, Cheryl L. (Cheryl Lynn), 1967-

  eBay Income: How Anyone of Any Age, Location, or Background Can Build a Highly Profitable Online Business with eBay / by Cheryl L. Russell.

      p. cm.

  Includes bibliographical references and index.

  ISBN-13: 978-0-910627-58-0 (alk. paper)

  ISBN-10: 0-910627-58-4 (alk. paper)

  1. eBay (Firm) 2. Internet auctions. 3. Electronic commerce. I. Title.

  HF5478.R87 2006

  658.8'7--dc22

                    2006000193

EDITORS: Angela C. Adams; Jackie Ness • jackie_ness@charter.net

PROOFREADER: Cheryl Morrissette • cheryl_morrissette@yahoo.com

ART DIRECTION, FRONT COVER & INTERIOR DESIGN: Meg Buchner • megadesn@mchsi.com

BOOK PRODUCTION DESIGN: Studio 6 Sense • info@6sense.net • www.6sense.net

Printed in the United States

CONTENTS

Chapter 8: Think Before You Click

Chapter 9: On Your Mark... Get Set... Auction!

Chapter 10: Congratulations... Now What?

Chapter 11: Other Sellers Clue You In

Appendix A: Becoming an eBay Member & Basic Site Navigation

Appendix B: Tools for Advanced Users

EBay Terminology & Index

FOREWORD

by Mardi Timm

*Business Consultant, eBay PowerSeller, and
Certified Education Specialist trained by eBay Website
www.youcansell2.com
Email: mardi@youcansell2.com*

Starting a business on eBay is fairly easy. Creating an eBay business that will make money and support your family is quite another thing. As a Business Consultant, eBay PowerSeller, and Certified Education Specialist trained by eBay, I am keenly aware of the pitfalls people encounter when starting their eBay business. I have personally made most of the mistakes that can be made.

I started on eBay in March of 1998 as a buyer. My husband and I wanted to expand our collection—and eBay did that beyond our wildest dreams. I quickly realized I could sell too! The first items I listed were three vintage sideshow postcards from the 1930s. I listed each one separately, and they collectively brought in over $86. I only paid $0.50 for all three! I was hooked and set about learning all I could about selling on eBay.

Since my business started as a hobby, in the beginning I didn't think much about the business of eBay. When I did decide to make eBay a real business, I found little help. Many of the business questions I had either went unanswered or were answered by trial and error. What I needed was a guide to help me make the decisions I needed to make and map my path to success. This book is the guide I needed when I was creating my eBay business.

Cheryl L. Russell walks beginners and seasoned professionals alike through the maze of the business of eBay and e-commerce. For business newbies, she explains the basic concepts of business in easy-to-understand terms, helps you understand eBay and the tools available to you, and shows you concrete ways you can build a business and earn a living on eBay. For the seasoned eBayer, she gives tips and ideas to grow your business and let people know you are there.

The difference between this book and others I have read is that this book focuses on the fact that doing eBay right is really doing a business right. You must have a solid understanding of business and good business practices in order to be a success on eBay. In other words, eBay is a business just like any other. By following the map that Cheryl has laid out, anyone can and will be able to create a successful online, e-commerce business on eBay and beyond. I am recommending this book to all my students!

Welcome to eBay!

It looked like one more forgettable Saturday garage sale like so many others that day. Lots of clothes with stretched-out necks or worn spots in the knees, the usual supply of pots and pans past their prime, maybe a videotape or two. That's what Joe surmised as he slowed and pulled up to the curb. Was it even worth getting out of the car to look closer?

Deciding that he had room in his trunk for a bit more inventory, Joe, who started his eBay business by selling his used VHS tapes, ambled over to the tables and began to scan them for anything of interest. He spied mostly boring merchandise of little or no value to a seasoned seller who can spot a good-old song-and-dance film ten yards away.

Wandering through the mishmash of wobbly card tables and boards propped up on sawhorses, some things caught Joe's eye. He had no idea what they were, but they looked old; that alone merited a closer investigation. The box contained old cards of some sort or other.

Joe hadn't ever seen anything like these before: turn-of-the-century scenes on finely pressed paperboard. Most of them were dated in the 1890s and were made by a company called Underwood & Underwood. They had images from all over the world: pyramids in Egypt, old warships, the Vatican, and the Philippine Islands. Each card had two of what appeared to be identical images on it, kind of like seeing double. Now that was odd!

Even though antiques weren't exactly Joe's interest, he had enough gut instinct to suspect when he'd stumbled across something that might be worth obtaining. There was no price on the box, so he asked.

"How much do you want for the cards?"

"I don't know; how much will you give me?"

Not wanting to offend the owner, he scrambled to think of a fair price.

"Five dollars?" he offered.

"Tell you what. Take both boxes and pay me ten."

Both? Joe hadn't even seen the second box nearby. Nodding his agreement, he paid for the horde and headed home to do some research. There were no vintage videos to be had at that sale, but within days he would be thanking his lucky stars that he stopped.

If you haven't already guessed, Joe (eBay user "whitebears") had stumbled across a cache of mint-condition stereoview cards. Popular in the late 1800s and into the 20th century, the Victorian-era cards were put into a binocular-type holder called a stereoscope that combined the slightly different images, making them three-dimensional, sort of like an early version of Mattel's® View-Master™ toys that first appeared in the 1940s and are still marketed today.

Joe picks up his story:

> *"Having researched the cards, I knew I had made a good find, and thought I might get $100 or even $150 for them. I listed them, not knowing I had hit the mother lode of stereoview cards."*

The two hundred or so cards were split up into lots, groups of 1 to 30 cards with a similar theme. The first lot listed included 30 cards with pictures from an exposition in Omaha, Nebraska, in the late 1890s. Bidding was fierce in the late hours of the auction, and Joe's eyes grew exponentially as the bids soared. When it was all said and done, that auction alone netted Joe nearly $1,100!

Some of the other cards fetched fifty dollars a piece, and by the time he'd exhausted his supply, Joe was giddy from his foray into the antiques market. He was more than $1,800 richer too. Not bad for a ten-dollar investment!

Joe has since become a PowerSeller, and while he still sells old VHS tapes, this experience helped catapult his diversity; suddenly he'd become a mini-expert at a new type of merchandise. Joe had inadvertently expanded his knowledge, his product line, and his reach to buyers on his favorite marketplace: eBay.

Does the thrill of the hunt before a Saturday of rummage sales and flea markets excite you to heights your spouse just doesn't comprehend? What about new merchandise: Do you see products lying lackluster on a store's clearance shelves, begging you to buy — and resell — them for a profit? Have you always thought someday you'd start your own business, complete with wholesale suppliers, a storefront, and a huge customer base?

If so, then this book is for you!

This book will guide you through the basic principles of starting your own small business, using eBay as your primary selling tool. In order to use this book most effectively, you should already have at least a little experience using eBay, either to browse or to purchase items.

For those who do not have that experience already, your best option is to read through the first three chapters and then take a detour to Appendix A, a step-by-step guide to setting up an eBay account and basic navigation around the site. This information has been separated for the convenience of those readers who have already been browsing or using eBay for purchasing purposes.

In fact, having some experience as a buyer is a great way to feel confident about becoming a seller, so go ahead and buy a few items to add to your collection or buy holiday gifts early this year. And of course, having some feedback to your credit before you begin selling is always a good idea (more about feedback in Chapter 10).

So with that in mind, let's take a brief stroll down memory lane and revisit a time when eBay, and the Internet as we know it, didn't even exist.

Understanding eBay

Many people have heard the simplistic, and not all-encompassing, story that eBay started as a way for the founder's wife to add to her collection of Pez dispensers. Pierre Omidyar takes this tale in stride. While it does have some basis in truth, his then-girlfriend (later wife) was one of his inspirations for an online auction and one of the first sellers, the entire story is far more interesting and inspiring.

Pierre Omidyar was born in France in 1967 and emigrated to the United States with his family when he was a young boy. He was in junior high school when the first personal computers from companies like Radio Shack came on the market. Immediately, Omidyar had found his life's passion and what would become his life's work: the world of computers. In fact, his fascination with computers was too strong to resist; he frequently skipped physical education classes to sneak off and use a teacher's computer during those early years. Even before finishing college in 1988, Omidyar began an early career in programming and was involved in various businesses that specialized in programming for Macintosh and Apple computers.

In the early 1990s, the Internet was a catch phrase that was spreading like wildfire on the lips of every computer geek in Silicon Valley. The epicenter of all things computer in those days, southern California en masse swooned at the thought of how the Internet was going to change the world and all the money there was to be made doing it!

Omidyar, too, was caught up in the excitement and even had some early Web sites devoted to such onerous subjects as the Ebola virus and a university alumni site. But when it came to making money via the Internet, his ideals about business and the free market inspired him to pursue equality for the common man in purchasing. For instance, he had become wealthy at a young age by buying stocks prior to an IPO (initial public offering) and then benefiting when the stock gained greatly just before the public had a chance to purchase it. This led Omidyar to wish that everybody would have the opportunity to buy low or bid the price up if the demand was there. He'd been lucky with his shortcut to financial success but wanted to even the odds for everyone else.

While Omidyar couldn't do much to change the way the stock markets operate, he could—and did—incorporate his ideals into his own hobby that turned into the world's largest business foray the Internet would know in its early days.

EBay, interestingly enough, was born in a quiet home office with very little fanfare. Over Labor Day weekend in 1995, Omidyar wrote the basic programming that would operate a simple auction site and named it AuctionWeb. The site was hosted on his Web site, ebay.com, and shared space with the previously mentioned Ebola virus information, as well as a couple of pages used by his fiancée and the alumni Web site.

The auction format was simplistic and far from the neat and slick eBay most people think of today. The block lettering and grey background was rather boring, frankly, and there were only a few options: list an item, bid on an item, and view an item. It was plain-Jane functionality at its best. However, prettiness aside, users immediately fancied the new way to buy and sell.

The first months of AuctionWeb weren't blockbusters by today's standards, but by posting information about his new site on other Web sites and Usenet newsgroups (some of the earliest sites on the Internet), business slowly picked up. Within four months, thousands of auctions had been set up on AuctionWeb, and the buzz about this new marketplace was spreading as quickly as the Internet itself.

Not content to merely provide a forum for buyers and sellers to do business, Omidyar made sure all users were aware of the ethical way he wished the site's users to treat each other. He posted a list of desired behaviors, such as being courteous and settling disputes politely. Thus were born the Community Values that today are still prominently featured in eBay's pages and discussion boards.

Initially, AuctionWeb charged no fees to the users, but when Omidyar's Internet service provider started complaining about his site's traffic, they forced him to bump up to a business account costing $250 per month. Hobby or not, that was a far cry from the $30 he had been spending, so the idea was born to charge just the sellers, not the buyers, starting in February 1996. Users paid final-value fees through mail, sending checks, paper bills, or even coins taped together. Right from the start, the collected fees covered the new expenses and even turned a small profit.

Omidyar knew he was on to something, and by the end of summer of 1996, he quit his full-time job and devoted himself entirely to turning his once-hobby into a thriving business. Others who came on board, including Jeff Skoll, helped shape the site in its early years. One of Skoll's most notable contributions was convincing Omidyar to drop the other Web pages that were existent on ebay.com and stick just to auctions. It was difficult, but Omidyar gave in and removed his prized Ebola virus page, along with the other non-auction pages, from the site. From then on, AuctionWeb became known by the handle eBay!

By the end of 1996, eBay had almost 10,000 registrants and had sold over one million items. In 1998 eBay became a public company with its stock traded on the NASDAQ. Estimates in late 2005 put the number of worldwide users at 135 million who were expected to buy and sell more than forty billion dollars through eBay in 2005.

A recent study indicated that nearly three-quarters of a million people in the United States rely on eBay for some or all of their income. While eBay has branched out to foreign countries, the United States is its most seasoned group of users and an important piece of its selling "pie." The gamut of eBay sellers runs from stay-at-home parents wanting to pad the family's budget to retired folks who know a thing or two about antiques. College students unload their old textbooks, and computer junkies hawk their outdated equipment. But the fastest-growing segment of eBay sellers seems to be those who are making it into a real business, steadily earning at least a portion of their necessary income without ever leaving the comfort of their homes.

Becoming the Icon

EBay has helped countless people realize their dream of owning a business and being their own boss. Although it may not be like the business their fathers' generation opened—and certainly is far different than their grandfathers' generation could have ever imagined—it is still a business, nonetheless. But why is this type of business so wildly popular?

Selling on eBay can be done with little or no overhead, inventory, and space. You don't have to rent an office, hire employees, or encounter many of the other traditional business headaches. Instead, there can be as little as a computer screen and a post office box, at least initially. Primarily, there is freedom, prestige, and a sense of accomplishment every bit as strong as those who operate more traditional (often referred to as brick-and-mortar) businesses.

Sure, there are still the same responsibilities as any other business. You must have a source of merchandise to sell (a product stream) and you must find ways to have a constant income (by generating sales). And despite popular myth, selling online doesn't release you from following all the laws that regulate businesses, such as reporting income and paying the appropriate taxes.

But if you were going to go into business anyway, the Internet — and eBay specifically — has made it entirely possible for you to make yourself a big business with relatively little investment compared to traditional methods of breaking into this world. There will still be investment needed on your part: a current computer, some basic software, a reliable Internet connection, and some basic office supplies, to begin with. But compared to the tens of thousands of dollars required to start a traditional business, the few thousand you'll need to start this one are attainable to most people today.

Ordinary people aren't the only ones that are clued in to the huge potential of eBay. Even big businesses are using the power of eBay to market their products. Some companies use eBay to unload surplus stock or launch new products, while others use eBay to increase their business, while not ever selling a single item.

One such company is the Golden Palace Casino, an online-only casino that has made itself a household name by purchasing outrageous items on eBay, such as the vehicle once owned by Pope Benedict XV. Even though they pay mightily for some of these offbeat items, the publicity they get by doing so is worth more than any ad campaign they could have bought for the same number of dollars. By standing out from the crowd of online gambling sites, they have managed to use eBay in a way that even Pierre Odimyar probably never imagined!

Other imaginative ways to do business and make money have cropped up with the help of, or because of, the success of eBay. EBay has helped shape the way we donate to charity, buy vehicles, rent apartments, and even hire employees. Countless Web sites have sprung to life in the past decade that take these everyday tasks to new levels.

The World's Online Marketplace, as eBay's motto proclaims, also cares about the world in which it operates. Charity auctions are highlights of the Giving Works site, which is easily accessed from eBay's main page. Current events have inspired waves of charity auctions, and eBay makes it easy to access these special auctions, often right at the top of the home page.

In 1998, before going public with its stock offering, eBay set aside more than 100,000 shares of stock to be put into the eBay Foundation, a charitable fund that to date has donated more than $8 million to non-profit charitable organizations all over the world.

Purchasing a vehicle will never be the same after eBay. While there are many sites on the Internet that specialize in vehicle sales, one of the first places that it happened was on eBay. Back when there was no category for listing a vehicle for sale, trend-setting sellers listed them under the category where toy cars were sold! EBay eventually clued in and created eBay Motors, which sells many motorized vehicles other than automobiles, and now accounts for a tidy share of their sales.

Looking for a new apartment? Rent.com is your answer. This site can even help match you with potential roommates and moving services. Half.com boasts one of the largest fixed-price purchasing sites on the Internet. While these two sites are eBay sites, they started out as eBay's competition — capitalizing on the amazing advances in online selling and servicing pioneered by their future parent company.

While it is neither created nor owned by eBay, **www.elance.com** takes the auctioning of services to new heights. It's actually a reverse-auction, wherein the company that is seeking to have work done will post its requirements on elance.com and the contractors (who are Elance members) bid on the opportunity to perform the service. Elance.com's pre-screened workforce specializes in everything from freelance writing to graphic design, software development, and engineering.

Using a strategy common to many large corporations, eBay has acquired other companies that provide services that are complementary to their own. This has given eBay an extremely broad range of appeal for sellers, buyers, and investors alike. In addition to owning all or a stake in many foreign auction sites, eBay acquired PayPal in 2002 to help facilitate auction payments. The software is so seamlessly integrated with eBay that it's almost silly to use anything else!

Another company that eBay has acquired and put to work servicing its own users is Kurant, a leading-edge company that specializes in software for e-commerce on small business Web sites. EBay used their products to create a new service for sellers that debuted in summer of 2005: ProStores. This extra-fee service allows sellers to set up an outside-of-eBay e-commerce Web site, complete with shopping cart and secure checkout through PayPal (of course!). Time will tell if this takes off with sellers, but it's a great addition to their already-burgeoning lineup of products and services.

Probably the most useful tool on the Web that facilitate eBay's services is PayPal. PayPal operates strictly on retrieving money from the buyer's PayPal account or other funding source and depositing it into the seller's PayPal account.

E-commerce in part hinges on one's ability to pay for the goods and services purchased online. Without these integral components such as PayPal and Bidpay, e-commerce would not have become what it is today.

Embracing E-Commerce

While eBay can't claim to have spawned e-commerce all by itself, anyone who was aware of the Internet in the mid-1990s will tell you that for many Americans at that time, eBay was synonymous with e-commerce. For many, eBay was their first try at buying anything online.

E-commerce, short for electronic commerce, has been around since the 1970s, when technology became available for sending documents over local and private networks. However, in a broader sense, it refers to anything done electronically that moves businesses along. This can include tracking inventory and the supply chain for a wholesaler, making an electronic funds transfer (ETF) for a customer at a bank, buying and selling through the Internet, a private network, or even a mobile phone.

For many non-techies of the world, e-commerce is more or less Web-commerce: the buying and selling of products and services via the Internet. This is the type of commerce that sites like eBay are created to perform.

The amazing thing about e-commerce is that it makes distances, even those spanning the globe, irrelevant. Imagine finding the means to open your own store in the heart of New York City — over 8 million people strong and millions of tourists annually. No matter how many years you were in business, it's simply not feasible to expect all those people to visit your store. However, thanks to e-commerce, your market includes not just New Yorkers and its tourists, but every one of those 135 million people who have already become buyers, sellers, and lookers. And that's not to mention the people who will join tomorrow and next week. You get the idea!

Web sites are the portals that make e-commerce as successful as it is. Many new business owners go overboard in buying all the gizmos and gadgets that they think they'll need right away, and this is especially true when it comes to Web sites. They're so necessary to e-commerce that people often run head-long into getting one before they really have any business, per se, on which to do it.

Obviously, Web sites are crucial for e-commerce, but in this case the Web site is already up and running for you: eBay! Having the tools already built into this amazing site is the time- and money-saver that every new businessperson needs! Like the old adage cautions: Don't reinvent the wheel.

Having your own personal domain and Web site might be slick and impressive, but it's not a true necessity at the starting gate, and slick and impressive can be costly. Spend some time building your presence on eBay, and when you are turning a real profit (after expenses) on a monthly basis, then look into it. Web sites are covered in Chapter 6 as well.

The e-commerce tools that you'll be primarily using to start an eBay business are e-mail (and other Internet messaging, such as instant messaging or text messaging on a mobile phone) and e-banking, such as a PayPal account, for sending payments to your suppliers or receiving payments from buyers. PayPal is covered in depth in Chapter 5, but for now, let's look more closely at business e-mailing.

E-mail is generally available through your ISP (Internet service provider), but if you don't want to use your personal e-mail address for your eBay business (which is a wise move), you can easily obtain another free e-mail address at a number of providers such as Hotmail and Yahoo. The competition in these sectors has become so fierce in recent years that the amount of storage space and additional features are quite nice compared to even a few years ago.

Merely having an e-mail address isn't enough, however. To really make your business profitable, you need to know how to get the most from your e-mail.

Professionalism

While you might really love your bulldog, you aren't going to impress business clients, suppliers, and lenders if your e-mail address is ILove-MySlobberingDog@e-mailprovider.com; unless, that is, you are selling dog-related products. However, even in that case, consider something a bit less dramatic. Poochproducts@e-mailprovider.com is more memorable, and isn't likely to turn anyone's stomach.

Signatures

Nearly every e-mail program today has an option for you to create a custom signature, which is a sentence or two containing virtually any information you want. Your signature will automatically be inserted at the end of every e-mail you send. It's yet another simple way to put the e-commerce components to work for you!

Use your signature line to promote your tagline for your business, "Selling the best in grooming and health products for your dog for ten years!" Get creative, but remember to be professional at the same time. Don't forget to include links to your eBay store or company's Web site when you move up to those levels!

Templates

This trick is one of the most valuable in terms of time saved versus time spent creating them. A template is a pre-fab letter for a specific situation. When an auction is complete, open your pre-fab "end of auction" letter (made and stored in a word-processing software such as Microsoft Word), copy/paste the contents into your e-mail program, add the auction number and title, and—voilà!—You can move on to your next task. Using templates greatly reduces your spelling and grammar mistakes, thus adding to the professional image you're trying to achieve.

Grammar

Yes, your high school English teacher was right! Someday, she predicted, your lessons in conjugation and spelling would come in handy. If you were one of those students who snoozed through English Comp, find yourself a good reference book on usage and style. To those customers whose grammar and spelling are above average to polished, nothing will make you look unprofessional faster than an e-mail full of errors.

Anonymity

The beauty of e-mail is that you can do it in your pajamas while sipping your morning coffee. When you're having a bad day, you don't have to speak to a customer face to face or via telephone. E-mail can give you a cheerful demeanor regardless of your mood at any given moment. Let e-mail be your poker face!

Opt-Out

E-mail is one of the slickest, and most annoying, marketing techniques there is. By law, if you are using e-mail for marketing, as opposed to auction-specific communications, you must include directions for opting out. You may as well include this important information in your template or signature so that you are not in violation of the law.

A simple opt-out message can be something like this: Unsubscribe: By unsubscribing, you are authorizing [your name/business] to discontinue all e-mail correspondence with you. You will not receive any information from [your name/business] via e-mail. Please send an e-mail to [your e-mail address] and type "unsubscribe" in the subject box.

Be very sure to follow through and remove the people who request an opt-out from your databases and address books. Keep a list of all persons who request this, so you don't accidentally contact them again!

Speed

E-mail is lightening-fast, and as such, people have come to expect speedy replies to their e-mails. Nothing annoys a potential buyer more than sending an inquiry for more details about your auction item and not receiving a reply until after the auction has ended! Answer all e-mails in a timely manner; the sooner the better. Even if the buyer doesn't purchase your product, you'll have left a good impression with a speedy and professional e-mail.

Alerts

One way to stay on top of incoming e-mail is to be alerted by your e-mail provider. Sign up for your provider's instant messaging program, and set it up to automatically sign in when you connect to the Internet.

File

Organizing your stored e-mails is critical. You can create folders to save e-mails, keeping your inbox clutter-free. Spend some time thinking about the best way to organize your folders for your use. Perhaps a different folder for every month or a different folder for each activity (shipping quotes, invoices, post-payment note, thank-you notes, etc.).

You can set many e-mail systems to automatically file items for you based on key words. Look into this, because the amount of e-mail that gets exchanged can become overwhelming if you're not organized.

You don't have to keep every e-mail for all eternity, either. Set a pattern of cleaning out e-mails related to an auction once feedback has been completed, unless there is some unusual reason to keep it.

Lists

E-mailing is a convenient way to announce a new product to your lineup or a sale on seasonal goods. Once you have completed a sale, you are privy to the buyer's e-mail address, even if not so beforehand. Set up a system (such as a separate group in your e-mail address book or a database) to record these addresses before you delete the e-mails, perhaps with a notation about what they purchased or notes about other correspondence you had with this customer.

For instance, if you note which customers purchased flea and tick shampoo from you last summer, the following spring you can e-mail them (by sending a message to all contacts in a specific address book or group) and announce that you're giving a discount on flea/tick products to repeat customers for one week only. Many people will be appreciative that you remembered them! Those who are no longer in the market or not appreciative of your efforts will use your "opt out" information (see page 18).

TIP — Don't Forget Your Manners!

Always begin and end a business e-mail with a note of thanks or appreciation for being a customer, a past customer, or with hopes for their future business. While business e-mail should be more formal than e-mail you send to your friends, people also like warmth and personalized service. The Internet can be impersonal and cold, so do your part to give it some heart.

You will find that your business communications will be simple and efficient if you take the time to use the built-in features offered by your e-mail provider and follow these guidelines to more professional business e-mailing.

This is also a good time to discuss some basics of Web safety. The Internet has its seedy side too, and it can be used for a tool to harm others as well as help them. Internet scams abound, and it seems that new ones pop up every day. Who exactly perpetrates these scams, nobody seems to know, but you need to stay on top of them. To follow is a brief list of security concerns and precautions to take.

Phishing/E-Mail Scams

This is a term that refers to unscrupulous persons who are "fishing" for your personal information in order to commit identity theft and fraud. They often use e-mail as their way to get to unsuspecting users by creating what appears to be a legitimate e-mail from someone you trust online, such as eBay, PayPal, even your personal bank!

The e-mail urgently requests your attention, and ironically they often claim that "someone has tried to access your account illegally" and that they are "warning" you of this. To protect yourself, the e-mail explains, just click the following link and enter your username and password to verify that you are indeed the correct user, or your account may be suspended altogether (for your own protection, of course). It all seems so friendly, so wonderful that your online business acquaintances are looking out for you.

But look out! Do not ever click the links in an e-mail like this! In fact, most places you do business with online state right in their policies that they will never send you an e-mail asking for your password. That alone should send up a serious red flag.

EBay recently started posting all e-mails that they send to you in your eBay inbox as well. So if you ever get an e-mail from eBay that doesn't quite seem right, open a new browser window and log in to your eBay account. If the identical message does not appear in your eBay inbox, then delete it or report it to eBay by forwarding the suspicious e-mail to this address: spoof@ebay.com. To report suspicious e-mail that claims to be from PayPal, forward it to spoof@paypal.com.

To learn more about how to combat suspicious e-mails, go to eBay's "Help" button on the navigation bar and type "suspicious e-mail" in the search field. Among the helpful information there is a tutorial that will teach you how to spot "spoof" e-mails and in-depth discussions on protecting your identity online.

Antivirus Software and Firewalls

Despite growing concerns about online fraud and identity theft, many people let their antivirus and firewall subscriptions expire or don't use them to their fullest potential. If you're going to be a serious businessperson online, you must stay on top of these issues. Merely having these protections is not enough; you must update them regularly. You can program any antivirus software to update automatically while you're connected to the Internet. Take advantage of this automation; having your system wiped out by a virus or having a hacker access your accounting, customer database, and personal financial information is devastating and could wreak havoc for your customers as well.

Operating System and Web Browser Updates

Another oft-forgotten item is the regular updating of your operating system and Web browser. These items, also, can be set up to update on a schedule, either at specified intervals or as updates become available. This is done differently based on your operating system and browser, but it's not hard to find out how to do this. Simply search the help files of your own computer or the Web sites of your software providers.

Passwords and User IDs

While it may seem like common sense to create passwords that are difficult to guess and unique for each Web site you log in to, it's probably not reality for most people. Unfortunately, many people use the same password for multiple sites to avoid having to remember or write down all the various usernames and passwords.

If you must, keep a log sheet of all your names and passwords, and keep it in a secure place that you can quickly access if you have a memory lapse.

EBay's "Help" sections can give you excellent suggestions on creating a good password. Although eBay doesn't prompt you to change your password periodically, it's a good idea to do so (and don't forget to update your log sheet!). When you change your eBay password, there is a password meter available that helps gauge the strength of your new password, so you can improve it before finalizing it.

Another password meter can be found at **www.securitystats.com**. Check out their password strength meter. If your passwords score as weak, then follow the suggestions they give for creating a better one.

System Backup

Newer versions of Windows operating systems will assist you in creating a set of "recovery disks" in case your computer is hacked or attacked by a virus or in case of a crash due to mechanical failure of your machine. Even things like smoke during a house fire can damage your computer, even if they don't burn it.

All your hard work, customer databases, and stored e-mails are at risk if you don't have your system backed up regularly. Your local computer dealers and repair shops can assist you in setting up an appropriate backup system.

The Better Business Bureau is committed to keeping e-commerce safe and combating scam artists. Their excellent Web site can help broaden your knowledge base about safety and e-commerce. It can be found at **www .bbb.org**. They are also one of many information sources that you'll utilize when setting up your business, as we'll talk about in the next chapter.

Don't skip the proper preparation in setting up your eBay business. You may even be doing damage by not making sure you've followed all the rules of setting up a business.

CHAPTER 2

Plan Ahead for Success

If you've already made a decision to start a business on eBay, then you probably want to get to the good stuff already: the auctions, the sales, and the income! Well, that's definitely what it boils down to: making money. However, you'll do yourself a big injustice if you skip all the proper preparation and move right to the selling. In fact, you may even be doing damage to your business by not making sure you've followed all the rules of setting up a business. Pleading ignorance in the future isn't likely going to win you any sympathy with the IRS or potential investors or lenders.

This chapter covers such tasks as writing a business plan, becoming an official business (as far as the government is concerned), accounting and inventory basics, and tax liabilities. It sounds worse than it really is, and since you're just beginning to plan and set up your business, it's much easier to do these tasks now than after the fact.

But wait! Aren't there tons of people out there who set up shop on eBay and haven't ever filed any paperwork or paid any taxes on their earnings? Well, yes. But the purpose of this book is to assist you in setting up a business. Those who sell without the proper setup are more like an online garage sale than a real business. If it works for them, that's fine. But if you seriously want to become a high-volume eBay seller with clout and credibility, you'd be foolish not to invest some time into the proper setup.

That being said, let's move to the most basic item: the business plan.

Writing a Business Plan

Think of your business plan as your company's résumé. As your company grows, so will the items that it covers. Initially, however, your business plan can be as simple as a bulleted list of objectives (goals) and strategies (how you'll accomplish the goals). If you are not planning to seek any financing (for startup costs or initial inventory), then you may be the only one reading your plan for some time. You can always polish it and expand upon it if the time comes that you seek financing or investors to grow your business.

If you are seeking financing or investors right away, then you need to write a polished and professional plan with proper grammar, punctuation, and terminology. There are numerous ways you could accomplish the task of writing such a specific plan, including online sources such as the following Web sites.

A business plan is specific and unique to one individual business. The plan contains information about operational and financial goals and explains how those goals will be achieved. The essence of a business plan contains the following elements:

- Begin with a simple statement of what you hope to accomplish with your business.

- Define what products or services your business will provide and to whom they will be provided. Include any supporting evidence you have for the need or desire for your product or service.

- Outline a plan of action for getting your products and/or services to your customers, including marketing tools.

- List the personality traits or strengths you have that will carry this project through, and identify those traits or weaknesses that may hinder you. Be honest; admitting your weaknesses is not a sign of failure. Just the opposite is true in business.

- Set a timeline for you to accomplish certain goals, in reasonable increments, to achieve that ultimate definition in your first paragraph.

- Project a statement of your financial situation at present and financial goals (future forecast of sales and expenses).

- Tie it all together with a brief recap or summary, using a positive tone that brings confidence to your endeavor. When things seem bleak in the future, you can pull out your plan and read it for a quick inspirational pick-me-up!

There are just about as many different ways to write a business plan as there are types of businesses, and do realize that if you're just starting out, you may not have a great deal to say in each of those categories. Just do your best for now, and keep working on it as your business grows and expands. Atlantic Publishing has recently published "How to Write a Great Business Plan for Your Small Business in 60 Minutes or Less;" available at **http://www.atlantic-pub.com**.

If you want to be more detailed and specific, check out the ideas about writing business plans at the following sites:

The Small Business Administration

Created by the United States Congress in 1953, this agency provides assistance in just about every aspect of starting and growing your small business. Their Web site, **www.sba.gov**, contains a wealth of information.

SCORE

Originally this acronym stood for the Service Corps of Retired Executives, but as this non-profit organization has grown and expanded since its inception in 1964; so has its name. Now the group refers to themselves as "SCORE: Counselors to America's Small Business," and by early 2005 they had assisted 7 million clients with their small business needs for advice and direction. Check out their templates and sample business plans in the "Business Toolbox" section of their site, **www.score.org**.

A Web search will turn up dozens of sites dedicated to helping small businesses. Peruse them, but be cautious; do not sign up for anything nor give out any private information without investigating first. Some sites claim to help small businesses but are only interested in selling you things that perhaps you don't really need anyway. Be sure to investigate, and if you have any questions about a site, contact the Better Business Bureau (**www.bbb.org**) for advice on determining its legitimacy.

As for the actual writing of a business plan, if you're able to verbalize your ideas and concepts but just don't have a flair for words, you can always hire someone to write it for you. Possible places to locate a writer include **www.elance.com**, which may be the way to go for thrifty reasons.

There are many software bundles full of tools for starting a business, such as Palo Alto's Business Plan Pro, MYob Business Essentials, and Quicken Legal Business Pro by Nolo Press. These software titles range in price from $100 to $300, but in addition to business planning assistance, they also contain many standard forms, accounting or legal advice and assistance, and other great features.

Another excellent resource is *How to Write a Great Business Plan for Your Small Business in 60 Minutes or Less* available from Atlantic Publishing for $39.95 (Item # GBP-01). To order call 1-800-814-1132 or visit **www .atlantic-pub.com**.

Becoming an Official Business

The eBay seller who has an official, legitimate business has both benefits and expectations above the seller who merely sells as a hobby. Unfortunately, merely writing your business plan isn't going to be the end of the paperwork. The good news is that you will save yourself a serious headache later if you do things correctly from the start.

First on your list of chores, once you've completed your business plan, is to decide on a business structure that best fits your needs. There are three basic structures to choose from, each with its own benefits and requirements.

The vast majority of beginning eBay businesspersons will choose to become sole proprietorships. This is the most basic, and therefore easiest, type of business to form. It simply means that you are the sole owner and solely responsible for the business. Your tax forms are filed under your own name and social security number, and you make quarterly tax payments (sorry, this isn't optional; Uncle Sam wants his piece of the pie quarterly) directly to the government.

In terms of legal responsibility, however, if someone sues your business, your personal assets could also be at stake. But for most beginners, this is a good starting point. You can always move up to a higher level at a later point, and it may be much easier to change structure types if you've been legitimate all along.

When you are a sole proprietorship, you can do business under your own name or file a DBA (doing business as) according to your local laws. To find out how to do this, and all these tasks in general, search for your state's business setup guidelines at Google or any Internet search engine. Simply search "start business [fill in your appropriate state]." A list of state Web sites is included in the back of this book, but as Web addresses change over time, you can always use the search method.

Another online source of information about many states' setup requirements can be found at **www.roninsoft.com/sitemap1.htm**. This site is a free information source for small business owners, and it is worth your time to bookmark it and become familiar with its contents.

While most eBay sellers will start with the sole proprietorship, it is good to know a bit about the other options as well. Partnerships are similar to sole proprietorships except there are two or more partners/owners of the business. This setup requires the assistance of an attorney, and as with the sole proprietorship, the business's owners are liable in the event of a lawsuit. Additionally, if one partner runs up huge bills in the business's name, the other partner is liable for the debts.

The final option is a corporation. The big advantage of being incorporated is that the liability for the company's debts and obligations is separated from the owner's personal assets. Tax advantages may differ from state to state, but it is generally believed that corporations have more tax advantages than other types of businesses. There are various sub-types of corporations; an attorney can advise you on these to choose the best kind for your company.

One of the less dreary parts of setting up a business is filing a business name. Many people who start a small business have a name picked out even before they seriously get started on the paperwork. It's kind of like naming your baby; people love to discuss names and give suggestions. Your company's name should encompass the products and services you wish to offer, but also be catchy or memorable.

Short is better than long, and alliteration or some rhyming is often helpful. Putting two words together is an oft-used technique (such as Wal-Mart, which is named after its founder Sam Walton, and mart, meaning market). A certain amount of misspelling is tolerated in business names, but don't get too carried away.

Avoid names that have meaning only to one nationality, culture, or regional location unless your business caters to that group or locality. Check around to make sure there are no names similar to yours that will cause confusion for your customers. And be sure to keep in mind that your business name will be tied to your eBay store name (when you begin one), so it needs to be something that will be easily remembered by your online customers.

Check with your county clerk's office to make sure nobody else in your county is using the name you choose, and you can also check online at **www.icann.org** for names registered online.

Your state's department of commerce is generally your best source for information on starting a business; however, don't forget to check with your county and local authorities as well. You may need to register your business with the county clerk's office, and you may need to have approval from your local zoning board to run a business out of your home. Don't bypass these steps, as pleading ignorance later won't get you very far if you're called on the carpet.

Once your business setup is in place, you can do several easier tasks to legitimize your business. Setting up a business bank account is really a necessity. Bookkeeping is time consuming enough without trying to separate all the business transactions on your monthly statement from your personal transactions. The IRS also will frown upon your methods if you don't have a separate account. Dream big: Some day your business might be large enough that you'll need to rent office space and buy large inventories at once. When it comes time to seek financing or investors, you will look really foolish if your business finances are co-mingled with your dry cleaning and doctor bills.

As a business, you have the opportunity to purchase your inventory or supplies to make inventory without paying sales tax on them. You do this by obtaining a seller's permit or resale license from your state. This varies greatly from state to state, but it's very important to have. Your state's department of revenue will be able to assist you in obtaining what you need to get started.

 **Get a Resale License**

A resale license may allow you to purchase your inventory or supplies to create inventory without paying sales tax, but you likely have to pay sales tax on supplies you need to run your business, such as printer ink, paper, and shipping supplies. Check with your accountant to clarify what exactly can be purchased without paying sales tax.

You may also need to get an Employee Identification Number (EIN), assigned by the IRS. EINs are assigned to businesses of any structure, but a sole proprietorship doesn't always have to have one. In that case, your Tax ID number isn't your EIN, but your SSN (Social Security number).

Even though you're probably going to be operating your eBay business from your home, you need to really start thinking in terms of separation for more than just your business bank account. If you're already an eBay and PayPal user, you need to start separating your personal transactions from those your business does. This is important for a professional appearance online, but also will be much easier for your bookkeeping. Consider starting a second username for eBay and PayPal. Depending on the username, you may choose to keep your old eBay name for your business or not.

It's best to have your eBay name reflect your business name or focus. In your "About Me" page, you can mention the reason why you started a second eBay name. Your feedback follows you if you change your ID on an existing account, so the good transactions you did prior to becoming a businessperson will still be with you. This is one reason for changing your ID name for your business (as opposed to starting an entirely new ID for your business, which will have zero feedback), as the feedback will do you more good for that than for personal buying.

Another way of providing a more professional appearance to your business is getting a separate business address. This generally will be a post office box as long as you're operating your business out of your home. Sure, it may be a bit of a hassle to go check your mail if you don't live near a post office, but realize that the vast majority of your transactions and correspondence are going to take place online. In addition to the U.S. Postal Service, there are independent sites where you can rent a mailbox, such as a UPS Store (formerly known as Mail Boxes, Etc.), and many other regional companies that provide these services. Having a separate address can also be a buffer zone in the rare case that a customer becomes angry enough to look you up online and, using your home address as a reference point, obtains your home phone number.

While you're at it, having a separate business phone number is also a good idea. Per chance your suppliers or shipping company need to contact you, it's probably wise that they call a number that won't be answered by your toddler or tied up by a chatty teenager. Both the fees for the post office box and a separate phone number may be deductible expenses, so make sure you keep all receipts and bills. Don't forget to pay for these items with your business account, for easier bookkeeping.

Checklist of Tasks:
Setting Up Your eBay Business

❑ I have written my business plan.

❑ I have carefully decided on a business structure and have determined what resources are needed to set it up.

    Sole proprietorship

    Partnership

    Corporation

❑ I have chosen a catchy, appropriate, or memorable name for my company.

❑ I have located the proper entity to file a DBA (doing business as).

❑ I have set up a business bank account.

❑ I have contacted my state's department of revenue for a seller's permit/resale license.

❑ I have determined if I need to file for an EIN or will use my SSN as a tax ID.

❑ I have separated my personal life online from my business life online:

    New e-mail address using my business name.

    New eBay name or converting current one for business use.

    New PayPal account or converting current one for business use.

❑ I have decided which address I'll use for business (home, PO box, etc.).

❑ I have a separate business phone number.

❑ I have done what I can to make sure my business records will be safe.

❑ I have called my insurance agent for assistance in insuring my business.

Keeping Track

You may have noticed the word bookkeeping sprinkled throughout Chapter 2, and for those of you who are petrified by numbers, this is a most crucial topic to consider. Basic bookkeeping is not as complicated as corporate accounting, but its importance can't be stressed enough. Most new businesses need assistance in filing their quarterly tax payments and annual tax forms, and your accountant will be forced to charge you substantially more in fees if your "books" (your recordkeeping) aren't in order. As your business grows and changes, you may find that hiring an accountant for your ongoing bookkeeping is a wise choice. Not only can they do the tasks faster and with more accuracy, but they can also help you stay abreast of changes in the laws and keep an eye out for tax deductions for you.

But as you're starting out and trying to keep expenses to a minimum, you probably can't afford the services of a professional accountant immediately. That's okay! Just set up a simple system right now and keep it updated with every transaction you make. When the time comes to get an accountant involved, he or she will be able to take your basic setup and incorporate it into his or her accounting software with relative ease. Your accountant will thank you for keeping good records from the start!

Accounting and a Simple Recordkeeping System

Recordkeeping is important for many reasons, the least of which is to back up your deductions and other data about your income or expenses. Having accurate records helps you get a sense of how your business is doing, whether or not your inventory is selling well, or whether or not you can afford to start a new product line.

Having neat and efficient records will also assist your future accountant, whom you will need as your company grows. You will also need to prepare financial statements (see the following list of accounting terms) about your company when you seek financing for an expansion or investors.

While you're starting your recordkeeping system, give some consideration to ensuring the safety of your business records. Even well-meaning spouses or family members may mess up a pile of receipts or accidentally throw away an important paper. If you have a completely dedicated room in which to set up shop, consider installing a new door handle with a lock, even if it's just a bedroom door. Not that you have anything to hide, but you have plenty to protect. A locked door will keep curious pets, kids, or visitors from inadvertently causing chaos.

If you invest in a filing cabinet, be sure to get one that locks. This extra layer of protection is wise for the few extra dollars you'll pay for that feature. And, of course, keep it locked and keep the keys in a safe place.

In order to use your computer's depreciation as a tax deduction, you need to have a dedicated computer as well (meaning it isn't used by other family members to surf the net or play games). Set up a password system so that nothing can be accessed without first logging in. Then make sure you remember to log out every time you leave the computer.

If your computer has a CD or DVD-writer, take advantage of it! Buy a supply of rewritable CDs, and use them to back up your data regularly (weekly, or daily if you have a lot of new data daily).

Of course, none of this will do you any good if you don't protect your computer from viruses or power surges that can knock out your hard drive. Spend the extra money for high-end surge protectors and the best virus and firewall protection you can find.

Another hazard that can wipe you out in a big hurry is a home fire. While saving your inventory may be low on your list of concerns in a fire, having your data all up to date and stored safely (in a fireproof safe or off-site) will give you what you need to file accurate insurance claims and start back up quickly. Good protection for your home, such as properly installed and serviced smoke detectors and a sprinkler system, are also good investments.

 **Insurance Coverage**

Check with your homeowner's/renter's insurance company about losses that would be covered by your policy in case of a house fire or other natural disaster, break-in, or other malicious act by others. If you aren't covered, your agent will be happy to amend your policy or sell you a different policy designed to cover your business.

There is simply no way that this book can cover all the intricacies of recordkeeping and accounting, so we will cover just a few things that you need to know or do in order to make sure you can accurately present your information come tax time. The recordkeeping and inventory-keeping systems shown here are likely different than what your accountant will set up for you someday, when your business grows, but they're sufficient for now.

The goal is not to show you how to do your accounting yourself, but rather to discuss keeping accurate records that will make it easy for your accountant to do the quarterly and end-of-year tasks for you, such as taxes. You'll find that keeping accurate data will have advantages for you, the business owner, by giving you a very clear picture of your day-to-day affairs.

 **IRS Guidelines**

*Go to **www.irs.gov**—download Publication 583, Starting a Business and Keeping Records. Print this 27-page document, and refer to it often during the startup phase of your recordkeeping.*

One of the first things you need to commit to in your recordkeeping is to do it daily. Getting caught up in the listing and selling on eBay is easy to do, but a fresh memory is your best ally when it comes to documenting your finances.

There are two ways you can choose to set up a system of basic bookkeeping: on paper or on computer. Whichever method you choose, the basic premise is the same. You need to keep track of all money coming into your business and all money going out of it.

Regardless of whether you do this on paper, a spreadsheet, or a formal accounting program on your computer, one way to start is to make a comprehensive list of all the possible sources of income you might receive and all the possible expenses you might incur.

Your sample list may look something like this:

Income

- Total eBay income (final bid amounts, "Buy It Now" amounts, and fixed-price auction amounts).

- Total eBay re-list refunds.

- Actual shipping fees paid by seller.

- Shipping and handling fees added (above actual shipping and handling).

- All sales tax collected.

- Bank interest on your business account.

Note that the Income column lists all the money received, regardless of whether you get to keep it or not. In the Expenses column, you'll then list all the costs incurred and items you must pay out from the money you received.

It might seem strange to think of a re-list refund as income, but in accounting terms, it is, because it's a credit given to you. The same is true of the shipping fees paid by the buyer. They are income because they were paid to you.

Expenses

- EBay listing fees (basic fees and fees for additional options).

- EBay final value fees.

- Fees to PayPal (not including postage purchased through eBay).

- Losses from fees on auctions that didn't sell.

- Money paid to shipping companies (including actual postage purchased through PayPal—it's really sent to USPS, not kept by eBay).

- Cost of shipping materials.

- Office supplies.

- Larger purchases (equipment, upgrades).

- Accounting or attorney's fees.

- Sales tax forwarded to the state.

- Cost of inventory (or raw materials to create inventory if you make your product).

- Your time/labor to create inventory.

- Your time/labor for other activities (packing shipments, doing paperwork, running errands, etc.).

- Bank fees on your business account (service charges, if any).

Note: Your list can get as detailed as you wish it to be. The best records reflect every aspect of the business, regardless of how small it seems to be. For instance, if you only record "expenses" in general and don't break them up into categories, how would you know if you are spending an excessive amount of money on office supplies every month? Wasteful spending is more easily identified once you can see in real numbers what you spend on each category in a month.

Additionally, under "eBay fees," you might want to track the different types of fees separately, such as how much of that amount was the actual listing fee and how much was for additional features (such as bold, gallery, extra photos, etc. — more about these fees in Chapter 5). This level of detail may not be necessary for tax purposes, but keeping good records will help you judge the soundness of your business over time. You may find that these extras are worth their money (by seeing a pattern: the listings with extras sell the first time around and don't need to be re-listed) or you may find that they don't necessarily attract buyers any quicker than listings without those extras.

Keep all documentation related to anything in these two columns. Then you'll need to figure out how to sort, organize, and utilize this information. A basic filing cabinet is all you'll need to store your paper trail, at least for now. Set up files in a manner that makes sense to you and isn't too complicated so you'll keep up with it. Here's a suggested list of files folders to start:

- EBay invoices, which are sent to you electronically every month, or you can print them out from the site.

- PayPal statements, which you can print out from their site.

- Individual summaries of each PayPal transaction (the monthly statements don't specify what each transaction was for) stapled to any other documentation for that particular auction, such as a delivery confirmation receipt or tracking numbers.

- Business bank account statements, with an envelope to put all deposit slips and other documentation for that month.

- Receipts for all inventory purchases.

- Receipts for all office or business supplies (shipping supplies, printer paper, etc.).

- Receipts for all shipping, including delivery confirmation receipts, insurance documents, etc. If you purchase shipping via PayPal, much of this information can be accessed by printing off the transaction record.

At the end of every month, staple, paperclip, or envelope all the appropriate items from each folder together so that they won't get mixed up with the next month's items as you place them in the file. If you're very careful to save and print out all supporting documentation, you should have all the information you'll need for your end-of-year tax filing.

 **Recordkeeping**

How long you need to keep records can vary from state to state or by business type, so be sure to ask the accountant or attorney who is assisting you for this answer. One thing to note: You may have to keep records for your insurance company or your creditors longer than you have to keep them for tax purposes.

Make a point of reconciling your business bank account as soon as the statement arrives. Your bank statements and your checkbook log are good documentation, but you will need your receipts as backup proof of your expenses. Another possibility is to gather all the receipts for the checks listed on your monthly statement and staple them to the statement.

Other statements you should make a point of reconciling are your eBay and PayPal statements. Although eBay and PayPal both have very accurate systems, comparing your invoices with your monthly spreadsheet/log sheet or accounting program is a good way to make sure you didn't overlook something. Make sure to mark invoices and bank statements as "reconciled" before filing, so you don't later second-guess yourself. You can download both eBay and PayPal statements and save them on your computer or import them into software, including Excel and most accounting systems.

If you plan to purchase a computer program to do your accounting for you, such as QuickBooks or Peachtree Accounting, then you would be well-served by hiring an accountant to set up the software for you so that you are keeping all the right information and entering it in a logical fashion that will give you the results you need.

An accountant can help you set up a chart of accounts based on the list of Income and Expenses you made earlier, with category titles and/or a numbering system (for ease of entering transactions). Accounting software is more efficient when you input as much data as necessary for proper reporting and tracking of income and expenses. If you have the financial ability to do this right from the start, it's highly recommended.

Another way to track expenses is with a spreadsheet program such as Microsoft Excel. Basic spreadsheets are not difficult to set up if you have some knowledge of how they work. This is a valuable program to learn, so consider investing in a tutorial program on CD-ROM. Numerous companies have them available, but probably the best source is Microsoft itself. They make a CD-ROM tutorial that sells for under $15. Of course, you have to have Excel; the program isn't included with the tutorial. Excel is standard in all versions of Microsoft Office, which is definitely a software packet that any business needs today.

If you don't yet have Excel or accounting software (or an accountant lined up yet), or the knowledge to put the software to work for you, don't delay in recording details of your auction transactions immediately. Set up your file folders and keep every piece of documentation. For analyzing your day-to-day expenses and income, you can always do it the old-fashioned way; that is, the way many small businesses did it until approximately 15 years ago!

Go to an office supply store and ask for a ledger book. This book will save your skin until you pull your accounting practices into the 21st century. A ledger book is simply a bound set of blank sheets with a pre-printed grid on it in rows and columns.

There are a number of ways to set up a ledger, depending on what you wish to track. For tracking individual auctions and the costs involved, use a simple setup like the following example.

Willy's Widgets 'n Gidgets – Ledger Categories		
Column	**Title**	**Explanation**
Re-List Y/N	Re-Listed Items	If this particular item had previously been listed and did not sell, then the loss would be on the ledger of the month it did not sell, but if I re-list in 90 days and it sells, I may receive a refund of some listing fees. I mark things that are re-listed with a "Y" in this column so when it sells, I can be on the lookout for the refund amount so I can fill in column J.
A	Acquisition Cost	This is the total cost that I incurred in obtaining or producing/making this product, including labor and materials if I made it myself. I have kept all receipts and records to verify this number completely.
B	eBay Listing Fee	This is the basic flat fee that I paid to eBay to post this item for auction. It does not include any extra services or charges.
C	eBay Listing Charges	These are the fees for optional services I chose for the auction. The code for the service is first, followed by the additional fee amount. See chart for list of codes for these services.
D	Final Value Fee	This is the incremental fee based on the sale price; will be -0- if item did not sell. See chart for structure.
E	PayPal Fee	This is the fee that PayPal charges to process the transaction between the buyer and me. 2% of the sale price + .30 for each transaction. This does not include any extra fees I incurred when buying postage through PayPal.
F	Postage	This is the amount of actual postage I paid to ship the item, including insurance, delivery confirmation, or other options chosen by the buyer or required by me. This does not include any fees I incurred while buying postage through PayPal.

	Willy's Widgets 'n Gidgets – Ledger Categories	
Column	**Title**	**Explanation**
G	Total Out	Since columns "A" through "F" are "expenses," they are in parentheses, which means they are "subtracted" from the income columns. Total these columns here (add all expenses together).
H	Gross Sold Price	This is the total amount the item sold for at auction, not including any shipping and handling fees/charges.
I	Total Shipping & Handling Charged	This column is the total amount paid by the buyer for shipping and handling. It may be more than column F, if I added a S&H charge when I started the auction.
J	Re-Listed Refund Amount	If I had previously listed this item and it didn't sell, and I'm now eligible for re-list refund, I enter the amount of that refund (eBay will let me know when I have received a refund).
K	Total In	Add columns H, I, and J, which are my income columns. This gives me my gross income for the auction.
	Net Profits	Subtract Column J's total from Column M's total. This is my *net* profit after auction-related expenses.
	Sales Tax	Even though sales tax collected is an income and sales tax payable to the state is an expense, for this type of chart it's easier just to set it aside immediately.

		A		B	C	D	E	F	G	H	I	J	K		
Inventory Number	Auction Start/ End	Re-List? y/n	(Acqui-sition)	Start/ Bid/ "Buy It Now" Price	(List Fee)	(Extras)	(Final v. Fee)	(Ppal Fee)	(Post-age)	Total Out (A to I)	Gross Sold $	Total S&H	Re-List Refund	Total In (H+I+J)	Profit (K-G)	Sales Tax
W001	1/1-1/2	n	2.00	.99/ 9.99	.25	bd/ 1.0 bin/ .05	.52	.71	3.85	8.38	9.99	4.25	0	14.24	*5.86*	-
G011	1/1-1/3	n	1.00	.99/ 9.99	.25	bd/ 1.0 bin/ .05	.52	.71	3.85	7.38	9.99	4.25	0	14.24	*6.86*	-
G012	1/1-1/8	n	1.00	.99/ 9.99	.25	bd/ 1.0 bin/ .05	.21	.54	3.85	6.90	3.99	4.25	0	8.24	*1.34*	-
G013	1/1-1/8	n	1.00	.99/ 9.99	.25	bd/ 1.0 bin/ .05	.47	.68	3.85	7.30	8.99	4.25	0	13.24	*5.94*	-
G014	1/1-1/8	n	1.00	.99/ 9.99	.25	bd/ 1.0 bin/ .05	.44	.67	3.85	7.26	8.45	4.25	0	12.70	*5.44*	-

Willy's Widgets 'n Gidgets Sales Ledger   January 2006

Willy's Widgets 'n Gidgets Sales Ledger   January 2006

Inventory Number	Auction Start/End	Re-List? y/n	A (Acqui-sition)	Start Bid/ "Buy It Now" Price	B (List Fee)	C (Extras)	D (Final v. Fee)	E (Ppal Fee)	F (Post-age)	G Total Out (A to I)	H Gross Sold $	I Total S&H	J Re-List Refund	K Total In (H+I+J)	Profit (K-G)	Sales Tax
W002	1/1-1/8	n	2.00	.99/ 9.99	.25	bd/ 1.0 bin/ .05	.52	.73	3.85	8.93	9.95	4.25	0	14.75	5.82	.55
W003	1/9-1/16	n	2.00	1.99/ 9.99	.35	bin/.05	.42	.66	3.85	7.33	8.00	4.25	0	12.25	4.92	-
W004	1/9-1/12	n	2.00	1.99/ 9.99	.35	bin/.05	.52	.71	3.85	7.48	9.99	4.25	0	14.24	6.76	-
G015	1/9-1/13	n	1.00	1.99/ 9.99	.35	bin/.05	.52	.71	3.85	7.48	9.99	4.25	0	14.24	6.76	-
G016	1/9-1/16	n	1.00	1.99/ 9.99	.35	bin/.05	.41	.65	3.85	6.31	7.85	4.25	0	12.10	5.79	-
W005	1/9-1/19	n	2.00	1.99/ 9.99	.35	bin/.05	.52	.71	3.85	6.48	9.99	4.25	0	14.24	7.76	-
W006	1/9-1/16	n	2.00	1.99/ 9.99	.35	bin/.05	.31	.60	3.85	7.16	5.95	4.25	0	10.20	3.04	-
W007	1/14-1/16	n	2.00	2.99/ 10.99	.35	s/.50 bin/.05	.52	.71	3.85	7.98	9.99	4.25	0	14.24	6.26	-
G017	1/14-1/15	n	1.00	2.99/ 10.99	.35	s/.50 bin/.05	.52	.71	3.85	6.98	9.99	4.25	0	14.24	7.26	-

Willy's Widgets 'n Gidgets Sales Ledger   January 2006

Inventory Number	Auction Start/End	Re-List? y/n	A (Acqui-sition)	Start Bid/ "Buy It Now" Price	B (List Fee)	C (Extras)	D (Final v. Fee)	E (Ppal Fee)	F (Post-age)	G Total Out (A to I)	H Gross Sold $	I Total S&H	J Re-List Refund	K Total In (H+I+J)	Profit (K-G)	Sales Tax
G018	1/14-1/21	n	1.00	2.99/10.99	.35	s/.50 bin/.05	.36	.62	3.85	6.73	6.95	4.25	0	11.20	4.47	-
G019	1/14-1/21	n	1.00	2.99/10.99	.35	s/.50 bin/.05	.31	.60	3.85	6.66	5.95	4.25	0	10.20	3.54	-
W008	1/14-1/21	n	2.00	2.99/10.99	.35	s/.50 bin/.05	.52	.71	3.85	7.98	9.99	4.25	0	14.24	6.26	-
W009	1/20-1/22	n	2.00	3.99/9.99	.35	bin/.05	.52	0.00	0.00	2.92	9.99	0.00	0	12.99	10.07	-
G020	1/20-1/21	n	1.00	3.99/9.99	.35	bin/.05	.52	.71	3.85	6.48	9.99	4.25	0	14.24	7.76	-
G021	1/20-1/23	n	1.00	3.99/9.99	.35	bin/.05	.52	.71	3.85	6.48	9.99	4.25	0	14.24	7.76	-
W010	1/20-1/20	n	2.00	3.99/9.99	.35	bin/.05	.52	.73	3.85	8.05	9.99	4.25	0	14.79	6.76	.55
W022	1/20-1/27	n	2.00	4.99/9.99	.35	bin/.05	.47	.68	3.85	7.40	8.99	4.25	0	13.24	5.84	-
G023	1/20-1/27	n	1.00	4.99/9.99	.35	bin/.05	.45	.84	5.40	8.09	8.49	6.00	0	11.49	3.40	-
Totals	22		34.00		7.45	9.65	10.68	15.10	86.25	164.23	203.44	95.25	0.00	299.79	135.56	1.10

A pre-printed ledger book is generally the same size as legal-sized paper, 8.5 x 14 inches, and will have many more boxes on it, so you can neatly print the numbers, decimals, etc. The ledger used in this example is a table in Microsoft Publisher, but it can also be done in Word and Works as well. Notice that in this example, Willy has set up a "legend" sheet, so he can refer to it if he forgets what goes in which column. Putting the wrong data in the wrong column pretty much negates whatever you were trying to accomplish. For further reference, Willy also made a few handy charts available to help him figure his fees quickly. Because of all the various things he wants to track on one ledger sheet, this would be printed on legal-sized paper. An office supply store can sell him a binder for this size, and he'll have his own custom-made ledger book.

If Willy were to fill this chart out accurately for every auction (either on the computer, or printing it blank and filling in by hand as he goes through the month), he will know exactly how much money he spent on every auction-related fee or function that month. He may also be able to spot some trends, such as whether or not adding bold to his auctions really earns him that much more in final sales price or just eats away at his profits. But mostly, he'll know how much money he's made this month after all auction-related expenses are deducted.

Column C Extra Features	Code	eBay's Cost for This Extra
Reserve Price	R	see below
Buy It Now	BIN	see below
Gallery	G	$0.35
Border	B	$3.00
Listing Designer	LD	$0.10
Highlight	H	$5.00
Subtitle	S	$0.50
Featured Plus	FP	$19.99
Bold	BD	$1.00
Gallery Featured	GF	$19.99
Scheduled Listing	SL	$0.10
Home Page Featured	HPF	$39.95
10-Day Duration	TD	$0.40
Gift Services	GS	$0.25

Column C Extra Features	Code	eBay's Cost for This Extra
List in 2 Categories	L2	see below
Add'l Pictures	XP	$0.15
Picture Show	PS	$0.25
Supersize Pic	SP	$0.75
Picture Pack	PP	$1.00

eBay's Fee Structure	
Starting or Reserve Price	**Insertion Fee**
$0.01–$0.99	$0.25
$1.00–$9.99	$0.35
$10.00–$24.99	$0.60
$25.00–$49.99	$1.20
$50.00–$199.99	$2.40
$200.00–$499.99	$3.60
$500.00+	$4.80

eBay's Final Value Fees	
Final Auction Price	**Final Value Fee**
Unsold	no charge
$0.01–$25.00	5.25% of the final price
$25.01–$1,000.00	5.25% of the first $25.00 ($1.31) plus 2.75% of the remaining balance
$1,000.00+	5.25% of the first $25.00 ($1.31) +2.75% of the amount up to $1,000 ($26.81) +1.5% of amount over $1,000

Fee Structure for Reserve & "Buy It Now" Options	
Reserve Price	**Fee (refunded if item sells)**
$0.01–$49.99	$1.00
$50.00–$199.00	$2.00
$200.00+	1% of reserve (up to $100.00)
"Buy It Now" Price	**Fee**
$0.01–$9.99	$0.05

Fee Structure for Reserve & "Buy It Now" Options	
$10.00–$24.99	$0.10
$25.00–$49.99	$0.20
$50.00+	$0.25

PayPal Fees

Standard Rate:
$0.30 + 2.9% per transaction

(incoming funds up to total $3,000.00 per month; more than that received, check into Merchant Rates, see PayPal's Web site)

Notes to Self
- Fees were current as of 10/2005. Ebay will notify all sellers before changes in fee structures
- Fees are based on *Auctions*—when I open an eBay store, the fee for *Store* items are different.

Realize, of course, that this isn't always money that Willy can then pay to himself. His expenses are more than the actual auction expenses (refer to list of expenses, above). He may have a service fee at his bank, he may need to purchase another supply of shipping materials, and he may need to refresh his supply of widgets and gidgets. He may have some sales tax he needs to earmark for the state and send on a schedule. Willy can't just go spending his profits, at least not until his business is strong enough that there are profits above all expenses. Then he can start utilizing another expense on his list: paying his own labor.

Here are some basic terms you need to become familiar with in order to work well with your accountant, attorney, or tax advisors.

Accounting Period: For most small businesses, this is the same as the calendar year, January 1st – December 31st of every year.

Accounts Payable: Expenses you haven't yet paid out.

Accounts Receivable: Income that hasn't yet arrived in your possession.

Assets: Every item of value that is owned by your company. Money in your business account, computers and office equipment, company vehicle, and accounts receivable are all assets.

Balance Sheet: This format displays your company's assets, liabilities, and equity, usually calculated from the time the business began to the present time.

Break-Even: The point at which your income minus expenses is zero.

Expense: All outgoing money, also called a debit.

Income: Money coming in, also called a credit.

Income Statement: This is a simple statement showing your business's income and expenses for a certain time period, usually from the start of the most current accounting period to the current time.

Inventory: The value of all merchandise in your possession that is currently unsold.

Liabilities: Every item that is "owed" by your company including accounts payable, business loans, any bills from vendors or utilities, and funds in your possession that belong to others (income tax due to the state).

Owner's Equity: This is what's left when you take your assets and subtract your liabilities. Hopefully this is a positive number.

Profit: The point at which all income minus all expenses is above zero.

In addition to all this organization of receipts, files, and sales data, you need to set up a system to easily identify and track your inventory. In the above example, Willy sells only two products: widgets and gidgets. Since he has multiples of each identical item, he uses a combination of numbers and letters so he can track individual sales based on the inventory number of the item. He uses W### for widgets, and G### for gidgets.

For those who sell a variety of items, new or used, assigning a number that stays with the item until it is shipped is a good way to go. You can use a two-stage system as well, if it doesn't confuse you and you want to track individual types of products. For instance, if you sell antiques but your two main products are old dolls and old postcards, you can number your dolls D1, D2, D3 and your postcards (or lots of postcards) as P1, P2, P3, etc.

That way, you can see how many items (or lots) of each type of merchandise you have sold. If you occasionally have other items that aren't either dolls or postcards, you can assign them to yet another category, such as miscellaneous, as M1, M2, M3. As long as the system makes enough sense to you that you can explain it to your accountant, it should be good enough for a start.

Regardless of how you decide to set up your inventory system, odds are that over time you'll fine-tune it and find other ways to make the system work better for you. However, you should start yet another spreadsheet (are you seeing how handy those things are?) or ledger sheet for yet another cross-reference and so that you don't reuse any inventory numbers.

Willy's Widgets 'n Gidgets Inventory Log for January 2006

Date Acquired	Descrip-tion	Category	Inventory #	Date Item Sold	Sold Amount	Buyer's Username	Auction #	Payment Type, Date	Date shipped	Shipping Method/ Confirma-tion Tracking #	Feed-back Given/ Received
1/1	Widget	W	001	1/2	9.99	buyer1		PayPal 1/4	1/5	Priority	y/y
1/1	Widget	W	002	1/2	9.99	buyer2		M.O. 1/13	1/14	Priority	y/y
1/1	Widget	W	003	1/16	8.00	buyer3		PayPal 1/16	1/17	Priority	y/y
1/1	Widget	W	004	1/12	9.99	buyer4		PayPal 1/17	1/18	Priority	y/y
1/1	Widget	W	005	1/9	9.99	buyer5					
1/1	Widget	W	C06	1/16	5.95	buyer6		PayPal 1/18	1/19	Priority	y/y
1/1	Widget	W	007	1/16	9.99	buyer7		M.O. 1/21	1/23	Priority	y/y
1/1	Widget	W	008	1/19	9.99	buyer8		PayPal 1/21	1/23	Priority	y/y
1/1	Widget	W	009	1/22	9.99	buyerA		PayPal 1/24	1/26	Priority	y/y

Willy's Widgets 'n Gidgets Inventory Log for January 2006

Date Acquired	Description	Category	Inventory #	Date Item Sold	Sold Amount	Buyer's Username	Auction #	Payment Type, Date	Date shipped	Shipping Method/ Confirmation Tracking #	Feedback Given/ Received
1/1	Widget	W	010	1/20	9.99	buyerB		PayPal 1/20	1/21	Priority	y/y
1/1	Gidget	G	011	1/13	9.99	buyer9		M.O.			y/y
1/1	Gidget	G	012	1/8	3.99	Buyer!		PayPal 1/10	1/12	Priority	y/y
1/1	Gidget	G	013	1/8	8.99	buyer1		PayPal 1/9	1/10	Priority Repeat cust!	y/y
1/1	Gidget	G	014	1/8	8.45	buyerC		PayPal 1/10	1/12	Priority	y/
1/1	Gidget	G	015	1/13	9.99	buyer@		PayPal 1/14	1/17	Priority	y/
1/1	Gidget	G	016	1/16	7.85	buyer10					
1/1	Gidget	G	017	1/15	9.99	buyerD		PayPal 1/16	1/17	Priority	y/y
1/1	Gidget	G	018	1/21	6.95	buyer&		M.O.			
1/15	Gidget	G	019	1/21	5.95	buyer*		PayPal 1/26	1/27	Priority	y/
1/15	Gidget	G	020	1/21	9.99	buyerE		PayPal 1/23	1/24	Priority	y/

Willy's Widgets 'n Gidgets Inventory Log for January 2006

Date Acquired	Descrip- tion	Category	Inventory #	Date Item Sold	Sold Amount	Buyer's Username	Auction #	Payment Type, Date	Date shipped	Shipping Method/ Confirma- tion Tracking #	Feed- back Given/ Received
1/15	Gidget	G	021	1/23	9.99	buyer11		PayPal 1/23	1/24	Priority	y/
1/15	Gidget	W	022	1/27	8.99	buyerF					
1/15	Gidget	G	023	1/23	8.49	buyerA		PayPal 1/24	1/26	Priority combined	y/
1/15	Gidget	G	024								

You may notice that there is some duplicated information from Willy's sales ledger. What information you store on your various ledger sheets is entirely up to you, so long as all of it is available one place or the other. Since Willy is obtaining his merchandise from only one source, he doesn't have a column to list the source of merchandise, but if you have several sources, you may want to track where items came from. Additionally, in the "acquisition cost" column, be sure to factor in any shipping costs you incurred while obtaining your products.

You are already familiar with Willy's numbering system from viewing his sales ledger. However, you may choose not to have a numbering system at all, if your products are each unique enough to be identifiable by their descriptions alone. However, many sellers do eventually turn to a numbering system.

Labeling your inventory has at least one huge benefit: You're less likely to accidentally list or sell the same item twice. It may seem almost ridiculous, at the outset, to imagine that you would ever do anything like that, but sellers report that it has indeed happened to them before they got organized. Another benefit of having a cross-reference number is that you are less likely to ship the wrong item to the wrong person. While you need to accept that a mistake is possible at any time, you'll be less likely to make silly mistakes like this if you're organized and efficient.

Sellers use a variety of methods to label their inventory. Some use adhesive notes to attach the assigned number to the item until it sells. Others place items in zippered storage bags and write the number on the bag with a permanent marker. If they are selling clothing that needs to remain hung, they may set aside closet space (this is handy if you're using a spare bedroom as an office) and wrap a piece of painter's tape (the blue stuff) around the hanger's neck with the pertinent information. There are as many ways to label your items as you can think of, but, generally, a simple system is best.

Willy has chosen to track the usernames of his buyers in case they have a question or complaint later on. He can easily scan this column for their IDs and have all the pertinent information at hand, including the confirmation or tracking numbers, in the next column (he will have stored all the actual delivery confirmation and tracking receipts in his postage file).

When you acquire inventory at estate sales, flea markets, or garage/yard sales, you likely won't be provided with a receipt for your records. In this case, pull out your little spiral notebook (keep in your car for tracking mileage) and write a receipt for yourself. When you return home, you can accurately record your acquisition costs of the items. If you purchase numerous items at one sale, you'll quickly forget how much you paid for each and could end up asking too little for an item later.

If you end up taking a loss on an item purchased secondhand, you'll need some documentation of what you paid for it in order to have that loss decrease your income for the month. Of course, this system requires a fair amount of honesty, but being dishonest about your actual costs paid will not give you a true picture of your business. It will hurt you in the long run.

Many accounting software programs, such as Peachtree, will also have a built-in inventory tracking system. If you are starting off with this advantage, be sure to have your accountant set up your inventory right away and teach you the proper way to input your merchandise. This will save you a lot of time in the future. For the rest of us, keeping accurate paper or spreadsheet logs is sufficient and could also be translated into data for a computerized inventory system at a later date.

Depending on your own personal interest in tracking things, you may want to set up ledgers/spreadsheets to track the business or office supplies you purchase. Set up one spreadsheet for those items you'll have to pay use tax for (see pages 62–63) and ones you bought in your own state. You could have a spreadsheet to list all your other deductibles (Internet service, PO box fees, storage/rent – if you're working away from your home or renting space to store inventory, etc.). The more detailed you are in your records, the less time you (or your accountant) will have to spend sorting receipts and totaling them all up every spring.

If you're the type who doesn't care to see every detail laid out like a magnificent buffet, then you will probably be content to file receipts appropriately and bundle them monthly. In this case, keeping just two ledgers (inventory and sales) will be sufficient for you. Either way is fine, so long as you're prepared come tax time.

Investigating
Your Tax Liabilities

In the same way this book presents accounting information, as a reference with simple tools to help you along the way, it also approaches tax information with the same goals. The entirety of tax law is far beyond the scope of this publication, and since tax laws change regularly, an accountant or attorney is your most accurate source of assistance.

With that in mind, familiarize yourself with these basic ideas and lists of sources to check out before tax time.

Probably the best resource for learning about small business taxes is the Internal Revenue Service's own site, **www.irs.gov**. This one-stop-shopping site is filled with publications, forms, advice, educational opportunities, and more for the small business owner.

Whenever you are exploring the topics of importance to you, the new business owner, be sure to pay attention to the gray bar on the left of the screen, which will continue to direct you to other important items about the topic you've chosen. A good place to start, right from their home page, is the "Businesses" link under the header "Information For." From that link, you will come across these excellent publications, articles, and charts to read or download and print.

- **Publication 334.** The Tax Guide for Small Business (for Individuals Who Use Schedule C or Schedule C-EZ).

- **Husband and Wife Businesses.** This brief article highlights some of the nuances of husbands and wives both working in the same family-owned small business.

- **Business Structure Chart.** This chart is excellent for reference, placing links to all the downloadable tax forms in columns based on the business structure. Print this page for future reference and file it with the other publications you should print off this site.

- **The forms you'll need.** Based on your business structure, you'll be needing the various forms listed on the Business Structure Chart. As with the informational publications, it wouldn't hurt to download these forms for future reference, especially if you are a sole proprietor and will be filing your business information along with your regular income tax forms. Remember that forms change annually, so don't use a form unless it is labeled for the correct tax year!

Other useful information you can locate includes tips about getting an Employee Identification Number (EIN). In a general sense, businesses should have one of these numbers, established by the federal government, if they are any business structure other than a sole proprietorship. Sole proprietorships can get them as well, but they're not as necessary because taxes can be reported under the owner's SSN. Search the **irs.gov** Web site for this topic for in-depth information about whether or not you need to have one of these, or call your tax professional.

Of course, every small business owner is concerned about taxes. There are three basic types of taxes you need to be concerned about at the federal level. The forms needed for each type of tax are listed on the Business Structure Chart, which is easily located by searching that phrase on the **irs.gov** site. These tax types are:

- **Income tax.** This is the same thing that is withheld from and sent to the IRS by your employer. Since you will be working for yourself, you must pay the taxes yourself. Quarterly tax payments are made using the appropriate form based on your business structure.

- **Self-employment tax.** This is how you contribute to Social Security and Medicare while self-employed. Like the income tax, the form you use for this differs based on your business structure.

- **Employment tax.** This is only applicable if you have paid employees, which most small businesses don't have to start out with. See the IRS's advice on Husband and Wife Businesses to determine if your spouse is an employee or actually a business partner.

 **Independent Contractors**

Look into using independent contractors for seasonal assistance or help with specific tasks. They provide you with an invoice for services and a W-9 form with their Social Security number. Then you can report the money you spent on their services as a deduction (be sure to send them the documentation—a 1099 form—so they can report the income).

Deductions are the "good news" of taxes. When you pay taxes as a legitimate business, you get some "bennies." Here are just some items that are likely deductible for your eBay business. Of course, double-check everything with appropriate tax professionals before taking a deduction.

Possible Deductions

- Depreciation on your office equipment, or purchases of new/upgraded equipment.

- EBay fees and PayPal fees paid.

- Fees paid to your attorney or accountant regarding your business.

- Home office space (though this is a tricky one, do so with professional advice only).

- Internet service.

- Office supplies and shipping supplies.

- Phone service (if you have a separate business line).

- Rent (if you rent storage space for inventory, rent an office, etc.).

- Traveling costs (mileage to/from your shipping point or for supplies/inventory).

- Utilities (if you rent space and pay for the heat and electricity, for example).

Keeping accurate records of deductible items is crucial, per chance you were to be audited by the IRS.

For mileage, keep a small spiral notebook and pencil in your car and log your mileage very carefully. Store these in a small, weatherproof container, such as a child's plastic flip-lid pencil box. This will not only keep them from getting separated in your car, but it also gives you a place to stash your receipts from the gas station. Unless you are using a vehicle strictly for business, you need to be able to show exactly how many miles you drove for business versus personal use. There are two options on deductions for vehicle use, standard mileage rate or actual expenses. Each option has its own rules, benefits, and requirements, so be sure to learn about those before filling out your annual tax forms.

Keeping receipts, bills, bank statements, and monthly statements/ invoices from eBay and PayPal will generally suffice for most other deductions. One issue that has come up in recent years is that receipts that are printed on the shiny rolls of thermal paper fade over time. In this case, photocopy or scan your receipts monthly and store those with the original receipts.

You bear the burden of proof in matters of deductions: You must be able to prove the expense in order to justify it. Here, again, you will be happy you separated your business and personal finances, especially when it comes to separating your personal eBay purchases from your business sales.

It can't be stressed enough how important it is to get appropriate tax assistance. While you can keep a majority of basic bookkeeping records yourself, interpreting the IRS's forms and instructions for businesses isn't as simple as the ordinary tax forms the average American files annually. Not to say you can't learn to file these items yourself, but be sure to hire a professional to guide and teach you to do them properly.

TIP — IRS Workshops

*The IRS is concerned about small business owners' understanding of tax laws and requirements. They would much rather help you get it right the first time than audit you. To do their part in educating small business owners, they offer workshops in every state. To find out when the next workshops will be in your state, search the **irs.gov** for "small business tax workshop."*

If you can't attend a workshop near your home, or simply don't have time to dedicate in one lump sum, you can also take online versions with streaming video from an actual workshop. This is a great alternative for those whose busy lives force them to do a lot of work late at night.

You can order or download some helpful products from the IRS, such as a tax calendar that will help you keep track of important dates in your tax year. They also have brochures you can view online or download with such titles as *Home-Based Business Tax Avoidance Schemes* and the *Small Business Resource Guide* on CD. To locate these and other items, search the IRS's site for "small business products order."

To help you stay up to date with tax issues, the IRS also offers a free e-mail mailing list you can join. Once the IRS knows about your business, they take the initiative to send you the appropriate quarterly forms in advance. This is just one way they try to make sure that business owners don't get behind or mess up accidentally.

Your own state also wants to do its part to make your business successful. To find information about how your state's taxation system works, search "state links" on the **irs.gov** home page. This page has a link for every state's basic information.

Don't neglect to register your business with your state and local authorities as well; you'll find that they are just as anxious for your business endeavor to be a success as the IRS. After all, you are helping your state's — and country's — economies to grow!

One more topic that falls under "taxes" is that of sales tax and use tax. As a legitimate business, you are required to collect sales tax on all sales to buyers in your own state and forward them to your state's department of revenue. Your state's department of revenue will be all too happy to assist you by sending you forms to use and reminders of the dates you must submit payment and verification. At this time, charging sales tax for sales in other states is not necessary, as your customers are required to report their purchases and pay the taxes themselves. This is called use tax.

You may have to pay use taxes to your state for all items, supplies, and other tangible goods that you purchase out of state (such as on eBay or from the Web sites of suppliers) and are using for your own business use. This doesn't apply to inventory you purchase for resale, but for the items that you normally would pay sales tax on if you had purchased them in your own state.

The companies who sold you these goods were not required to collect sales tax from you, but you may be required to pay it yourself. Keep a separate spreadsheet or ledger page listing the items you buy that are subject to use tax and make copies of applicable receipts for verification. Your accounting professional, or your own state's department of revenue, can help you determine if you must pay use tax.

When you contact your state department of revenue, be sure to get the details on all of these topics:

- How often do I need to forward sales and use taxes?

- What specific items are or are not taxable?

- What is the tax rate?

- What is the process for forwarding taxes?

- What assistance is available to me by way of forms or advice?

If you collect payment for auctions through PayPal, you can program it to automatically collect sales tax within your state. Beware, though, PayPal's fees are based on the entire amount of money sent by the buyer, and they don't exclude sales tax in that figure. So, technically, you will be paying PayPal fees on the sales tax you collect. To make up for this, you may wish to add a few pennies more to your shipping and handling fee when you set up an auction.

The long and short of it is that taxes can be complicated matters that require professional assistance. The penalties, interest, and headaches incurred when mistakes are made are just far too costly for most small businesses. They can sink your ship before it sets sail or leave you deserted on an island of debt. The information contained here is only of general nature and should not be considered the definitive answer to any of your tax questions.

While it may seem overwhelming to consider all these issues — setting up an official business, recordkeeping and inventory, bookkeeping and taxes — don't be discouraged. Everyone involved wants you to become a successful business, and even though there are many rules to follow and taxes to pay, they will do what they can to steer you away from pitfalls and failure. The rest is up to you: do it right the first time, take the time to learn the rules and follow them, and be prepared to spend some money for the tasks you can't do yourself.

Once you have your business structure set up, with your business plan down on paper and your recordkeeping and inventory systems set up, you're ready to nail down some important details. You will need to obtain a product to sell, choose how you'll receive payments and ship items, and learn how to promote your business.

Checklist of Tasks: Setting Up a Recordkeeping System and Learning About Tax Issues

❏ I have thought about, and made a list of, all of the possible expenses and income sources I might have in this venture (my early chart of accounts).

❏ I have determined how I want to file receipts, invoices, and bank statements, and made a list so I can set up my filing cabinet right away.

❏ I have decided how I will track my auctions, inventory, expenses, and income:

> By hand in a purchased ledger or computer-made ledger-type form.

> By spreadsheet program, which I know how to use or will get assistance in setting up.

> By accounting software, which I know how to use or will get assistance in setting up.

❏ I have given some thought to how I will store and label my inventory.

❏ I have contacted an accountant or attorney for advice on how to deal with tax issues when starting a new business.

❏ I have become familiar with the various online resources at **irs.gov** and my home state's business startup Web site and am comfortable with what's required of me:

> Quarterly income tax payments.

> Collection of sales tax for sales to others in my state.

> Documentation and payment of use tax for items I purchase online.

Obtaining merchandise, choosing payment and shipping options, and advertising are all part of the strong foundation you are building for your business.

Stuff to Sell

You're getting closer to the reality of starting your own business; perhaps you've even got a good start on the tasks in Chapters 2 and 3. If so, then you're on the right path to success!

Before you delve into setting up those auctions, let's explore some other things that are better to have figured out sooner than later. While these tasks may not be as crucial as the legal issues and tax obligations discussed previously, they are all part of what will make or break your business. This includes things such as obtaining merchandise, choosing your payment and shipping options, and advertising yourself. All of these tasks are part of the strong foundation you are building for your business.

Obtaining Merchandise

This is one thing that most people have some idea about when they first consider opening their own business on eBay. Part of it is pure logic: sell what you like. If you're an avid collector of Hummel figurines, for example, then you'd be a good seller because you know your merchandise well. If you worked all through high school in a sporting goods store, then you may want to put that knowledge to work for you and sell sporting goods.

However, simply selling what you know isn't the final word on what you should sell. You may have several specialties or interests, or you may have a product you want to make yourself. But the question is this: Are these things that people are buying on eBay?

Spend some time searching current (tips on searching, Chapter 7) and completed listings to see if the item or types of items you want to sell are currently being marketed. This will give you a good idea of whether or not your product will generate some interest and what sort of price you can expect to ask.

Determining the price you'll be asking for your product is dependent on being able to obtain your product cheaply enough to make a profit for yourself and still give buyers a good price. If you can't do that, you probably won't sell much. See what your competition is charging for the same, or similar, products on eBay.

Remember that you'll have to acquire the product and maybe pay some shipping fees to receive it. Then you'll have to spend money on eBay fees (remember Willy's Widgets 'n Gidgets Sales Ledger) and still turn a bit of profit in the end. Simply the price of the product doesn't give you a full sense of how much profit you'll have in the end.

Whether or not you've already decided on a specific product or type of product to sell, you'll want to be checking into buying from wholesalers and distributors. This can be the difference between very low profits and decent profits. Especially if you are planning to make your product yourself, you'll absolutely have to purchase your supplies through wholesale avenues. When you have a reseller's permit then you'll have the opportunity to do business with wholesale dealers without paying sales tax. Some of them won't do business with you unless you have the proper permits.

How do you find a wholesaler who sells the type of products you want to sell or supplies you'll need to make your product? The Internet, of course! You may not have to go far at all, since many wholesalers sell on eBay. Just do a search for "wholesale lot" or "resale lot" and you'll have dozens of pages of deals to sort through including everything from power tools to lingerie to baby basics.

There are countless wholesalers who have Web sites as well; search "wholesale + [your item]," (such as: widget, jewelry, tools, etc.) or "wholesale list," to locate sites that merely list wholesalers. Beware that some Web sites want you to pay for access to their site or to obtain a list. Investigate these offers before putting out any cash; you may be able to find the same information for free elsewhere. Other search terms you might try include "liquidation," "closeout," "overstock," "clearance."

Each search will net you pages and pages of sites to investigate. Be sure to do just that: investigate. Unless you know someone who has dealt personally with an online company, be sure to take basic precautions to be sure your money doesn't buy you nothing. Most sites have an "About Us" page. Check it out and look for an address. Note this information and check the Better Business Bureau's Web site at **www.bbb.org**. If there is a phone number listed, consider calling the number (to be sure it is an actual working number) and asking the company for some references or verification of their business practices. Any reputable company will not be offended by such requests.

Try also to distinguish if you'll be buying directly from the manufacturer or if the wholesaler is a distributor. Going straight to the source (getting items directly from the manufacturer) is going to cost you less than through a distributor, although even that is cheaper than buying retail. Some manufacturers don't wholesale their merchandise, but most of them will give you names of authorized distributors. Check out all your options before deciding on a supplier.

 **Wholesale Merchandise**

Wholesalers deal in bulk merchandise, so be sure you are clear about the minimum quantity you must order and what the price-per-item is at the quantity you plan to order. Sometimes their advertised price is based on a huge quantity ordered, so don't just assume that the advertised price is the price you'll get.

Buying wholesale can definitely put you into a much nicer profit margin, but there are downsides to buying this way. The most obvious issue is that of potentially having five thousand of any one item on hand. Do you have room to store that much merchandise? Is the demand going to be strong long enough to sell that many of one item? You may be smart to pay a slightly higher cost per item and not have so much stock.

Before buying up cases and cases of an item, check with the manufacturer to see if a newer product line has been developed recently. People may not want an older model if a newer model with more features can be had. Unless, that is, they can get it at a substantially lower price, making those newer features not worth the extra cost.

Another thing to consider is this: Are eBay buyers going to pay shipping and handling for really small items? Perhaps you can get five hundred baby rattles with a popular cartoon character on them for fifteen cents each. These should easily sell for a dollar or more. However, who will pay the shipping cost for one small rattle? Unless it's a very popular cartoon character whose merchandise happens to be difficult to find, you may have a hard time getting people to buy them, no matter how good the deal.

Here's a suggestion: If you've found such a good deal on baby rattles, see if you can snag a deal on some burp cloths, teething toys, receiving blankets, sleepers, and other baby basics. If you can get together several such items, you can sell them in lots. Make up a package of one or more of each item and sell them as a group (lot). Put in a little creativity and you might have yourself a nice product. Try getting some tulle (inexpensive netting, like what's used to tie up rice bags at weddings, can be found cheaply at fabric stores) and ribbon. Arrange your group of items neatly in a circle of tulle (pink or blue) and tie up neatly with a piece of ribbon.

Locate some wholesale gift tags or greeting cards and include a "baby shower" card for the buyer. Presto: a pre-packaged baby shower gift, just sign the card and go! If you're not wild about the idea of venturing into a fabric store to find tulle, locate a wholesaler for wrapping paper and include a package of pink or blue in with the lot. Those little extras are what makes an item worthwhile and will build you a grateful customer base. This is just one example of how you can use multiple items from wholesale lots to create a unique product that will have more appeal than just the individual items alone would.

Since buying wholesale might require a great deal of storage space, you may wish to look into using a drop shipper. This is a system whereby you sell the merchandise and the drop shipper stores and ships it for you. There are numerous suppliers who are willing to do drop shipping for you. They may have an account setup fee that you will have to pay, so be prepared for some investment, but always investigate all costs before agreeing to pay anything. An online search is a good way to locate suppliers who drop ship, but beware that there are numerous companies who are more interested in making money from you than in helping you make money.

Some things to investigate before starting a relationship with any drop shipper include the following:

- What will the drop shipper charge you for the merchandise, including any handling charge they pass on to you for shipping the item?

- How will charges be processed? Are you expected to pay as they ship each item, or do they invoice you monthly?

- Do they accept returns from your buyers, should the merchandise be damaged?

- Do they actually stock the merchandise themselves or are they merely a middle-man for yet another drop shipper? (Hint: Avoid these companies; the more middlemen there are, the smaller your profit.)

There are also companies who sell lists of drop shipping companies. Like with lists of wholesalers, you may very well get the same information for free at another source.

Other services that charge fees may help facilitate drop shipping. One such company is **www.wholesalemarketer.com**. This company is an eBay certified service provider and calls themselves a "value added product sourcing partner." By paying a membership fee, you gain access to 90,000 wholesale products. This company uses the buying power of many to negotiate deals that you may not be able to negotiate on your own. However, you'll need to weigh the membership costs against the extra purchasing power.

Another resource that's an eBay-certified service provider is **www.worldwidebrands.com**. This Web site was created by an eBay Radio's Product Sourcing Editor. There is plenty of free or very low-cost information on this site, in addition to the membership they want to sign you up for. As with all services that will cost you money, investigate before investing and weigh the costs against what you stand to profit.

One of the better options for new sellers in terms of drop shipping is an arrangement with a local artisan or small-town manufacturer. Perhaps you live in Oregon but have a cousin in Baltimore who makes beautiful handmade birdhouses and feeders. He sells them in his front yard, mostly. Maybe he even goes to an arts and crafts fair a couple times a year. However, his exposure is limited. That's where you come in.

It would be silly for your cousin to mail birdhouses and feeders to you so that you could photograph them, sell them, and then re-ship them to the buyer. That's a waste of time and money. Drop shipping is a good arrangement in this case: you set up the auctions, collect the payments, and send your cousin's share to him. Your cousin ships the item to the buyer directly.

If there is some latitude in your cousin's profit—he generally makes a handsome profit and is willing to share some of it in exchange for your eBay marketing and he is willing to ship the product before receiving his share of the profits—then this could be a great opportunity for you to create some business for both of you. One way to make sure he gets his share right away is for him to have a PayPal account that you deposit his share (plus the shipping cost he'll incur) as soon as you receive payment.

Any such business arrangement, even with family members, should be put on paper and properly documented in a manner suggested by your attorney. You want to build strong, trusting relationships with your drop shippers, but you also need to make sure all parties are working for the same goal and agreeing to the same things.

 **Arts, Crafts, and Copyrights**

Check with any artists or crafters to be sure that they are not making their products from plans or patterns that are copyrighted, nor are they copying a registered or trademarked product from another company. All artistic and handmade items should be made using the crafter's original ideas and designs.

Drop-shipping arrangements can be made with local manufacturing firms as well. Smaller family-owned companies make products all over the country, and yet they often don't have the world-wide exposure they'd like to have. Set up some appointments to meet with these local businessmen and women to see if you may be able to do business with each other. You may be able to develop an exclusive right to sell their products on eBay, which is always an advantage to you.

Your hometown may be the source of several hotspots where you can obtain merchandise as well. Flea markets, estate auctions, rummage sales, and thrift stores can all provide you with items you can resell for a profit. These sources may be less reliable in terms of product stream; you can't always count on getting some great merchandise every time you go to an auction.

Additionally, in the colder parts of the country, flea markets, auctions, and rummage sales are a seasonal occurrence, so your product flow would be interrupted unless you buy enough in the warm seasons to last you all year long. Some cities have indoor flea markets and auctions even in the winter, and the prices may be more reasonable at that time of year due to reduced competition, so if you're going to secure your inventory through these methods, check around for the winter sale locations.

Estate auctions can be a virtual goldmine of merchandise, depending of course on how well the auctioneer knows his business. Most auctioneers are pretty well versed in the major categories of antiques, but where you'll find some of the best deals are in the "boxes of junk" that often are auctioned off at the end. These boxes contain odds and ends found in junk drawers and jewelry boxes. Stuff that didn't merit being auctioned off by itself gets tossed into cardboard boxes, and the entire contents of the boxes are auctioned off. Usually these items are sold at the end of the sale, which is a bother because you may have to wait around for hours on end. But the later the bidding begins, the less competition you may have. It's not unheard of to get a box of "goodies" for a single dollar.

Many auctioneers will get the highest bid they can and then let the winning bidder choose which box from the group of boxes they want. Some will even let the winning bidder take as many boxes at the same price as desired before beginning the bidding again. So if you're the high bidder at four dollars a box, you can select out the cream of the crop right away. Some boxes may not look as promising, so then you may wait it out to see if you can have some of the other boxes for two dollars or less.

Since you don't often have a chance to completely inspect the contents of a particular box, you may not even know what you'll find until you can get it home and empty it onto your kitchen table. It's kind of like emptying your pillowcase of goods on Halloween when you were a kid!

And since you paid little or nothing for the box (boxes that just can't get a bidder are sometimes even left deserted for the taking by anybody), you won't be out a tremendous amount of money if there is nothing saleable. But before you toss out that old slightly tarnished ladies' compact, double-check to make sure it wasn't made by Dorset, Fifth Avenue, New York City. It may look tacky to you, but it may be collectible to the right person!

Some people just don't have the patience to wait through a long auction, and others don't like the competitiveness of live bidding. If you aren't shy and you love to haggle for a bargain, then try auctioning. You may even become hooked!

Flea markets and antique dealers can also bring about some surprising finds, but beware that many flea market vendors (and nearly all antique vendors) do know the actual value of their wares. Unlike the auctioneer who must sell all the goods in a single day, the antique dealer and flea market vendor can be patient and wait for the right customer to come his way. He may be willing to bargain with you somewhat, but there are limits to just how low he'll go sometimes.

Rummage sales are utilized by a surprisingly large number of sellers. Even if they sell new merchandise or a specific product line, every now and again you'll see a bargain they picked up second-hand somewhere. Rummaging has become almost faddish; everybody's looking for a great bargain, and more and more it's for resale purposes! Unlike flea market vendors and antique dealers, the odds are in your favor that the people who've cleaned out their closets don't really have a handle on the possible value of their "junk" but are more concerned about not having to put it back into their closets or haul it to a charity's thrift store.

Use this to your advantage when bargaining; ask for a discount if you purchase numerous items. Most people expect to lower their prices if asked, and later in the day (especially on the last day of the sale) they are generally more than willing to give in to your requests. But don't be too pushy; you don't want to offend them by insinuating that their junk is merely junk!

TIP — Rummage Sales and Auctions

If possible, have someone you know available to do a quick Internet search for items while you're out rummaging or auctioning. You may have a hunch about an item, and knowing if an item does or does not sell well on eBay is a smart move before buying.

This tip was shared by Joe (eBay user "whitebears") who snagged himself a good deal thanks to his cell phone. Admittedly, cars aren't Joe's thing. "I know about as much about cars—model cars or the real thing—as Celine Dion knows about heavy metal," he admits. So when he saw an old die-cast model car at a garage sale for $15, he flipped it over and noted the word Gama on the bottom. His brother-in-law, who collects old die-cast model cars, had told him that in general they fetch around thirty dollars. Noting that it had some minor flaws, even though it was intact, he figured that the profit margin would be too low and passed it up.

As he drove away, he called his wife on his cell phone and mentioned the car to her. She immediately did a search on eBay and told him that there were completed auctions for Gama cars that sold for over $200.

Joe high-tailed it back to that sale, and luckily the car was still there. The elderly ladies having the sale were glad to get their full, asked-for price. Within a couple of days, Joe's research had revealed that this was a model of a German-made Cadillac that had been sold in the 1950s. It was rare. Seven days later, at the close of the auction, the car sold for $648.

"And that," concludes Joe, "is why I love eBay!"

Thrift stores, such as those run by charities, can be a source of good deals as well if you know what to look for. Become familiar with the various brand names that are popular, and know which "store brand" labels are from the discount chain stores (such as Wal-Mart, Kmart, etc.). Even if the item is in great condition, you may not get much for it if it was a $10 Kmart buy to begin with.

Across the country there are several different franchises of what's known as the "dollar store," where literally everything in the store is $1. These stores don't always carry the same merchandise, so what you can pick up for a buck locally may or may not be available at a dollar store four states away. Other "discount" stores have $1 aisles; these places can also be sources of merchandise, especially if you can also get items on clearance.

Like with combining wholesale items, you can often combine a group of similar items from one of these dollar stores to create a lot that will be attractive to buyers. Party supplies, for example, are one item easily found at dollar stores. If you purchase an entire grouping with a popular theme (such as a cartoon character, race-car theme, or seasonal theme), you may be able to sell the entire grouping for a nice profit. This is more likely if you include a nice variety, such as tablecloths, plates, cups, cake topper, goodie bags, and party favors. Your odds increase if you are current on the trends in children's birthday parties, so doing some research on existing party supplies on eBay is a smart move.

If your city or town has any you-store-it types of businesses, you may want to give them a call to see if they have regular auctions on any abandoned property. Most storage rental companies have at least an occasional customer who never paid the rent or never returned to claim their items after the rental term was complete. In this case, the storage unit's owners have to abide by laws that require them to attempt to locate the owner, and after all else has failed, they may dispose of the stored items to recoup lost rent or to clear up the space for other renters. You may or may not get to look at the actual items stored, and you may have to purchase the entire lot to win the auction, but it's a chance that may be worth taking.

Other businesses, such as dry cleaners, may also have opportunities for you to claim abandoned items—that are already cleaned and pressed!

Even your local newspaper can become a source of merchandise. Regularly scan the classified listings or place an ad stating what type of used items you want to purchase. You may find someone with an entire collection of vinyl records that she inherited from Uncle Bernie twenty years ago and now just wants them out of her closet. The "legal notices" section of your paper may also clue you in to auctions of seized and abandoned property.

 **Better Business Bureau**

*Look for the Better Business Bureau's Online Reliability logo on Web sites of wholesalers, distributors, and drop shippers. Clicking on the BBB's logo on these sites should take you to the Better Business Bureau's Web site. There you will see a message stating the company's compliance. If the logo doesn't take you to the BBB's site or it takes you to a site that doesn't begin with **www.bbb.org**, then report it immediately to the Better Business Bureau.*

- EBay has nearly thirty Certified Service Providers—companies who provide a variety of fee-based extra services to eBay sellers—at this location: **http://developer.ebay.com/programs /certifiedprovider/catalog**

Your own home may be a source of merchandise, at least initially. Often people begin selling items such as their kids' outgrown clothing or items that have been stored away or are no longer being used. If you have a large collection of items that you're no longer interested in, selling them may be a way to test the market and hone some skills in writing auctions (more in Chapter 8). However, unless you've been a serious pack rat all your life and now want to permanently downsize, you'll soon run out of inventory, so this isn't generally considered an ongoing product stream.

You also may purchase individual items from eBay and other Internet auction sites because you can get such a super deal that you can resell that item for profit. Like selling your own personal items, this isn't the best strategy for a product stream, but it never hurts to keep your eyes open. Plus, keep in mind that your acquisition cost for the items you buy online has to include the shipping you paid to get it to you.

To locate items on auction sites that may be had for less than the going rate, perform searches on eBay using commonly misspelled words or search the title and the auction text both for keywords. When the vast majority of lookers can't find an item due to an error on the seller's part, you'll have less competition and better odds at snagging a bargain.

While eBay is the largest of the online auction sites, there are others that may have deals you can resell on eBay. Some of these are Bidz.com, Yahoo! Auctions, Ubid.com, Overstock.com, etc. There are dozens of auction sites online, but the same rule applies to every one: Do your homework to be sure they are reputable and fair.

When considering all the sources of merchandise available to sell, don't overlook your own ingenuity and creativity. Yes, you could be your own best supplier of inventory, whether it be a handmade item or a less tangible e-book.

Writing and selling e-books is a growing trend, and one that can definitely be a money-maker if your product is good. If you have some special knowledge of a topic that would qualify you to write an e-book, you can do so with only basic software. E-books are e-mailed to the buyer upon payment, and Adobe Reader format (PDF files) is the most common format used.

There are software packages available to help you set up your format; add zip with graphics, charts, or illustrations; and other issues that may make your head swim. There are also companies that will (for a fee) assist you. You can even purchase books (paper and e-books) on the subject as well. Just search "write e-book" in your Internet search engine.

- Warning! Read the fine print on any resources you enlist for your e-book venture. Some of them require you to sell and distribute your book through them or will charge you royalties for every copy sold. Make sure you retain the full reseller's rights and copyrights. Be sure that you are the one making the money, not the company that assisted you!

Other types of e-information include booklets, pamphlets, or informational packets. You don't need to have a large enough topic for an entire book for it to be worthwhile to someone else.

If writing isn't your cup of tea, then perhaps you have a unique hobby that produces one-of-a-kind (commonly abbreviated as OOAK) products. Perhaps you've made them for family and friends over the years, and everybody has loved them. People have been telling you for years, "You should make and sell these; they're wonderful!"

While making items can be very time consuming, many buyers appreciate the efforts of custom-made goods. For one thing, they know that their neighbors' children won't be wearing the same exact sweater as the one they bought from your hand-knit supply.

Or perhaps you enjoy woodworking and have a nice workshop set up. Don't hesitate to create some unique items and photograph them well. Save photographs for a portfolio, which you can e-mail to prospective customers to let them see the other wonderful projects you've done.

Your handmade items can be made in advance so you have a supply available to ship immediately, or you may make the items as the orders are placed and paid for. If you choose the latter option, make sure you give a time frame in your auction listing as to the expected delivery after payment is made. If it takes four weeks to make it, be sure your customer knows that. While this may turn away some buyers, it can help you to avoid investing a lot of time and materials in a product that may or may not sell.

Also consider adding a note similar to this one in every auction:

> *"If you like my work but have something in particular in mind or a special request, I'll be pleased to custom make a product for you for the same cost as the 'Buy It Now' price listed plus an additional $XX.XX for _____."*

State the additional cost you charge for doing custom work, and in the blank space, enter what the extra charge will cover (specialty fabrics or yarns needed, higher grade of wood to be used, special paint colors, etc.).

One item previously mentioned that bears repeating is that you must be aware of and follow all copyright and trademark laws when you hand make items and sell them for profit.

This is especially true when making items of clothing. There's nothing illegal about buying a Butterick® sewing pattern and making a cute outfit for your niece. But if you use that same pattern to make an outfit you're selling on eBay as your own OOAK creation, then you are in violation of copyright law. The same is often true of knitting or crocheting, quilting, and woodworking patterns. If you have any questions, contact the pattern maker.

Additionally, when using fabrics, you must be sure that the fabrics you're using are acceptable for commercial use. For example, fabrics with Disney characters on them are not allowed for commercial use. They generally are stamped along the selvage (finished edge) with a statement such as "For home use only; commercial use is prohibited."

If you have any questions about the legality of any particular fabric, contact the manufacturer listed on the selvage or on the bolt's label. The salespeople at the fabric store or your wholesale dealer may also be able to assist you in determining which fabrics are acceptable for commercial use.

For sewers, this can present some problems, such as where to get patterns. There are several good computer software programs that will allow you to create your own custom patterns for commercial use. Unless you can draw the patterns you use freehand, you'd be wise to invest in software to assist you. An Internet search will reveal companies who provide pattern-making services to you for a fee. Compared to the fines you can get for violating copyright laws, this may be the more economical of your options.

Whatever product you personally plan, produce, and sell is also copyrighted. Consider marking your items with copyright information. By law, it's not required that you do so in order for a copyright to be in effect, but it's a smart choice to do so. Use the copyright symbol ©, the year it was created, and your name or company's name. For example: ©2006 My Company Name. Doing so will definitely make it easier to defend your rights in the future if it becomes necessary.

 **EBay VeRO Program**

If you are an artisan or crafter who is selling your original product on eBay, be sure to register with eBay's VeRO program (see Chapter 7) to protect your rights from infringement by others on eBay.

Now you've got some ideas on how to locate merchandise to sell or have been inspired to produce your own product, whether through e-books or OOAK merchandise. Spend as much time as you need on this step, because what you sell ultimately determines your profit.

Once you've made the contacts necessary to secure inventory or a drop-shipping relationship or you've secured a supply of wholesale materials to produce your product, then you're ready to tackle the next set of decisions.

Checklist of Tasks:
Obtaining Merchandise

❑ I have made a list of subjects that I am proficient in or have special knowledge about to consider as possible product lines.

❑ I have done some research to determine if the things I know about are being bought regularly on eBay and, if so, approximately how many people are selling these items.

❑ I have evaluated how much space I have at my disposal for storage of inventory to help me decide if I can work with wholesalers who sell in bulk or if I should consider a drop-shipping relationship with a supplier.

❑ I have made a list of local manufacturers or distributors who may be sources of merchandise.

❑ I have considered the pros and cons of purchasing used items locally (rummaging, estate sales) and decided if I'll include these as a merchandise source.

❑ If I am planning to create custom products for sale, I am aware of all copyright laws and how they may apply to the items I'm making.

Nail Down the Details

Next on your to-do list is choosing how to receive payments and ship items. Don't wait until after you've posted an auction to think about these things, as items may sell very quickly and you'll have a buyer waiting to pay and no idea how you want him or her to pay. If you put something such as "payment and shipping to be determined by the end of the auction" in your item description, people will know you're a newbie and will treat you accordingly (read: buyers are hesitant to do business with people who simply don't know what they're doing). The more savvy the buyer, the less likely they are to be bothered with a seller's incompetence (or unwillingness to do the work ahead of time).

There are numerous ways that you can receive payments from your buyers, and each has its pros and cons. Being aware of all the options can help you make an informed decision that will lead to your company's policy on payments. How you accept payment is up to you, but it's wise to maintain the same policy regardless of the auction item.

The six basic ways to receive payment are this: cash, personal checks, money orders, cashier's checks, escrow services, and PayPal.

Cold, hard cash may seem like a logical choice, but few sellers will accept this payment type, even though they can avoid any PayPal fees and other nuisances (such as check-clearing time) by doing so. For one thing, if you, the seller, never receive the money, the buyer may not believe you or might accuse you of receiving it and not shipping the product (on the flip side, the buyer has no way to prove he sent the cash, and risks appearing like a scam artist if he demands the product be shipped anyway). No seller wants or needs to be put in that predicament. There is no way to track cash, so consider it a risky payment method at best. When sellers do accept cash, often you'll see this notice in their payment policy: cash at your own risk.

Personal checks are another payment form not commonly accepted on eBay. When sellers do accept them, they generally have a disclaimer in their payment terms stating that they will hold merchandise for ten days to assure that the personal check has cleared. Most buyers accept this requirement. The good thing about having a buyer send you a personal check is, like with cash, you avoid any fees from electronic transfers. For the buyer, it's cheaper (and easier) than going out of the way to purchase a money order or certified check.

If you aren't comfortable with personal checks, then consider accepting money orders and certified (bank) checks. Money orders are less secure than bank checks, but both are still considered more secure than personal checks. Most sellers don't hold off shipping until these items clear. However, be warned that there have been many reports of counterfeit Postal Service money orders in the past year or so.

- The FDIC (Federal Deposit Insurance Corporation) Web site has a special bulletin about counterfeit money orders and how to determine if a Postal Service money order is authentic. See **www.fdic.gov/news/news/SpecialAlert/2005/sa2305.html** for this bulletin.

There are numerous companies that sell money orders, so to protect yourself, a good policy is to ship all items after your bank has accepted the money order for deposit. Your bank will be happy to examine any money orders for you.

Cashier's checks are generally considered a very safe form of payment, although most people don't want to pay the extra fees for them (they are often more expensive than money orders) unless you demand it. If you are selling a very expensive item, consider asking for only electronic payments (such as PayPal) or a cashier's check. It's always possible that even these types of checks can be counterfeited, especially if it's from a bank on the other side of the country that you've never heard of. Here again, presenting the check to your bank is the quickest way to be assured that it's legitimate.

Another way to secure payment for those expensive or rare items is by using an escrow service. An escrow service is a third party who receives the money from the buyer and holds it while the seller (knowing that his or her money is secured) ships the product. When the buyer has had a chance to inspect the purchased item, he notifies the escrow service to release the funds to the seller. There are fees involved and the process can take some time, but eBay recommends using an escrow service if the auction price is over $500. Search eBay's help directory for "escrow" to see a list of suggested escrow companies and to read more about the process, fees, and terms.

The final payment option is the electronic payment company, PayPal. This system performs most of their functions directly through the Internet.

PayPal, found at **www.paypal.com**, works by obtaining funds from the buyer's bank account, credit card or debit card. Buyers can choose the funding source(s) they wish to utilize. However, for sellers, this can cause some major headaches.

PayPal has three levels of accounts. There's the personal account, which is primarily meant for eBay users who are buyers. It doesn't work out very well for sellers, especially if you do any volume of business at all. The personal account offers the basic ability, within restrictions, to send and receive money at no charge to buyer or seller.

The restrictions state that sellers can only receive funds from the buyer's registered bank account (this is called an EFT, or electronic funds transfer) or via an e-check (electronic check), which could take several days to clear the buyer's bank. Sellers can also accept funds directly from the buyer's PayPal account, if the account happens to have a standing balance (from auctions the buyer sold, for example). You cannot accept payments made from the buyer's credit or debit card.

Where this gets confusing is this: Everyone knows that debit card funds come directly from a buyer's checking account, right? But the point is that whether debit or credit, PayPal is going to incur fees from the credit card companies for processing these transactions, because debit cards are processed using the numbers on the face of the card, same as credit cards.

And if PayPal incurs fees, you will too.

To ensure you can accept payments from buyers' credit and debit cards, you must sign up for a premiere account. This is a good choice if you're only doing business under your own name, as opposed to a company name (that is, if you've filed a DBA—doing business as—with your state or local government and you're going to be doing all your business under that name, then you'll want to go straight to the business account, page 89).

There are several benefits when using a premiere account, shown on the chart on page 89. The major benefit we'll discuss here is that with a premiere account, you can accept debit and credit card payments as well as EFTs, e-checks, and PayPal funds.

Oh, but there is one little catch: PayPal will deduct a commission before depositing the money into your PayPal account. For sellers who have $3,000 or less coming into their account every month, that fee is a flat 2.9 percent + 30 cents for each transaction. The 2.9 percent is taken from the entire amount of money transferred to you from the buyer—including any shipping and handling charges and sales tax you collect.

 **Payment for Multiple Items**

If you have a buyer bidding on multiple items from you, ask them to hold off paying until all the auctions they are bidding on have ended. Then they can pay all at once and you will only be charged the thirty-cent transaction fee once.

When your sales really take off and you are having more than $3,000 per month routed through your PayPal account, then be sure to check into PayPal's merchant rates, which are lowered percentages (the 30 cent fee is the same). You need to apply for this rate; PayPal doesn't automatically start charging less.

If you want to have the funds in your PayPal account transferred to your bank account, there is no charge, but the process could take several days. This makes it almost easier to purchase postage and business supplies through retailers who accept PayPal payments.

Sellers who only have personal accounts are constantly having to reject payments from buyers who submit from their credit or debit card and ask them to resubmit them by using an EFT or PayPal funds only. This is a headache for buyers and sellers alike.

Some of the blame (if it can be termed as such) lies with PayPal itself. PayPal advertises "choose how you pay," without mentioning that the seller may not be able to accept every one of those payment choices.

Even though PayPal "knows" you have a personal account, the system will "accept" the credit and debit card payments from the buyer and submit it to you — along with a notice that you can't accept this payment unless you agree to bump up to a premiere account (which is what they ultimately want you to do — that's where they make their money!). This puts sellers in the precarious position of going back to the buyer and saying, "I'm sorry, I can't accept your payment."

Buyers, who thought they successfully paid for their item, can get irate over being told that they must either re-submit their payment using a different funding source (such as an EFT or PayPal balance, as opposed to using a debit or credit card) or pay through one of your other approved payment methods.

Buyers who are not also sellers for the most part are insensitive to the seller who doesn't want to pay fees to PayPal. Buyers just want to pay for their items, and PayPal didn't reject their credit card, so why should you? If you reject their payments because you don't have a premiere account, you're likely to find yourself haggling with a buyer who may turn to negative feedback to vent their frustration.

The best advice is this: Suck it up and get the premiere account. It's just part of the cost of doing business. It's simply not worth trying to explain to buyers why you can't accept their payment.

 **PayPal and Credit Cards**

*If you display the PayPal logo in your listings and state that you accept PayPal payments, you cannot state in your listing that PayPal payments made via credit card will not be accepted! This policy can be found at this link: **http://pages .ebay.com/help/policies/seller-non-performance.html***

One strategy that some sellers have tried is to have both types of PayPal accounts and then separate their transactions, so that if the buyer is already planning to pay with PayPal funds, an EFT, or an e-check (the types allowed with a personal account), the seller can avoid paying PayPal fees by directing the buyer to submit payment to his or her personal-level account.

Conversely, if the buyer is planning to pay with a debit or credit card, the seller will then direct the buyer to his or her premiere account and pay the appropriate fees to PayPal. In theory, this is a reasonable plan, but it can cause some serious confusion.

Recall that buyers who aren't also sellers don't differentiate between paying with their debit cards and paying directly out of their bank accounts. To them, it's one and the same. If you have both types of accounts, odds are that you'll still encounter buyers using the wrong account, and then you'll have to reject the payment and ask them to re-submit it to the other account.

Another strategy I've seen in conjunction with this is to insist that the buyer e-mail you before paying, indicating their intended payment type. Then, the seller directs the buyer to the correct PayPal account (rather than expecting the buyer to choose the correct one from information in the auction listing).

However, many buyers actually pay for their items before the seller even knows they've been sold! Having to e-mail the seller and then wait for a response before being able to pay is just plain-old antiquated and it will result in some annoyed and angry buyers. The end result is still this: negative feedback. As a new seller, that's exactly the kind of advertising you don't need.

When it comes to PayPal, you'll be between a rock and a hard place if you try to run any kind of serious business without having the premiere or business account. If you start selling with any volume, trying to manage and direct buyers to different accounts all the time will not only add to the chaos, but really add to your recordkeeping and accounting tasks as well. Is it really worth it to avoid the PayPal fees? You'll have to answer that one for yourself as you learn the ropes and build your business.

The business account is yet another option PayPal offers. It isn't terribly different than a premiere account, but it is necessary for businesses that operate under a business name, as opposed to operating under the owner's name.

Feature	Personal	Premiere	Business
Offer PayPal logo/promo on all listings	X	X	X
Offer "PayPal Preferred" tagline on listings		X	X
End-of-auction e-mail to winning bidder	X	X	X
History log	X	X	X
Downloadable log	X	X	X
Monthly statement		X	X
Refunds to buyers w/ fee credits	X	X	X
Buyer Protection Service	X	X	X
Seller Protection Service	X	X	X
Web site e-commerce tools		X	X
Instant (real-time) payment notification		X	X
Multi-user access to the account		X	X

BidPay was another popular payment option; however due to a corporate buyout, the service is temporarily unavailable. Services are expected to re-launch sometime during summer 2006.

Brief Explanation of Features

PayPal logo and taglines. PayPal can do this automatically, or you can insert a set of logos manually. Go to the "Auction Tools" tab in your account for detailed instructions on setting up either of these options.

End-of-auction e-mail to winning bidder. This is a nice service, because even if you're not online to see your auction actually ending, PayPal will notify the winning bidder and then (if you've already set up your shipping options properly) the bidder can pay immediately via PayPal if he or she wishes. This slick feature benefits PayPal too; by being the first in line to accept the payment, buyers don't have to even think of choosing one of the other options.

History log. The history log lists every transaction for the previous three months, sorted by date. To access it, click on the "History" tab in your account. You can select from several different options for searching the history, by transaction type to searching by date.

Downloadable log. This is a great way to speed along your recordkeeping. Download this log monthly and keep it with your monthly sales ledger. Backing up your data in your sales and inventory ledgers is always a wise move.

Monthly statement. Make sure you sign up to get a monthly statement (go to the "Profile" tab and click "Link") and then go to the site to print it monthly (new statements available on the 15th of the month). Keep it just as you would keep your monthly bank statements. Reconcile it by comparing the totals with your ledger, and if there's any discrepancy, you can compare your downloaded log, transaction by transaction.

TIP **Print PayPal Statements**

PayPal statements are only available for three months back, so if you forget to print one, don't wait too long or it may be gone!

Refunds and fee credits. If you need to make a refund to the buyer, go to the specific transaction. If it's not listed on the "My Account" tab page, then click the link at the bottom of that box that says "All Activity." This takes you to a screen where you can pull up information from the past three months. You can make refunds for up to 60 days after the transaction first took place. Simply click on the transaction you wish to see and click the refund button. PayPal will walk you through the rest of the necessary steps.

If you refund all of the buyer's payment to you, PayPal will refund the fees that they charged. They do not offer a refund of fees if you only make a partial refund to a buyer.

Understanding Buyer and Seller Protection provided by PayPal. You'd be smart to thoroughly read all the information on PayPal's Web site about Buyer and Seller Protections, as this information is just a quick snapshot of the programs. You'll find detailed discussions about these features under the "Auction Tools" tab when you're logged in to your account.

Buyer Protection is available with all account types, but in order for the buyer to be protected, you (the seller) must have done certain things first. Some of these requirements include:

- Your eBay feedback score must be at least 5.0 with 98 percent or better positive feedback.

- You must be a verified member of PayPal.

- You must be a seller in 1 of 20 listed countries (United States and Canada are on the list).

- Your account must be in good standing.

- You must have the "Buyer Protection" icon displayed in your Seller Information box on eBay.

- You must use a shipping service that allows you to track the shipment, in case of a claim that the item was never received.

Buyers also have requirements they must meet, including time limits; they must make their claim within 45 days of the PayPal payment. The buyer also must have paid using the seller's e-mail address as stated in the listing.

Why would a buyer file a claim? If the buyer never receives the item or, as PayPal's Web site terms it, if the item is "significantly not as described." Merely being less than thrilled is not an excuse for filing a claim. Buyers are limited in the number of claims they can make per year as well.

Of course, buyers and sellers are always encouraged to work things out between them first without resorting to filing claims, which should always be a last resort.

PayPal cares about the sellers they serve as well. They offer a Seller

Protection plan that helps prevent fraud. They work hard to prevent fraudulent chargebacks and will help you fight a chargeback if you have sufficient documentation to prove that the chargeback isn't necessary.

Some tips that they offer to help you defend yourself include the following:

- Use tracking tools with every shipment. These can include delivery confirmation (which is required for every shipment when you purchase postage through PayPal), insurance, and actual "tracking" (if you use UPS, FedEx, or other carriers).

- Ship to the buyer's confirmed address only. Be suspicious of buyers who want their items sent to different addresses (especially in different countries). In the transaction details, it will say "Confirmed" after the address.

- Check to see if the buyer's PayPal account is verified, which means that his or her bank account has been confirmed by PayPal. You can check the status of a buyer right from the transaction page. Simply click on the link for Details. Look for this: *Payment From: Seller's Name (the sender of this payment is Verified).*

- Check buyers' eBay feedback for a general view of their reputation.

Web site (e-commerce) tools. If you have your own Web site, PayPal has many features to assist you in collecting payments through their system, right from your own site.

Instant (real-time) payment notifications. PayPal notifies you immediately when a buyer has paid you.

Multi-user access. If you have employees, you can assign them each different levels of access.

PayPal has so many features that, like its parent company eBay, this topic could almost fill a book. It really is important that new users learn as much as they can about PayPal when they first get an account, and even seasoned users may well learn a thing or two by going back and reading up.

One place that all users really should become familiar with is the "Profile" tab on your account page. Here, you can manage every detail of your account and even see what other services or features you may not be using (such as creating custom templates for invoices). It's well worth spending a little time clicking all the links just to learn what you can about how PayPal can work for you.

With over 78 million accounts, PayPal is by far the largest fish in the online payment pond. And because it's an eBay company, it is super easy to use. It is available in 45 countries and in six different currencies. Plan on accepting PayPal for a good share of your payments. Get to know all of the options and utilize all the tools available for your account level. If you make it work for you, your account fees will be well spent.

Getting a handle on payment choices is a large task, and hopefully you'll have that one under control before you start your first auction. Trying to scramble and set things up after the fact won't help you project a very professional image.

Another detail that takes some thought and planning is choosing your shipping provider(s). There is no rule that says you must ship via one provider or the other. The choice is pretty much up to you and may be based on which provider you can most easily access. The three most common shipping providers are the Unites States Postal Service (USPS), Federal Express (FedEx), and United Parcel Service (UPS), although there are several others. Let's take a brief look at each provider's basic features, the tools they offer eBay sellers, and some of the intricacies of shipping internationally. We'll look at how you list a buyer's shipping options in auctions in Chapter 9.

Of course, you'll have to be flexible when it comes to shipping, to a certain degree. Some buyers may have only a post office box, and neither FedEx nor UPS will deliver to them. Others may have a very rural address that is difficult to find, making the USPS a better choice. Additionally, with USPS there are different levels of pricing, from the economical Parcel Post all the way to the zippy (and pricy) Overnight services. Buyers may not care if they don't receive the item for two weeks as long as they can save money on shipping costs, so be prepared to offer as many choices as you can without being counterproductive.

Another decision you'll have to make is how frequently you'll ship items.

This varies greatly based on what shipper you use and if they'll do home pickups of packages or if you have to haul them to the shipper. Some sellers pick certain days of the week that they'll ship (such as Monday and Thursday) while others ship every single weekday. What you're capable of must also be balanced with the level of customer service you hope to provide. Obviously, buyers want their items shipped fast, preferably within one business day of sending payment. Determine what's feasible for you, and make sure you state your shipping schedule clearly in your auction listing (more in Chapter 9).

The United States Postal Service (USPS, found at **www.usps.com**) has really worked hard to secure their piece of the Internet shipping pie. They are a preferred shipping provider for eBay and are nicely integrated with eBay's shipping calculators (when you set up auctions) and PayPal. In 2005, USPS and eBay paired up to offer eight "eBay Day Small Business Tour" workshops to eBay sellers around the country. These one-day workshops were offered free and gave sellers a chance to get one-on-one assistance on building a business, selling, and shipping.

Whether you plan to take your packages to the post office yourself or purchase postage online through the USPS's Web site or PayPal, you'll need to know how much shipping is going to cost. Buyers are accustomed to having shipping costs stated outright or being able to use the shipping calculator, right in the auction listing, to determine their choices and costs. Gone are the days when "contact seller for shipping quote" is the standard phrase on all auctions. Buyers want accurate information before bidding, in most cases.

There are a couple of reasons for this. The main one is that they need to weigh the cost of shipping against going locally to a traditional store and purchasing the item. Sure, you may sell an item not available in just any store, but odds are that it is available elsewhere, even if online. If your shipping costs aren't competitive with another Web site, you may lose the sale. Comparing shipping costs is standard in Internet comparison-shopping nowadays.

The second reason is that a buyer wants to assess your shipping and handling fees. When you add a shipping and handling fee (while setting up the shipping calculator, Chapter 9), the buyers don't see this fee separately; it's all tabulated in the total cost given when they enter their zip code into the calculator.

However, many buyers aren't fooled by the fact that they can't specifically see the shipping and handling charge. If you are selling a paperback book and the media mail quote comes back at $8, the buyer is going to know that you heavily padded your shipping and handling. There are differing views on shipping and handling charges, and you're going to have to make your own decisions about what your policy will be.

See what other eBay sellers have to say about shipping policies and how they handle their shipping and handling charges (Chapter 11). Join the eBay discussion boards and ask others to tell you their feelings about the topic. Then make up your own mind about how you'll handle this choice. Shipping and handling charges will also be discussed more in Chapter 9.

However, it is imperative for you to know what the item you're selling will cost to ship. This can be done easily on the USPS's Web site under the "Calculate Postage" link. This easy-to-use tool prompts you for the necessary information, which generally is the type of item (envelope, box, etc.), the weight, and the zip codes of origin and destination. Then it will present you with all your options and the applicable costs. It's as simple as that. Bookmark this tool and use it to calculate postage on any item when you know the destination zip code.

 **Flat-Fee Shipping Rates**

If you want to offer flat-fee shipping (same price for everybody) via USPS, use their online calculator and enter a "From" zip code on one end of the country (such as New York City, NY 10001) and a "To" zip code at the other end (such as Beverly Hills, CA 90210). This will give you the maximum postage needed for that package coast to coast.

This tip was offered by eBay seller Linda (username "LindaCatNH"), who lives in New Hampshire. When she calculates shipping this way, she enters her zip code and then a zip code in California. That's about as far away from New Hampshire that you can get, postal zone-wise, she notes. Add a note in your auction for buyers in Hawaii and Alaska that the cost will be recalculated before they pay.

Linda is known by her customers as an honest seller, partly because she has occasionally had a buyer who happened to be in a neighboring state, or even closer. When they're that close, she sometimes recalculates the flat-fee shipping cost and refunds a portion of the shipping fee. Call it nepotism for Northeasterners, if you will!

Generally, you won't know the destination zip code until your auction is complete and the buyer has been identified. When setting up your auction, if you have an accurate weight for the parcel, use that to set up the shipping calculator. Then the buyer can enter their zip code themselves and get an accurate shipping quote.

Obviously, in order to get an accurate shipping weight for an item, you'll have to have it boxed up with the packing material (crumpled paper, packing peanuts, bubble wrap, etc.) already in as well. It may not be wise to tape up the box just yet; a bidder may want an additional photo or you might later put in a thank-you note or a receipt for the buyer.

One of the first items that you will need to purchase for a successful eBay business is a modern, digital, postage-type scale. These items are reasonably priced and can be easily found at an office supply store or right on eBay. Giving your customers accurate shipping quotes right in the auction listing is simply the easiest and best way to go. When you weigh the box, add two ounces or so to the weight on the scale and use that as your shipping weight. Merely adding a receipt or note and tape can bump the box up to a completely different weight, and you may end up eating excess postage charges because of it.

For your boxing needs, the USPS has a line of co-branded boxes that you can obtain for free (co-branded, meaning that they have an eBay logo as well as the USPS logo on the box). There are three sizes available, plus two sizes that are flat-rate boxes (meaning the price is the same for shipping regardless of destination or weight). With all of these boxes, there are certain restrictions, so be sure to read up on them on eBay's Web site. All of these boxes are free to sellers to obtain (on eBay's site), but note that they cannot be used to ship items for any other mail class than Priority or Express (depending on the particular item), nor can they be used for anything but mailing auction items.

Other USPS (not co-branded) items (including tubes, labels, delivery confirmation forms, etc.) are available at their Web site. Generally, there is no cost for these items, but the boxes, tubes, and envelopes are for Priority or Express mail only. You'll still have to supply your own boxes for other mail classes or for items that don't fit into the standard box sizes.

You can also purchase USPS postage (including extras like insurance and delivery confirmation) right through PayPal, and then track the package right from your PayPal account as well.

If you purchase Priority postage, there are no fees in addition to the actual postage and insurance fee. Delivery confirmation is free with Priority Mail and only $0.13 for other mail classes (as opposed to $0.55 if you were to take that same package to a post office and purchase postage there).

When you purchase postage online through PayPal, you also have the opportunity to schedule a pickup by your local post office. This is especially nice if you don't live a stone's throw from a post office or if you're going to be away from your home but you want to make sure that the boxes get shipped.

If there is going to be inclement weather or if it's not safe to leave an unattended package near your mailbox, then you may have to get creative. If you have a covered porch, you can call your local post office and give them instructions on where the package will be (or tape a note to your mailbox), or get a plastic storage bin with a tight-fitting lid and set it next to your mailbox.

For people who live in condominiums or apartment complexes, often the manager's office will serve as a drop-off location for outgoing packages.

Call your local post office and ask them for suggestions as well. They are happy to help you in any way possible and want to make sure your items get there securely and quickly.

Just a few quick ideas about shipping supplies: Linda in New Hampshire (eBay user "LindaCatNH") also has a good suggestion for obtaining free boxes (if you're shipping items that don't fit in the free boxes from shipping providers or using services such as Parcel Post or Media Mail). She says that she isn't ashamed to go "dumpster diving" for boxes that have been discarded by retailers, but she also notes that most store owners are happy to have her take them even before they are put in the dumpster, to avoid having to recycle or dispose of them themselves.

To make a box appear less like a case of frozen peas and more like a new container, she separates it at the glued side and flips it inside out, re-taping securely. This gives her a clean slate for the postage and address label and also gives the box at least one more use. Recycling is important to Linda, and she hopes that her rejuvenating efforts pay off and people continue to re-use that same box.

Packing materials such as Styrofoam peanuts or bubble wrap can be expensive and environmentally unfriendly as well. I have found that my local newspaper will sell what they call "end rolls," basically the end of the huge roll of paper used to print newspapers on, for a very reasonable fee. This paper has not been used, therefore there is no ink to get on your hands or on the merchandise. The rolls vary in size, but for the small fee there is no more economical packing material around. Check with your local newspaper or printing presses about end rolls or other materials you could recycle into packing materials.

 ## Create Your Packaging Materials

Even your ordinary "junk" mail can become packing material. Purchase a small shredder (not one that does crosscut shredding, just the one that shreds in strips) and shred your junk mail (not anything with sensitive information on it) as needed. When you need packing material, just reach into the container and grab a handful! If you have kids, this is a good way for them to earn allowance; plus, they feel like they're helping you with your business. Let them make an invoice for their fees, and you'll be teaching them how to do business themselves!

Many eBay sellers have found creative ways to store any packing materials that come into their home (or friends' and families' homes as well) to re-use for their auction shipping. Go to the eBay "Community" tab (on the top toolbar) and check out the discussion boards. There's even one dedicated to packing and shipping questions. If you don't find what you're looking for on the first couple of pages, then ask a question; you'll get plenty of suggestions on how to obtain, recycle, and store shipping materials.

If there is one thing that the USPS doesn't do as well as their competition, it's tracking. Delivery confirmation and insurance, while nice for the protections they do provide, are not tracking. Since you don't receive any verification that the package arrived (you merely use your delivery-confirmation receipt or insurance receipt as a tool to ask for proof of delivery if the buyer claims they did not receive it or it was damaged), you don't even know if the package arrived until the buyer leaves feedback (or contacts you otherwise). For sellers who like to be privy to every little detail, this can be annoying.

With the USPS, tracking is available only for Express Mail packages. For other classes, you need to purchase a signature confirmation or return receipt, which will add significantly to your shipping costs. And while they don't provide tracking, at least you are notified when the package is delivered. But if you are shipping an item via Priority, Parcel Post, or First Class, and you have to know when it arrived, these are your only options other than going to another shipper.

Federal Express (FedEx) focused on the overnight-delivery market in the early years of their business, but now they also serve the world's slower shipping needs with their FedEx Ground service as well as standard overnight service. Their Web site, **www.fedex.com,** can direct you to all your shipping options. Go to the "Welcome Center" (left-hand side of home page) and click on "New Customer Center" to set up an order and learn about all FedEx will do to gain you as a customer.

Their Web site is easy to use and has excellent drop-down menus to let you navigate quickly through the tasks you'll need to perform. Their online tracking system is excellent, letting you see details such as when the package arrived in a certain location, and even when it's out on a truck for delivery! FedEx also has shipping materials available online, or you can pick up materials at any FedEx location.

FedEx's online calculator walks you through simple steps, asking you how soon the package needs to be delivered, general weight, and other information. It gives you sample prices based on examples (such as New York to Los Angeles, 1 pound, $X.XX). While it may not be an exact quote for you, it gives you an idea what ballpark you're looking at.

Paying for your FedEx shipments is made simple by a variety of choices. You can be billed monthly or set up your account to do an EFT to pay for a shipment. There are other options as well, which you will learn about when you set up an account.

If you're going to use FedEx on any regular basis, it's worth getting an account and handling all the options online rather than going to a physical location.

The **United Parcel Service** (UPS) is not about to be outdone when it comes to online services, either. Their user-friendly Web site boasts all the great features of their competitors: online tracking, online shipping calculations, and more. From their home page (**www.ups.com**), click on the "Business Solutions" link, and then the link that says "I am a small business owner" to learn about all the ways that UPS is anxious to be your shipper of choice. Just a few of the tools they offer include:

- Storage of your customers' addresses online. If you have a lot of repeat customers, this could be a nice time-saver.

- Advanced tracking tools for business owners.

- Arrange for pickup.

- Create shipping labels for up to 20 packages at a time on their site.

- E-mail notifications of deliveries, so you don't have to check tracking.

While the USPS seems to have got the lion's share of business on eBay, the other shipping companies have some great features that make them worth looking into. Depending on your product, you may find that one shipper far exceeds the others in ease and service. Like the USPS, you can purchase and print UPS labels right from your computer, for both domestic and international shipments (including the customs forms). Especially for items that are too large for USPS requirements, this handy feature makes UPS very competitive with the USPS in that regard.

All three shipping companies we have been looking at can assist you in your international shipments as well. For sellers who are just starting out, the mere process of shipping internationally could make your head swim. However, with some patience and practice, you'll soon be writing up customs forms like they were last week's grocery list.

EBay's policies state very clearly that it is the responsibility of the seller to be sure that their items are legal to sell in any foreign country that they are offering to sell in. Don't let this policy scare you away from considering international sales, however. It's not very difficult to determine what is prohibited or restricted in other countries around the globe. Every country has its own rules about what its occupants may import. To get a handle on what could otherwise be a very confusing topic, bookmark and check the USPS's International Mail Manual, found at **http://pe.usps.gov/text/imm/welcome.htm**. If you discover that your product is prohibited or restricted, then it is not acceptable for you to even offer to sell it to the country with the restriction/prohibition.

 **International Selling**

EBay has the answers to many common questions about international selling and shipping. Explore the link **http://pages.ebay.com/globaltrade/index.html**. *Plus, they have assembled an International Selling Toolkit for you to download. This ten-page PDF file is part of this list of tips:* **http://pages.ebay.com/internationaltrading/sellertips.html**.

The USPS's International Mail Manual discusses shipping with the expectation that you are utilizing the USPS's products and services, but regardless of what shipping company you are using, the Index of Countries and Localities will be useful to any seller who ventures into international shipping. If reading the information in the manual is more confusing than reading a foreign language, then print out the information for the country you need to ship to and go to your local post office. Someone will take the time to explain the relevant items that you need to know for that country. (Note: if your post office is generally a beehive of activity, call ahead to see when their slower times are or ask to make an appointment.) Much of the information in the index won't apply to your occasional eBay shipments. The more educated you are about this topic, the less frightening this will be.

For example, who knew that you can't sell a watch to a buyer in Mauritania? Or that you simply cannot ship photo albums of any kind to Italy? Checking these lists against any countries that you are considering shipping to will save you time. If your product is prohibited in one country, it may well be in many others.

If you're really interested in the details of shipping to countries all over the world, check out the World Customs Organization's Web site at **www.wcoomd.org** and then click on "Customs Web Sites" on the left-hand side of the home page (if everything is in French, go "back" one page and find the link to the English version of the site). The "Customs Web Sites" page will help you explore the Web sites of customs departments all over the globe.

If you choose not to offer international shipping, it's polite to say so right in your auction listing or templates. A simple statement such as "We are only able to ship to locations in the United States only" or "We are not able to ship internationally at this time" is probably sufficient.

While most international bidders will respect your policy, there may be some who will either not read your listing closely enough or will bid and, if they win, hope that you'll go through the trouble to ship it to them anyway.

If you are willing to delve into international shipping, be sure to fill in the international shipping calculator when you set up your auction so that buyers will be able to see up front what their costs will be. Another thing to make clear in your auction text is that any duties (taxes paid to the country of destination) are the obligation of the buyer. Most international buyers understand this, but it never hurts to cover this base in case you get a novice buyer. For their part, buyers may be able to determine what their customs fees will be in advance of bidding. This should always be strongly suggested.

Regardless of what shipping company you use, you'll have to provide documents for customs. All packages sent to other countries must have certain information, such as a declared value of the contents, so standard forms have been developed to provide that information.

USPS Form 2976 (also known as the short form) is used for shipments weighing less than four pounds. USPS Form 2976-A (which is the multi-part longer form) is used for parcels over four pounds. When using this second form, you'll also need to use a 2976-E Customs Declaration Envelope. You can get these forms at your local post office or order them from their site, if you do a lot of international shipping.

While the USPS and other shipping companies may have their own forms, they cover pretty much the same information, so once you're familiar with one version, the others will be easy to use as well.

Tips for Filling Out Customs Forms

- Fill them out in English. If you are fluent in an officially-recognized language of the destination country, you may provide a translation for the "contents" section along with the English (U.S. customs officials need to be able to read it too).

- Describe the "contents" briefly, with no abbreviations or American slang.

- Fill in the "value" in U.S. dollars; the customs agents will do any conversion if needed.

- Make sure you've checked that your item isn't prohibited or restricted.

- Don't forget an address label; customs forms don't do double-duty.

- Attach the completed form to the lower left side of package top (same side as address label).

- You may be required to enclose the recipient's name, address, and/or telephone number inside the package; check with your shipper for details.

- Insure your package, if at all possible.

The USPS's Web site allows you to fill out the customs forms online at **http://Webapps.usps.com/customsforms/welcome.htm**. This page also has a link to the Index of Countries and Localities already mentioned as well as a rate calculator available right there. The lookup of postal codes is also built in, so you don't have to go searching the site for the tools you'll need to complete the form. Both forms are available on that page, as well as the military versions (for mailing to APO/FPO addresses).

FedEx and UPS also assist you in completing customs forms online and printing them. This saves time when you drop off your package and is necessary if your package is being picked up at your location. These two companies, however, offer mostly "expedited" shipping in foreign countries. Unless your buyer wants the item fast and is willing to pay for it, you may not find any useful choices with these carriers, but it doesn't hurt to ask!

TIP Custom Forms

Some countries require that a copy of the invoice be included in an envelope with the customs form, even though you have declared the "value" of the item on the customs form. Be sure to check this out before heading to your shipping company's location, or you may waste yourself a trip. Make it a policy to include one with every international shipment.

International buyers have been known to ask sellers to lower the value of the item to reduce their tax assessment (duty) in their own country. It is illegal (and against eBay's policies) to misrepresent the value of the item for this purpose. The value of the item is exactly the price they paid for it (minus shipping and handling they paid). Your invoice should reflect exactly what the buyer paid.

Marking the item as a "gift" is also against everyone's rules. The only time that this might be appropriate is if you are sending a replacement for damaged goods. However, check with your shipping company to see how they would suggest you mark the package in this event.

If you are selling an item that is new and has a price tag on it with a significantly higher amount than the actual sales price, you may remove the price tag if the buyer wishes. This is to avoid the buyer having to over-pay their taxes should customs agents open the package (which they can do at their discretion). Removing price tags that do not reflect what they buyer paid is not illegal.

For more information about eBay's policies regarding international sales, including numerous helpful links to agencies and Web site that are able to assist you with special situations and general information, see this site:

http://pages.ebay.com/help/policies/international-trading.html.

Now that you've covered payment and shipping options, let's move on to something a little more exciting: promoting yourself and your business! There are so many ways to get the word out, from old standbys to the outrageous. How you choose to portray yourself and your business has a lot to do with your future success, so choose wisely based on your product, your budget, and your own personal preferences.

Checklist of Tasks:
Choosing Shipping Providers

❑ I am aware of all the possible ways to receive payments, including the pros and cons of each, and have decided on which ones I will accept in my eBay business.

❑ I will be fair when adding a handling charge to the cost of shipping.

❑ I have (or will) purchased a digital scale for determining the weight of items so that my customers can obtain accurate shipping quotes right in the auction body.

❑ I have (or can) located sources of reclaimed or recycled materials for packing to save the cost of purchasing new materials, if possible.

❑ I have researched international shipping and made a decision about whether or not I will offer this option. If not, I can always offer it later.

Advertising: Blow Your Own Horn

If you're still reading, you are obviously very serious about getting your business off on the right foot! Though these tasks are a time-consuming aspect of being your own boss, doing research (such as reading this book) and taking time to set things up properly is really the only bona fide way to go about this.

Next on our ever-growing list of details is how to advertise yourself on and offline. If you were starting a traditional business in your hometown, there are numerous things you'd do to spread the word, but placing an ad in your local newspaper probably isn't going to get the word out to, oh, 135 million people worldwide!

So how are you going to let the entire eBay community know you're there, ready, willing, and able to sell? There are many ways to make you more visible on eBay. Even small things can make a difference, so consider using all the resources you have available at little or no cost to you.

First, let's take a brief look at the free marketing strategies you should be employing. Ebay offers every seller these five free ways to make your listings stand out.

Cross-Promotions. This is the box at the bottom of your listing that says "Other Great Items From This Seller," and it doesn't cost you anything to have it. To get it, go to your "My eBay" page and click on "Preferences" (under "My Account") and click the link that says "Promoting Similar Items on eBay Pages and E-mails." Edit your promotion preferences here. If you're utilizing all the cross-promotions available, it will say "Participate in cross-promotions" and then "Yes in all available areas" after that. That's it: free help from eBay to drive lookers and buyers to all your other listings (and your store: a link to your store is placed in that box as well).

Some of the places that your cross-promotions will be displayed include the e-mails sent to non-winning bidders letting them know they did not win the auction. When someone places your item on their Items I'm Watching page, they will see some of your other cross-promoted items as well. Even when a buyer pays an invoice through PayPal, they'll again be shown a choice of items that they can purchase from you!

Check Out My Other Listings. Even though eBay puts up a nifty box of your other auctions, it is at the bottom of the auction page, and sometimes it just doesn't get noticed. So while you're writing out your auction text, make sure to add a link (you'll learn how in Chapter 9) to your other listings.

Cross-Promotion Connections. You can make arrangements with other sellers to promote each other's items. This is great if you sell widgets but not the specialty cleaner that keeps your widget looking new! Cross-promote with the sellers who sell complementary items, not competing items. Check out the information under "My Account" and "Cross-Promotion Connections."

"About Me" Page. Every eBay member has the opportunity to create an "About Me" page at no cost to the member. Some people post pictures of pets, local tourist attractions, or themselves, giving their customers a "face." Others are more businesslike, sharing information about their merchandise or customer-service philosophy. If you haven't yet made your "About Me" page, do so soon.

To create your page, go to "Community" (on the top toolbar) and scroll to the bottom of the page, where you'll see a link inviting you to create a page. The step-by-step instructions walk you through a series of boxes where you type in your text, make your choices, and preview your page.

You can use your own HTML, if you're lucky enough to know that already (Appendix B is an HTML primer, so be prepared to learn it eventually). Enter your HTML simply by clicking on the "HTML" tab.

If you're like many new sellers and haven't been exposed to much HTML yet, never fear. All you have to do is use the drop-down menus to choose your font type, size, and color. The buttons for bold, italic, underline, numbering, bullets, etc., are all pretty much standard (they should look just like those in any word-processing software you use).

Spend a little time making your page interesting to look at. Don't use a font that's too small or too large (it will appear as if you're shouting). Use different colors for the different sections (such as personal information, business information, policies, and customer service).

You can also link to photos that you have stored online or your company's logo, if you have one already.

Even if you just put up some basic information, at least it's a start. Surf around eBay and look at other seller's pages (there isn't any way to search "About Me" pages; you need to just click on the "me" logo after any seller's name you encounter on the site) to get ideas for your own page (don't steal any logos or photos, though!).

Personal information should be friendly and interesting, but perhaps not too personal. You don't want to offend potential customers by stating any views on controversial topics. Additionally, for security reasons, it may not be wise to get too detailed about where you live or the identity of other family members, especially any minors who live in your home.

Pets, however, are definitely a good thing to talk about and share photos of. Also, your travels, the seasonal scenery in your part of the country, or a photo of your workshop might be appropriate. If you make your product by hand, show an item in different stages of completion and perhaps a description of how the item is made with care and attention to details.

Business information you might want to share could include your mission statement (from your business plan) and your customer-service philosophy. If you haven't yet put one to paper, here's a good time to do so. Your statement might read something like this:

Our goal is to serve all our customers in a timely manner with fair prices, speedy delivery, and service after the sale! We want to make every customer a repeat customer. If there's anything about our service that you feel needs improvement, feel free to e-mail me personally at WillysWidgets@e-mailprovider.com.

If your product has any exemplary features or has won any awards, praise, or good reviews, cite these (and the source that you got this information from) as well. For example:

Our widgets are made by the finest facility in North America. The *Widget Review* (July 2005) states that "these widgets outperform every other model on the market. You can't go wrong when you invest in this easy-to-maintain and quiet-running model!"

EBay will also ask you to choose if you want any current items listed to appear after your text. You can even choose how many items you want to provide links to. Additionally, you can have your last 10, 25, or more feedback listings displayed, with a link inviting the reader to go to your member profile and view all your feedback.

Good feedback is something that sellers are proud of, and you should always take the opportunity to share your well-deserved feedback rating. More about feedback in Chapter 10.

You'll also be able to insert links to Web sites, including your own company's site, with certain restrictions that are clearly laid out (click the link on the "About Me" creation page), and HTML images (use the same method for inserting photos in your listings, see Chapter 9). To further personalize your page, you can choose from one of three layouts, and then preview your information in the chosen layout. If you want to see the other layouts, simply go back and choose again.

 **Editing Your "About Me" Page**

Editing your page follows the same process. To edit your page, go to the page and scroll to the bottom. There you will find a link directing you through the editing process. Keep your page current, and edit it anytime you have a new product line or announcement to make about your business. Also, try changing the photos seasonally; this helps those looking at the page know it's current.

When your page is complete, eBay will provide you with a link to your new "About Me" page, which you should make a point of writing down. Add it to your e-mail templates or signature so that every business e-mail you send points prospective customers to your page, which highlights your product and your feedback. Are you starting to see how it all connects together to form a chain link of marketing?

Linking to and from eBay. Promote your eBay store, your "About Me" page, and auctions on other Web sites or via your e-mail. In addition to using your "About Me" page link (above), you will be able to link people directly from their e-mail to your store when the e-mail is opened. When you link from your "About Me" page, make sure you are within the requirements of eBay's policy; linking from your "About Me" page to your own personal Web site (or domain name, see below) is really important.

You can't link from your "About Me" page to another auction site that you also may sell on; it must be to your own personal Web page. However, on that Web page, you can link to other sites you auction on as well. Check out eBay's policies thoroughly before linking; you certainly don't want to offend the company who is helping your business get a good running start!

Linking is an important part of Internet marketing via e-mail and message boards, which are also considered "free" marketing techniques. We've looked at e-mail before, but it bears repeating: use e-mail to its full potential. It doesn't cost anything to add links to your eBay store, your "About Me" page, or your personal Web site in an e-mail. Use the signature section (an option you need to actually use and fill out in your e-mail provider's setup) to place this information in every e-mail for you, so you don't have to retype or copy/paste the links all the time.

Start saving your customers' e-mail addresses right away. Use your address lists to announce new products or other big news from your business. You don't want to bombard your customers with e-mails, as you may then be relegated to their "blocked senders" lists, but you don't want them to forget you, either. Seasonal e-mails can be a happy medium. For every season, e-mail your customer list with a new announcement, product promotion, and a wish for their happiness in the months to come until you e-mail them again. Make sure to express your sincere desire to do business with them again!

Don't forget the "opt-out" message (see page 8). All businesses must be sensitive to customers who don't wish to receive e-mail, so keep your own list of those who contact you and wish to opt-out.

You should probably also include a statement about what you do with your collected customer e-mail addresses. Be sure to let customers know that you value their business and that you have no intentions of ever selling, renting, or trading e-mail addresses with anybody else.

If you're looking for a way to supplement your own customer database, you can purchase e-mail address lists that are generated from "opt-in" clauses on Web sites. These are generally considered more reputable sources of e-mail addresses than some other lists you can buy, but beware that you still may be regarded as spam by the recipients. Be sure to make clear in your e-mail title that you are not spam. Many companies also offer to actually do the e-mailing for you, using opt-in lists they have on file. There are scam artists posing as reputable marketing companies who simply send spam with your company name attached to it. Tread very carefully when contracting with any other company to do the e-mailing for you.

For the most part, at least for now, obtain your e-mail list from your own customer base and guard it carefully. Your customers will thank you for protecting their privacy and not adding to the spam in their inbox every day.

Another possibility for your seasonal e-mail is to use a "newsletter" format, with advice on other products compatible with yours or of a general nature. For example, Willy's winter e-mail might be a newsletter format with a list of the "Top 10 Ways a Widget or Gidget Can Make Your Life Easier During the Winter Months" and maybe include general tips on how to conserve electricity and cut heating bills. Even though widgets and gidgets may have nothing to do with heat or electricity, this information is almost universally applicable in the winter.

Sprinkle little tidbits of interest in a newsletter; a very brief poem, humorous quote, or anecdote from one of your customers. If you feature a customer's comment or quote every time, you may find your customers giving you material just hoping to be featured in the newsletter.

To make a newsletter universally readable by your customers, you'll have to use a software that will transpose your format (whether your use something basic like Microsoft Publisher or Adobe Acrobat) into a PDF file. There are reasonably priced programs available to do this (of course, if you're using Adobe Acrobat, you won't need separate software) and one of the best (in my opinion) is found at this site: **www.pdf995.com**.

This software is available for free. You will have to tolerate a pop-up box asking you to purchase a package of products, which is very reasonably priced, every time you use it, but even if you choose not to purchase the additional products, the basic product will convert your Publisher, Word, or most any other file to a PDF format.

You'll also need some graphics for your newsletter. Microsoft products contain built-in connections to their Web site where you can search through literally thousands of clipart and Web images. There are many clipart studios that you can purchase at any software retailer that are worthwhile as well. When comparing, make sure you purchase one that allows you access to the company's Web site and any new clipart that is produced after the discs you purchase were made.

Since your newsletter will be sent via e-mail, you can offer special discounts to these valued customers. Insert a link to a current product in your store and offer a discount, such as free shipping, for those who buy in the next 48 hours. Instruct them to delete the shipping charge during the eBay checkout process. You can compare their e-mail addresses to those on your list to make sure they are customers who had received your newsletter, and not a new customer who accidentally deleted the shipping charge.

Internet chat rooms. Internet chat rooms and message boards can also be a way to spread the word about your eBay business. Check around for eBay-related sites that aren't affiliated with eBay. There are dozens of Yahoo! Groups devoted to eBay, some of which exist only for members to post their listings, specials, and links to their store. There is no cost involved to you; just a few minutes of your time to post the information. Try looking for message boards and chat rooms devoted to your particular product, as you'll probably not generate much interest in your heavy metal music sales if you're posting ads on a board of senior citizens who are looking to buy travel-related products.

These suggestions aren't all-encompassing in regards to marketing yourself for free. Check out the eBay "Community" discussion boards on this topic; you'll learn some tricks of the trade without having to figure them out the hard way!

Few businesses can survive solely on the free marketing that they can do. While it's important to utilize every possible opportunity you get to advertise your business for free, you will probably have to pay for some services as well. Let's look at some marketing ideas that are worth paying for next.

As with the free marketing ideas listed above, we'll begin by looking at the for-a-fee services that eBay offers first. It only makes sense that if you're using eBay as your primary selling tool, you'll also utilize every possible option eBay has to market your business and products.

Probably one of the most common tools used by sellers is the **eBay Store**. The fees for having your own eBay store are reasonable, if you were to compare the price for renting a traditional store space or regularly placing ads in the local newspaper. Once you are a registered eBay seller and have earned a feedback score of 20 (more about how feedback is calculated later in this chapter), you're eligible to open a store.

EBay suggests that you open a store when you're ready to sell regularly. This isn't really a good choice for the occasional seller because there are ongoing fees. Also, you should have sufficient inventory and a regular product stream set up. The basic eBay store can be had for just $15.95 per month, with the first 30 days at no cost to you.

The benefits of having your own eBay store are numerous, including:

- A professional presence on eBay that says "I'm not just an occasional seller."

- Lower listing fees for store inventory items.

- Longer listing times (or never-ending listings) for store inventory.

- Categorize your merchandise how you choose; five pages in your store.

- A place to showcase all your listings, including current auctions.

- Selling Manager software use for free.

- Cross-promotions in more places for store sellers.

- Link a domain name directly to your store.

- Final Value Fee credits if your off-eBay referral buys from your store inventory.

- Accounting Assistant (software that works with QuickBooks).

- Free e-mail marketing tools.

- Sales reports for your store and other listings.

- Special features for upgraded store types (Featured and Anchor Stores).

Having an online presence is very important, and having a permanent storefront is one way to achieve that. Whether you have the basic or the Anchor Store, you can use eBay's tools (or your own HTML) to create a great looking store that showcases your merchandise. It takes time to set up a store that "looks" zippy and professional, but if you take the time to read all the associated help files and utilize the built-in tools, you'll soon have a great-looking store that will be appealing to look at and not appear just like another auction listing page.

Your store will show all of your current listings, whether they are fixed-price listings, auctions, or "store inventory" listings (which are sold through "Buy It Now" only). What do you choose to put into inventory and what to auction?

Well, there are differing theories about this, and really it will depend on your product. If you sell primarily the same products over and again, then you should always run some auctions, because when lookers do a search from the home page (at the top right), they'll see auctions, including fixed-price listings, in their results, not store inventory.

If a looker's search turns up thirty or fewer results, then up to thirty store inventory listings will appear after the auction listings. If the search turns up more than thirty results, then there will be a link at the bottom of the page letting buyers know that the same items can be located in eBay stores. All they have to do is click to be taken to a page of store listings.

If a search turns up no auction or fixed-price listings matching the searcher's criteria but there are store inventory items that match, then up to thirty of the store inventory items will be displayed with a gallery photo (a photo that is displayed in the actual search result, as opposed to the green camera icon that normally displays unless you pay the extra fee for the gallery photo).

So what's the difference between a fixed-price auction and a store inventory item? Primarily, the number of days that it is available for sale. Fixed-price auctions run the same as regular auctions, for one, three, five, seven, or ten days only. In your store, you will be able to set up your inventory items to be for sale for 30, 60, 90, or 120 days (or for all eternity... or until you cancel it). You can convert any store inventory item back to an auction item at any time, if you wish to do so.

Why would you want to have a listing never expire? This is for items that you always stock or always produce. But don't start mentally adding up the listing fees just yet; when you list store inventory items, the listing price is currently two cents for a whole thirty days! The Final Value Fees are higher for store inventory items, though. See the charts of eBay store fees at the end of the chapter.

You're thinking *Yippee!*, right? Just hold on a second; don't forget that your store won't get the same type of exposure as auctions in the buyer's basic search (there is no way for buyers to specify that they want to search store inventory only or in addition to auctions), so you would be wise to still run auctions. Think of them as a tool to drive people to your store.

Not to say that stores are entirely without their own promotion. Your store will be listed in the directory of all stores, which can be easily accessed from the home page. Some people prefer to buy from a store rather than wait it out in an auction, so they search by going to the eBay stores page first.

On the "eBay Stores" page, the buyer can search by store names or by matching items. So for Willy, if a buyer wants to find out who's selling gidgets in an eBay store, they can search "gidget" and the search will return a list of stores that currently list a gidget in their inventory. This is the only place on eBay that lookers can go to search specifically in store's inventory.

But don't rely on buyers always doing a search on the "eBay Stores" page; write a sentence or two that you will always include in every auction text, suggesting that the looker could find much more variety and choice in your store. Save your text in a word-processing software and insert it into every auction (you'll learn how to do this in Chapter 9) and make sure to put it in your Turbo Lister templates (Appendix B goes over this free software from eBay). The point is to get lookers to check out your store, even if they're not as interested in the auction item once they've seen it.

One word of warning, however: Let's say you want to promote your store in every one of your auction listings, as suggested above. That's a great thing to do, but you have to be sure you don't engage in what's known as keyword spamming. In short, your invitation to view your store can't refer to your store items by their brand names or even their keywords.

Your invitation must be generic in nature. You can't say "Be sure to view my store for more great items, including purses by Louis Vuitton, Manolo Blahnik, Gucci, and more!" Even if that particular auction is for one of those designer purses, you cannot list other brand names in your auction text, not even in an invitation to view your store or other auctions.

Let's say your auction is for a Gucci purse; the invitation to your store can say, "Be sure to visit my store for more great designer items." You didn't mention purses, any particular designer, or brand name.

You may wonder why this is such a strong issue on eBay. An unscrupulous seller will insert popular keywords in his auction text so that when a looker searches "Manolo Blahnik," the seller's auction will show up in the search results, even though their auction has nothing to do with that keyword. They do this in an attempt to gain more exposure for their items.

This isn't really fair to the looker who isn't interested in the other item being misrepresented, and it seriously affects the integrity of eBay's database and search results. EBay is constantly on the lookout for violations of this policy, but it can't be all places at all times. It's up to all sellers to be aware of this underhanded method of promoting listings and make a commitment never to engage in keyword spamming. So be sure to play fair and promote your store in a way that showcases your integrity as a seller. Buyers look for and really appreciate honest, trustworthy sellers.

When you use appropriate cross-promotions to attract buyers to your store, they merely have to glance at the left-hand side of the screen to see the neatly categorized list of all your items. Perhaps they're not interested in spare bike parts, but you've also picked up a nice wholesale lot of porcelain dolls. If they see a category for porcelain dolls, they can avoid paging through all your items and go straight to what they're interested in.

When you are a store seller and your looker bids or buys, you also have cross-promotions presented to the bidder/buyer. Of course, one of the best ways to promote your eBay store is to get a domain name (for example, Willy might want to get **www.widgets4sale.com**) and then have it go straight to your eBay store when anybody on the Internet clicks on it. There are costs to have a domain name, but they are fairly reasonable, especially if you don't actually have a Web site there. Think of a domain name as a portal for now, with the potential to be yet another selling tool (an off-eBay Web site) in the future.

One good reason to get a domain name is eBay will give you credits on final value fees on sales of your store inventory (not auctions, even though they, too, are listed in your store) if the buyer got to your store from outside eBay through your own marketing efforts. So that domain name you're considering can actually pay for itself if people use it to get to your store and then make a purchase! Be sure you understand eBay's policies on this so that you meet all the requirements properly.

 **Advertise Your eBay Store**

When you have an eBay store, consider advertising it locally the same way you'd advertise a brick-and-mortar store: newspaper, the Yellow Pages, radio ads. These may be especially effective if you also have a Web site address (domain name) to advertise along with it.

There are also four additional goodies you'll be able to use free when you open a store: Selling Manager (free with your store), Accounting Assistant (works with QuickBooks), e-mail marketing, and Sales Reports.

Selling Manager is a program that makes your "My eBay" page's "All Selling" tab slicker, more productive, and more useful. It's a strongly suggested selling tool for medium- and high-volume sellers. It usually costs $4.99 per month, but it comes with a free 30-day trial, so consider trying it for the 30 days before you open your store.

One of the nice features of this program is its ability to track your sales contacts. Remember that e-mail database you're planning to keep? Selling Manager can help you with that task. It also includes some nice e-mail templates, plus templates for invoices and shipping labels too.

You can even create templates for feedback comments that you can store and use for your customers. Have you ever wondered who has the time to write out those fancy feedbacks that look more like art than wording? They're saved templates, more than likely, and now you can make them too.

This software will archive four months of your listings, unlike the standard in "My eBay," which shows only those listings for sixty days back. There is also a tool in there to help you download your selling history, which can be helpful for your bookkeeping.

For those of you who set up your books in QuickBooks right away, **Accounting Assistant** will interface with QuickBooks to make all those tasks easier.

E-mail marketing is very important, as we've already determined. And since you'll have Selling Manager keeping track of all your sales contacts, you can use the free e-mail marketing techniques to send up to one hundred e-mails monthly to your contacts if you have a basic store; upgraded levels get more. If you need to send more than one hundred e-mails through this system, there is a one-cent charge for each additional e-mail.

While this may not be a cost-effective way to send out thousands of e-mails a month (when you only have the basic store), do take advantage of it at least monthly until your contact list reaches one-hundred buyers. EBay provides a step-by-step guide to help you set up your strategy and system.

Sales Reports are a good way to get a quick glimpse of your overall sales, the percentage of your sales that come from auctions, store inventory, or the sales for each of your store's categories.

The features and freebies of the basic store are really great for the fee charged. Sellers who truly immerse themselves into their eBay selling and learn to utilize all the tools available to them (no doubt there are even more than what we were able to cover here) will never regret paying their eBay bill at the end of every month!

At some point, you'll be successful enough to upgrade to a **Feature Store**. Priced at $49.95 per month, it's still not unreasonable because you'll be privy to these additional benefits:

- Your store's name and brief description will be rotated among all feature stores and shown on the "eBay Stores" page in the center (not top box, but one below it).

- You get up to ten pages that you can fully customize by category or by price, have a page for promotions/specials, a dedicated home page, etc.

- The ability to minimize the eBay header on all your pages, giving you more room for your own information.

- Traffic reports that give details about what buyers are looking at most and from where they entered your store (your own domain, eBay, etc.).

- More detailed sales reports than with the basic store.

- Your inventory listings are more likely to appear at the bottom of the page where a buyer searched for auctions with certain keywords.

- $30 per month to use on eBay's keyword program.

- Selling Manager Pro is included free ($15.95/month value).

An **Anchor Store** will give you premium exposure and services on the "eBay Stores" home page, but this little venture will put you out $499.95 per month. Suffice it to say, this is something to write down and post on your wall as a goal: I will someday upgrade to an Anchor Store!

The term **keywords** has two meanings in eBay lingo. The meanings are related, but must be differentiated or overall chaos can ensue. Let's start with the simple meaning for keywords.

When buyers search for listings, they type in words that they think might be in the title of something they want to purchase. If they're in the market for a very expensive watch for Grandpa's retirement gift, they might type in "Rolex" or some other high-end brand name of watches. In that case, then, Rolex is the keyword that connected the buyer with Grandpa's new watch.

The second meaning for keyword is basically the same: a word or phrase that is searched. EBay allows sellers to bid on the right to have their store's advertising displayed when their chosen keyword is searched by buyers. Have you ever noticed that if you perform a search for "Rolex watch," you'll get auction listings for Rolexes, and just above the first auction listing, there are a couple of boxes that magically pop up, trying very hard to entice you into clicking on them and check out their Rolexes. If you click on one of the boxes, you'll be taken to that particular seller's store, more than likely.

This is how the higher-volume sellers who can afford more than the minimum advertising in their budget keep their merchandise in the front of your vision (or in this case, at the top of the list). They also can then make a sale without having an auction at the top of the list (which, by default, shows auctions ending first).

Many top sellers swear by this technique, and when you have a Featured or Anchor Store, you'll have an allocated amount of money to spend on the keywords program. You are only charged for your banner at the top of the page every time a customer clicks on it. So while your banner might display fifteen times in a twenty-four hour period, you'll only be charged the fee for the two times that it was used to enter your store.

You can also purchase keyword banners if you only have a basic store, but there is an upfront fee charged in addition to the per-click fee. When you have your store set up, go to the "Manage My Store" link and click on "Purchase Keywords" to learn about the fees and restrictions.

The search engine Google has a keyword per-click program called AdWords. Once you start using keyword banner programs and feel you have a sense of how to best use your keywords to drive business to your eBay store (or your domain name, which in turn drives customers to your eBay store), then check into this program as well: **https://adwords .google.com/select/Login3**.

Your own domain name, as we've already discussed, can be used without an actual Web site attached to it; it can be used as a stand-alone product that merely refers potential customers to your eBay store. But once you have the income (and time) to devote to setting up an off-eBay Web site and maintaining it, then you should look into getting your own Web site/store.

The cost for this can vary greatly depending on a number of factors, such as your ability to create the site yourself (using a software such as Microsoft FrontPage, Adobe GoLive, or Macromedia Dreamweaver) or have a friend or family member who can assist you with this task.

If you prefer to hire someone, you may find a big price difference when you check with several companies. Sometimes small in-home businesses will create sites cheaper than the "big guys." Just be sure you're getting the best Web site and hosting deal for your money, including things like a secure server with shopping cart, etc. There are companies online that will design an original site for you as well, so don't limit yourself to only local companies (although, keeping your business local may be something you like to do).

Your hosting company will also be able to submit your site to all the major search engines so that people can find the site when they search for words that are applicable. One good thing about Web site search engines is that they'll also search the content of your site so that matching phrase and words will be shown, not just matches in your site's name.

Having your own Web site can lend itself to yet another new marketing opportunity: affiliated marketing. This is a method whereby you loan out space on your site to another company's banner and in return, if customers go to the other site via your site, you get either a per-click fee or a percentage of the profits when the customer purchases something. Affiliated marketing is very popular and should definitely be considered when you get to this level of sales and marketing. Be sure to check into having your banner ad on other Web sites as well.

You can use your Web site for a variety of purposes. You can conduct product sales on your site, in addition to conducting them from an eBay store. You can use your Web site as an information portal as well, merely providing information about your product and directing all sales back to your eBay store.

Willy might set up a Web site to sell his widgets and gidgets, without paying eBay fees to do so. But since he can earn some credit on his final value fees by directing his Web site traffic to his eBay store, he may also choose to focus on maintenance of your widget or showcasing the newest models of widgets and gidgets, which can be purchased in his eBay store. Either way, when potential buyers search the Internet for "widget," "gidget," or any other related word, they will be directed to Willy's site. These are just a couple of ways that you can add a Web site to your existing sales approach.

Other less expensive but worthwhile marketing items are **business cards and giveaways**. Business cards have become downright cheap in the past decade, and you can even print them yourself on cardstock (and then cut them out by hand) or buy pre-perforated paper that will let you quickly separate them. Search for companies on the Internet that have volume discount pricing; however, be sure to ask about the weight of the cardstock that they use, as that can vary. You don't want to be passing out business cards that are not much thicker than regular paper. Standard cardstock comes in thicknesses starting at 65-pound weight. Make sure any business cards you order are at least that weight or higher.

If you get a really good deal on business cards, order them in a large quantity and be liberal about passing them out any chance you get. Tack up a few on the bulletin board at your local grocery store, gas station, or anywhere else that you are allowed to leave items like this. Don't litter and don't leave them in places where solicitations aren't welcomed, as that will decrease your professional image.

In addition to business cards, you can order literally thousands of products with your company name, eBay store name, Web site address, or company logo on them. You can get everything from baseball caps to pens and pads of paper to small toys, all with your information on them.

Pass out these items to your family and friends (but maybe not as their birthday gifts) as well as at gatherings such as parades (simply walk through the crowd; you don't have to be in the parade itself) and community gatherings (picnics, your child's tee ball game, school programs, the county fair). Don't make a pest of yourself, but if you're excited about your product, your store, and your business, people will want to hear about it and pass the word along for you. You just never know where your next customer will come from.

 **Send Business Cards with Orders**

These are also nice items to tuck into an order, as a way to encourage your buyers to come back soon. You could also send along a business card with a message on the back "Pass this card on to a friend who will receive a 10 percent discount when placing an order," and then when you get a customer who mentions having a card of yours, ask which customer gave it to them. You can send the referring customer a thank-you e-mail with an invitation for 10 percent off their next order as well.

Other traditional advertising methods might serve a purpose for you, such as newspaper and radio advertising. If your product is heavily used or highly desirable in a particular geographic location or among specific populations (such as in warm climates, during the summertime, or popular with college students), then consider ads in publications that they read.

If your product is popular with college students, contact college newspapers, which often have very reasonable rates and are starved for advertisers. Trade journals are a good place for ads if your product is applicable to one particular field, such as for use by medical professionals. Regional magazines that are published for a local readership may have good advertising rates, as well as helping you target your audience in that region.

Local radio stations might be willing to pursue an advertising campaign for you. Look into sponsoring a particular hour of the day, such as rush hour, when people stuck in their cars might be more likely to listen in. Try offering a product as a "prize" once a day to "caller number five." Pay to have the station's deejays wear shirts and hats with your company logo at local functions and pass out some of your giveaways to the crowd.

There are many ways radio stations can help you build your company's name locally, and while you may not have but a small percentage of your sales locally, if everyone in your county knows about your company, they'll be more likely to refer their friends and family to your site as well.

These ideas are just some of the ways that you can advertise your eBay business, ranging from the free to the frivolous. Name recognition is what it's all about; even if people can't always remember your name or your phone number, if you can implant your Web site address in their subconscious, you've succeeded.

Now that you've got some ideas on where to obtain your merchandise and how to set up payment, shipping, and advertising plans, you're close to starting up the actual business of selling! Let's take a quick look at the differences between your old eBay status (as a looker, buyer, or occasional seller) and your new relationship with eBay: serious seller.

Store Type	Monthly Fee
Basic	$15.95
Featured	$49.95
Anchor	always free
First 30 days	always free

Length of Store Listing	Insertion Fee	Additional Surcharge	Total per Item
30 days	$0.02	None	$0.02
60 days	$0.02	$0.02	$0.04
90 days	$0.02	$0.04	$0.06
120 days	$0.02	$0.06	$0.08
Good until cancelled	$0.02 / 30 days until cancelled	None	$0.02 / 30 days until cancelled

Note: Fees for store inventory are based on the duration, not the quantity. See eBay's policies to gain a thorough understanding of store fees, as this is merely an overview.

Selling Price	Final Value Fee
$0.01–$25	8% of the final sale price
$25.01–$1,000	8% of the initial $25 ($2) + 5% of the remainder (over $25)
Over $1,000	8% of the initial $25 ($2) + 5% of the amount between $25.01 and $1,000 ($48.75) + 3% of the remaining balance (over $1,000)

All the other features and extras offered by eBay (listing designer, bolded title, etc.) and all the photo options have different pricing for store inventory as well. You can find the complete breakdown of store fees at **http://pages.ebay.com/help/sell/storefees.html**.

Checklist of Tasks:
Planning Your Advertising

❑ I have set up my eBay preferences to utilize cross-promotions effectively.

❑ I have created my "About Me" page.

❑ I have set up a place to securely store my customer database so that I can e-mail specials or newsletters to my customers.

❑ I am aware of the benefits of opening an eBay store and will consider doing so when I have a regular product stream and the financial ability to move ahead.

❑ I understand eBay's policies against keyword spamming and choose to be an ethical seller who will not engage in this behavior.

❑ I understand that I can advertise on sites like Google for a per-click fee when my budget will allow me to do so.

❑ I will consider a domain name, for the purpose of directing traffic to my eBay store and ultimately to have as an e-commerce site, when I am financially able.

❑ I will utilize common techniques such as business cards, giveaways, and local advertising to help drive customers to my eBay business.

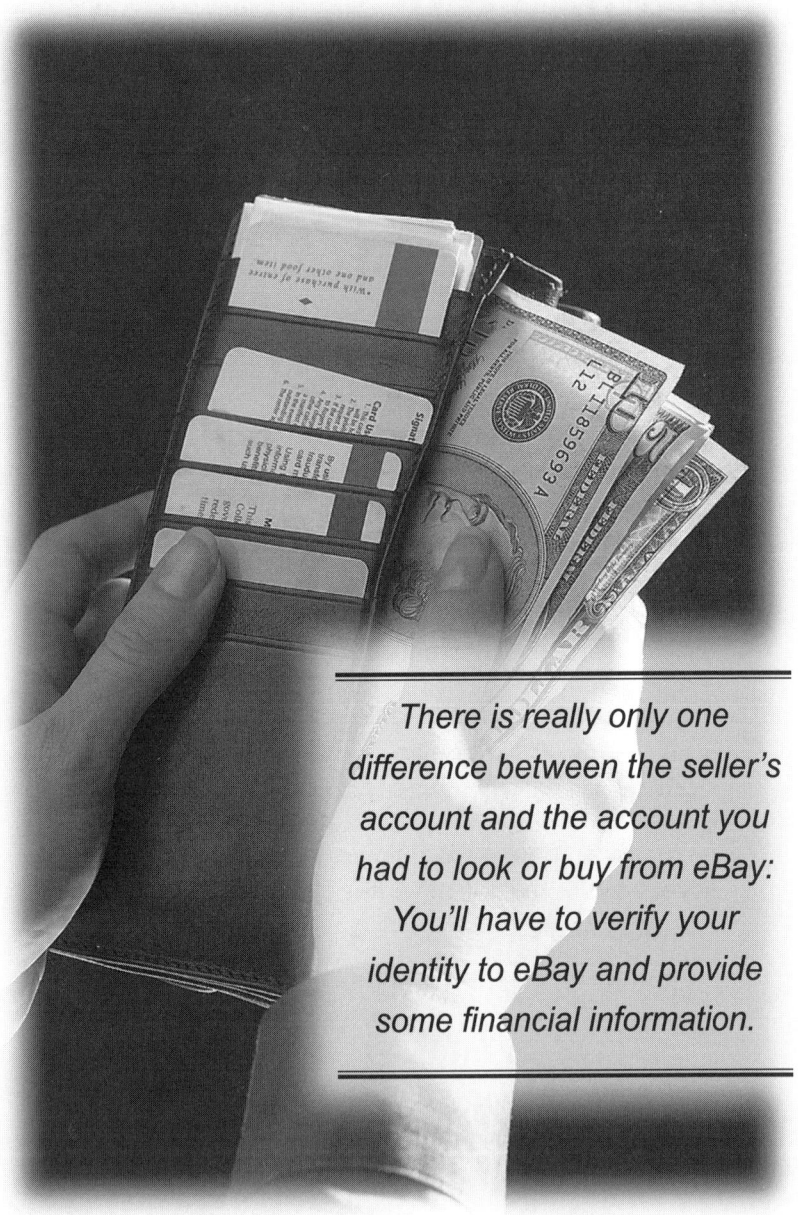

There is really only one difference between the seller's account and the account you had to look or buy from eBay: You'll have to verify your identity to eBay and provide some financial information.

CHAPTER 7

Join the Club!

When you join the ranks of the millions of eBay sellers around the world, the first thing you'll have to do is open a seller's account. There is really only one difference between the seller's account and the account you had to look or buy from eBay: You'll have to verify your identity to eBay and provide some financial information.

Moving from a Looker or Buyer to a Seller

This is usually done by providing a credit card number and information about your checking account (at any U.S. bank). There is no cost to become a seller, so your card will not be charged nor will there be any withdrawals from your checking account, unless you also designate one of these accounts for paying your monthly eBay invoice.

If you've already set up your business checking account, be sure to use that account information for your seller's account setup and also arrange to have your invoices paid automatically from that account.

If you don't have (or don't want to provide) a credit card number for verification purposes, you can choose to become ID Verified, which means that for a $5 fee (charged to your eBay account) the secure system will cross-check your name, address, and telephone numbers against various databases to help prove that you are who you say you are. Even if you're going to use a business address and telephone number for your customers' information, use your home address and phone number for this process.

Once you have completed the verification process (actually, this is a good thing to do, even if you register as a seller by providing credit card information to eBay), you'll have the ID Verified symbol in your profile.

There are a few other tasks that you should complete before starting up your first auction, including starting a PayPal account, if you haven't already been using one for your purchasing on eBay (and, if you have, setting up a second one). EBay will prompt you to do this when you set up a seller's account.

You'll want to make sure that you use your business checking account information in PayPal as well so that you can transfer funds from your PayPal account when needed.

TIP — Paying eBay Invoices

When eBay sends you an invoice (via e-mail), you don't have to wait for the funds to be withdrawn from your checking account. If you have funds in your PayPal account, go ahead and pay your eBay invoice if you want.

Now that you're an eBay seller, you'll also want to review your preferences to be sure that they accurately reflect the way you want to receive information and view your selling information. Go to "My eBay" and click on "Preferences" under the "My Account" header. When the next page opens, on the right-hand side you'll see a link that says "Show All"; click this to see all the preferences laid out on the page.

For instance, if you have located a Web site to store your photos on (so you can enter multiple photos without paying extra fees to eBay), you'll want to edit the category "Use This Picture Service" and enter the site or service you'll be using. If you don't want buyers to be offered an eBay checkout, then you'll have to change the pre-set "Yes" to a "No" by clicking the "Edit" link at the top of that section.

At the bottom of the "Selling Preferences" section, you can edit your preferences for blocking particular bidders/buyers. In case you ever want to block whole groups of people from you auctions (such as those with unpaid item strikes against them or those in a foreign country you do not ship to), then this is where you'll need to make that change.

In the years that I've been using eBay, I have only seen one auction where the seller opted to block all bidders who did not already have a PayPal account. This would be useful if your only payment option is PayPal (although, you need to really consider the needs of your customers before making such a drastic decision) and you don't want to be bothered by buyers who ignore your requests for PayPal only. Some buyers will ignore information such as that and just assume or hope that you'll accept their payment form once the auction's over.

In order to block certain people or groups of people from you auction, you'll need to go here: **http://offer.ebay.com/ws/eBayISAPI .dll?bidderblocklogin**.

You can also require that bidders be pre-approved before bidding. This is not a commonly used technique in selling except under special circumstances: **http://offer.ebay.com/ws/eBayISAPI .dll?PreApproveBidders**.

 **Learn How to Change and Edit**

Take a few minutes and click on all the possible things you can change or edit, just to see if you fully understand what all your options are. You will also find links to explanations of these items.

If you've already decided that you'll use some of eBay's software applications, such as Selling Manager or Turbo Lister, then download those and spend some time getting to know them before you begin posting auctions. In Chapter 9, we'll go through setting an auction step by step using the traditional auction setup, and in Appendix B, we'll review the basics of Turbo Lister.

Even though you haven't even received your first invoice from eBay yet, let's review some of your contractual duties to eBay as a seller. If you didn't take the time to actually read your User Agreement when you first created an eBay account, take the time to do so now. There probably won't be anything earth-shattering in there, but you will have a better understanding of how eBay views their relationship with you, the new seller.

In particular, sellers have the following duties when they list an item for sale on eBay:

- You must be the legal owner of the item, or have permission of the legal owner, and you must be of legal age to enter into contracts (18).

- Your item must be described accurately (as possible) and honestly, with all terms of the sale disclosed in the listing.

- You can't put content on their site that doesn't specifically deal with the item you're listing.

- You must use the appropriate categories for listing items; you can't put something in a category that's currently "hot" just so people will see it.

- You must not knowingly sell prohibited items. A comprehensive list of prohibited items is on the site.

- If you're selling multiple items (Dutch Auction), all of the items must be identical.

When your listed item receives bids or sells, your obligations are these:

- If you receive even one bid at or above your minimum price (or your reserve price), then you must sell the item at the highest bid, even if it is the minimum price unless:

  - The buyer fails to follow through with your pre-set requirements, such as paying within a certain time frame.

  - You can't verify the buyer's identity.

  - If the listing falls under the Non-Binding Bid Policy (such as real estate auctions).

- You must not fail to provide the goods as described in a timely manner by:

  – Refusing the payment (see Chapter 5 regarding eBay's policy on PayPal credit card payments).

  – Failing to ship the item.

At all times, you have the following obligations:

- You are not to commit any type of fraud on eBay or its users, including:

  – Manipulating the price of any item.

  – Interfering with another seller's auctions or sales.

  – Shill bidding (artificially raising the bids on your own items, by either bidding with another username or having a friend bid on them).

  – Cancelling listings to sell directly to someone who found your product through eBay.

  – Offering to sell or buy off-eBay to avoid fees.

  – Fee-avoidance techniques (see **http://pages.ebay.com/help /policies/listing-circumventing.html** for a thorough explanation and online tutorial on this topic).

  – Falsely claiming a "final value fee credit" (see **http://pages.ebay .com/help/policies/fvf-abuse.html**).

- You are not to commit any fraud upon the owner of a copyright, trademark, or owner of intellectual property including:

  – Selling items by using a brand name in the auction, when the actual item is a knockoff or imitation.

- Selling items made using a copied or copyrighted pattern, design, or instructions.

- Selling handmade items using materials that have copyrighted designs (i.e., fabric with Disney characters, stating in your auction that this is a Disney item, when it was neither made by nor endorsed by Disney).

To assist owners of intellectual property and copyrights from infringement of their rights, eBay has created the Verified Rights Owner Program (VeRO) program. The five thousand or so participants have registered with eBay as intellectual property holders or copyright/trademark holders. If you misrepresent a product in your listing and the owner of the copyright, trademark, or intellectual property you have incorrectly used or misused notifies eBay, then your listing could be revoked. If you repeatedly infringe on the rights of others in this manner, your eBay privileges could be revoked. EBay takes the rights of copyright/trademark holders very seriously.

For example, let's say that Willy sells widgets and gidgets that are made for him by Acme Widget Manufacturers of America. Acme's main competitor is the Winning Widgets of America Corporation. Let's say that Willy has found that even though the widgets are pretty much identical in every way, he sells them faster if people think that they may be made by the Winning Widgets of America Corporation.

He doesn't actually say that they're made by Winning Widget, he merely implies it, by making an auction titled, "Widget, Winning My Auction Is Easy!" Now, perhaps anybody who wasn't a widget connoisseur might not even know that "Winning" is an indirect reference to another company that makes widgets or, specifically, the company that did not make the widgets that Willy is selling. But the avid buyers of widgets know, and so does the Winning Widgets of America Corporation. In fact, they are a registered VeRO program member, and they regularly scan the listings of every seller who has the words "widget" and "gidget" in their listings, looking for any unscrupulous sellers who are looking to capitalize on their Winning product's name.

Willy, being the honest seller that he is, didn't realize that he was infringing on the rights of the other manufacturer. He was just trying to make a zippy title, and knowing that most widget buyers are familiar with the Winning name, he added it to assist searchers in finding his widgets. Okay, so eBay will be forgiving—once. But believe me, the

Winning Widgets of America company will be watching his listings for a while, just to be sure.

For a complete breakdown of the VeRO program, copyright infringement issues, and intellectual property, see these eBay pages:

- **http://pages.ebay.com/help/confidence/vero-rights-owner.html**

- **http://pages.ebay.com/help/policies/questions/vero-ended-item .html**

- **http://pages.ebay.com/help/policies/replica-counterfeit.html**

- **http://pages.ebay.com/help/policies/trademark.html**

 **Do Not Violate Trademarks**

In the above example, Willy was not only violating the Winning Widgets of America Corporation's trademark rights but also engaging in keyword spamming. By putting the other company's name (even part of it) in his title, he was inadvertently causing the search results of potential customers who were searching for widgets made by Winning Widgets to display his listing as well. Keyword spamming is covered in Chapter 9 as well.

There are a number of other equally important items in the User Agreement, so take some time to read up on it. Even if you have every intention of being an honest, upright seller, it's always good to be familiar with this information, in case you ever need to refer to it later for a question. You want your customers to take your eBay business seriously, so you need to make sure you take seriously your obligations to eBay and your customers as well. Review and print (for future reference) the detailed information about all of eBay's policies for sellers at this site: **http://pages.ebay.com/help/policies/listing-ov.html**.

Now that we've spent some time reviewing your duties as a seller, let's turn our attention to a few more specifics about eBay that you may want to keep in the back of your mind, should the opportunity arise for you to turn these places into potential markets for your product.

EBay Motors is fairly well known as the used car lot of the Internet. There aren't just used cars there, but new and used vehicles of all sorts. Probably the only type of vehicle that hasn't ever been listed there is a spaceship! There are airplanes, campers, race cars, muscle cars, sailboats, and powerboats. While vehicles may not be your product, there is a section for "Parts & Accessories" in the eBay motors site too, listing everything from repair manuals to bunk-hanging hardware for a sailboat.

EBay Business is another specialty site accessed from the home page that shows listings of industrial equipment and supplies. The listings are divided among general industrial categories such as "Agriculture & Forestry," "Construction," "Food Service & Retail," "Industrial Electrical & Test," "Industrial Supply," and "Manufacturing & Metalworking." Some of the categories (such as Agriculture>tractors, Construction>trailers, etc.) have a twenty-dollar insertion fee in this section, so check out the categories that have higher fees before listing here. Search "eBay business fees" in the "Help" directory to learn more.

Want It Now has been a fairly recent addition to eBay's plethora of innovative ways to keep people visiting, and buying from, their site. "Want It Now" is chock full of listings from potential buyers stating what they want to purchase but haven't found in the auction listings or stores (or didn't want to take the effort to look for it).

You can search by general categories or type in a specific word or phrase (just like searching for auctions) and see what pops up. You may find your buyers this way, instead of having them find you!

ProStores is the latest full-service station on eBay. This service assists you in turning your domain name into an e-commerce Web site, complete with shopping cart and secure checkout—the works! You can do business on this site and drive business to your eBay store as well. There are various fee levels based on how many services you want, but the most basic fee level is $6.95 per month. You can learn all there is to know about ProStores in this link: **http://pages.ebay.com/merchantsolutions/ prostores/index.html**.

Starting up a Web site with ProStores is probably not something you are going to delve right into, but keep it on your back burner; it might be the perfect way for you to expand your business when the time is right.

Just when you thought you've seen it all on eBay, you'll stumble across the "Everything Else" category where you'll find zany sub-categories such as "Mature Audiences," "Mystery Auctions," and "Weird Stuff." Not just ordinary weird stuff, either. EBay manages to have three categories of weird stuff: the slightly unusual, the really weird, and the totally bizarre.

"Mature Audiences," as a category, probably doesn't need any explanation as to what type of merchandise is available there. However, in order to even enter that portion of eBay, you must be ID Verified and go through an additional sign-in session or agree to the terms of use and have your information verified. If you have products you wish to market in this area, they will not be seen by the general auctioning public, to protect minors. This can make it somewhat difficult to market items in this area, so unless your item is explicitly "adult" in nature, you may want to list it in non-mature audiences categories first.

"Mystery Auctions," are just that: a mystery. In this type of auction, the bidder "purchases" something such as an empty cardboard box of a certain size, shape, etc. However, the contents of the box (which are a mystery) are given to the buyer as a gift, at no additional charge. These auctions often cite "eBay rules" that they are following, but the "Help" files do not contain any such reference. So whether this is part of the whole storyline or simply an urban legend of sorts is, well, a mystery.

The outrageous stories that go along with these boxes are like online soap operas. They seem to take on a life of their own and some of them have developed almost a cult following. There are jilted lovers disposing of their former flame's possessions, ex-roomies who got stiffed on the lease, and even babies hawking goods! Some people even try to turn it into a real mystery: you'll receive this envelope with instructions on where to locate a treasure. Whatever the sob story (real or fictitious), there seems to be a certain faddish following going on there.

Hints are often provided every time the auction reaches a new level of bidding, such as with every $50 increment. There is no data that I could find to support whether or not these auctions really do bring any amount of business (or whether or not the buyers even pay for them), and so I wouldn't go pinning my hopes on getting rich by posting these auctions. However, if you need a good laugh after a long morning of posting auctions and updating your accounting files, this might be your source.

The "Weird Stuff," however, may indeed be the strangest things to hit the Internet auction sites. There are plenty of just plain-old-stupid auctions and even auctions that really aren't weird at all, but there are truly some interesting things as well.

Like the "Mystery Auctions," there may not be much actual business value in listing here, but they're sure good for a giggle once in a while. Despite eBay policies against having sexually explicit material on the general site, the "weird" categories can contain much of that material, so be cautious about letting minors explore these categories.

A recent foray into the "weird" turned up a "Buy It Now" offer for purchasing one square inch of land in a particular state. The price? Just $9.95 plus $1 to ship your authentic deed to you. A set of plastic wall hooks that screw into wood. Oh, did I mention that they're shaped like an appendage and cost just $6.95 plus $4.95 shipping?

If those items are too mundane for you, how about a pewter-look statue of the Grim Reaper? Looking for the most unusual jewelry? Try on an enchanted ring from India or a necklace where the pendant was carved out of the eggshell of a very large bird. If you're searching for something profound, you can purchase a prayer or a bobble-head of a major religious figure.

You might only be able to conclude that it is true: eBay is the world's marketplace, including just about anything for just about everybody on the planet.

Seeing the Big Picture

Now, getting back to business, we'll review some tactics you need to master before you start auctioning. You'll need to be adept at searching current and past listings so you can do some price comparisons to know how to price your auctions, as well as quickly navigating around your "My eBay" page.

And, even though your mind may be spinning still from the discussion about the "User Agreement," there are a few more policies you need to be aware of, including eBay's list of banned items.

Searching current and past auctions isn't terribly difficult, but you'll likely be doing a lot of it (unless you sell the same merchandise repeatedly) so it's worth learning the tricks to good searching. When you do a basic search, you may be confronted with ten pages of results that you don't have time to sort through. Narrowing down your search and utilizing keywords will help you find the listings you need to compare.

Basic keywords are those that would be in the title such as the brand name (Levi's), manufacturer (Hewlett-Packard), year made, size, or color. Think of how you are planning to title your auction and search for those same words. Don't make your search term into a full sentence, though, as your results will have to match every word in your search.

If you have a wholesale lot of infant sleepers to sell, your basic keywords might include infant sleeper, baby sleeper, or newborn pajamas. When you search multiple words, simply leave a space between the words. This tells the search engine that you want the title of the auction to contain all those words, in any order. If you want the word order to remain the same as your search, which is useful for a title of a book, then put quotations around the phrase.

Perhaps you aren't picky about the word order, but you want to find listings for any down jackets, but not green ones. So you might search "down jacket -green" or "down coat -green." Put the minus sign before the word for which you do not want to get results for.

Suppose you want to find those same jackets, but not green or purple ones. Your search would then be "down jacket -(green,purple)" or something similar. Put the terms you don't want to see in parentheses separated by a comma but no space, and put the minus sign directly before the parentheses.

Willy wants to find past auctions of widgets, either made by Winning Widgets of America or Ace Widgets of America. So he'll search this way: "widgets (winning,ace)" to include all widgets where either Winning or Ace was also used in the title.

If you're looking for a word that may be misspelled, use the beginning of the word and an asterisk (*) to search for all titles containing that string of letters: "adv*" will bring up listings for anything with "advanced," "advertising," "adventure," "advantage," or "Advent" in the title.

TIP — Quotation Marks in Searching

EBay will automatically include items in your search that you didn't specify, such as common misspellings or two spellings for the same basic word (grey/gray), or add an "s" to the end of your term (boot/boots) to give you more results. If you don't want the search engine to do this, put your term in quotation marks.

EBay provides a list of keyword search category expansions that you can view on their site. Just search the "Help" directory for this term.

Other tips from eBay:

- Search titles and descriptions by checking the box below the search field.

- Be specific. Searching "doll" will get you a thousand. Searching "porcelain Cinderella doll" will get you a lot closer to what you're looking for.

- Try searching with and without the "s" on a word that could be plural.

- Don't use punctuation in a search unless it's part of the term (Dr. Seuss).

- Browse categories where you might find what you're looking for and study the titles for ideas to assist your searching.

Navigating around your "My eBay" page isn't rocket science, but there are a few things that you might not be familiar with. It seems that everywhere you click on eBay, there are dozens more links with even more information and even more links. You just don't have time to explore every link, so perhaps you haven't seen some of these spots in "My eBay."

When you click on "My eBay" (from the top toolbar), you'll be taken to your "My Summary" page. Notice that to the right side of the page is a link called "Customize Summary." This is the quickest way to review all the available content on this page. Change it up to suit your needs; it doesn't have to be the way eBay set it up by default.

For instance, when I got to the point that I had more than ten auctions going at once, it drove me just batty that the "Summary" page only showed the ten ending first; every time I went to that page, I had to click "Show All" and wait for my browser to reload the page. Then I discovered that I can opt to have up to fifteen items shown, and I can also move around the order of the items on that page. If my current auctions are more important to me than actions I'm currently watching or bidding on, then I can move my selling auctions to the top of the page. You even have choices in what columns of information you want displayed. For the current auctions, I chose to display the number of unique bidders that auction had. This lets me know if there are several bidders or perhaps just two having a bidding war. There isn't any strategy involved in knowing this, just pure curiosity.

Notice that each section has its own customize display link, in case you want to just change that particular section. Additionally, each section listed in the box on the left-hand side of the page is customizable to suit your needs. You're going to be spending a lot of time on your "My eBay" page, so it may as well be user friendly!

On your current listings, notice that each item has a drop-down menu at the end that says "Sell Similar." This is a shortcut to starting another listing of a similar nature. It doesn't have to be an exact duplicate, because you can edit or change anything in the listing, including the category it's listed in, the price, duration, or description. It saves you having to input things like shipping policies and general information.

Other options you have with that drop-down menu are to revise that listing, add to the description (meaning to revise just the item description portion of the listing), end the item listing, or end promotions on the item. Some of these features can't be accessed when the item has a current bid on it or if the listing ends in the next twelve hours.

Current listings are shown both on the "Summary" page and the "All Selling" page. On the "All Selling" page, it also shows your previous listings that did not sell. The drop-down menu on those items offers to re-list the item with the opportunity to revise anything in the listing you choose before it is resubmitted to the active listings. We'll review re-listing in Chapter 10.

 **Getting Re-List Refunds**

In order to qualify for a re-list refund (if your item sells the second time around, eBay will refund your second listing fee), you must have initiated the re-list from this screen. That is the only way eBay can track that it's the same item/auction.

Spend the time clicking on all the customizable sections of your pages and getting to know what your options really are. When your "My eBay" pages serve you most efficiently, then you know they are customized correctly.

Many of eBay's policies have been pointed out as we've gone along, in topics that they apply to. However, eBay's banned items list is one thing that you need to be familiar with.

The list contains more than eighty categories where all or some of the items are restricted or prohibited. There are the obvious items, such as human remains and counterfeit items, but did you know that used clothing is allowed for sale only if it's been properly cleaned according to the manufacturer's instructions? Used cosmetics are never allowed to be sold because of the U.S. Food and Drug Administration's rules. The lists are too comprehensive to reproduce here, but spend some time reviewing any category that is applicable to your product line. Search eBay's "Help" section for "Prohibited and Restricted Items: Overview."

Other informational lists you may want to read through or print out for reference are the "eBay Glossary" and "eBay Acronyms." There are a number of terms and abbreviations that are unique to the Internet and online auctioning, and you'll want to be able to understand and use them appropriately.

EBay's "Prohibited and Restricted Items" list can be located at **http://pages.ebay.com/help/sell/item_allowed.html**.

The "Glossary" can be located at **http://pages.ebay.com/help/newtoebay /glossary.html**.

The "Acronym" list is found at **http://pages.ebay.com/help/newtoebay /acronyms.html**.

Keeping Your Eye on the Enemy

In addition to all the other tasks that you will be juggling as a small business owner, you'll be smart to keep an eye on the enemy — your competition. This is not to say you can't be friendly with other sellers; by all means do not alienate them, because they may be the only people who can answer a query you place on the message boards.

However, it's always a good practice in business to know what your competition is up to. On eBay, you can view your competition's listings and compare their prices, their shipping rates, their warranties, or other customer-service policies. Make sure you're up to snuff with your competition, because you can bet potential buyers will do some of the same comparing.

 **Do Not "Re-Use" Auction Items**

Do not ever take or use photos or item descriptions from another listing to use as your own. This is a violation of that seller's intellectual property rights and could be reported as a VeRO violation. This also applies to the "look" or "feel" of someone else's "About Me" page.

Check out the competition regularly. There are a few shortcuts for doing this. First, you can add another seller to your "Favorite Sellers" list and get regular reports on their new listings. Or to see many sellers' items at once, perform a search using your keywords and then save the search to your "Favorite Searches" list. On your "My eBay" page, you can quickly pull up your favorite searches with just a few clicks.

Of course, you'll probably see your own listings amongst the favorites in the search, but that's actually a good thing. Try to put yourself in the buyers' shoes. What's different about your listing? Does it stand out? Are the photos previewing properly? Are your photos better quality than the competition's? Is your shipping cost (or the option to calculate shipping) right on the search page? How does your title compare to the other auctions?

If you spend some time honestly assessing your listings against other companies' listings, you can learn a lot. You don't want to copy the competition (and certainly not their photos or text, as that is against eBay's VeRO policy), but you want to make sure that your listings are as polished, professional, and informative as theirs are.

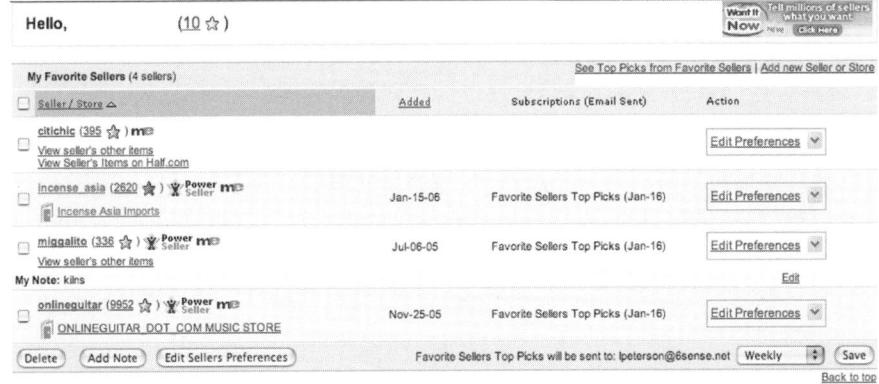

Staying on Top of Trends

Keeping up with the competition isn't the only thing you'll need to be regularly monitoring. Things change on eBay very quickly; new features are added constantly, upgrades to services are being tested, and new educational opportunities are offered.

One spot that you'll want to become familiar with is the "eBay Pulse" page (the link is on the left-hand side of the home page, just after the list of categories). This page has information on the top search terms (keywords or phrases) that day, the top five largest stores by number of active listings at that time, and the most watched items at the moment. At the bottom of the page, follow the link to the page showing all eBay categories, and from there, you will get to each category's "pulse" page, showing the top searches in each category and the top watched auctions in each. This might give you some idea what, within the categories your products are listed, people are looking for.

The pulse pages are gaining quite a following. The most-watched auctions shown on the "eBay Pulse" main page are often featured on other Web sites that show unusual or interesting auctions. This has created a desire among many auctioneers to have slicker, fancier sites than the next guy, and more outrageous and unusual auction items, just hoping to be featured on eBay's pulse page and on other sites.

However, that's not the only reason why people create outrageous auctions that get featured on the pulse page. One seller has turned outrageous auctions into a slick marketing technique that drives people to his real business. Read his story, "Keeping His Finger on the Pulse," in Chapter 11.

Another way to keep ahead of the crowd is by utilizing the **eBay University** and **Seller Central**. With eBay University, you can take courses in selling, from beginner to advanced. The "Selling Basics" course is for the real newbies, and it will prepare you to do basic transactions. For those who are already somewhat experienced with the concept of selling on eBay, there is the "Beyond the Basics" course. This course will assist you in creating a better-than-basic listing, help you utilize some of eBay's online tools, and familiarize you with PayPal.

For the seller who wants to really delve into the business aspects of eBay, try the "eBay for Business" course. This will give you additional information about taxes, inventory, accounting and recordkeeping, finding merchandise, and marketing yourself.

The first two classes are available either live (check the schedule on eBay's Web site for a location near you), online, or via a CD-ROM that can be purchased. The business-level course is currently only available at the live sessions. If you have a chance to attend, you may be able to do more than just learn; these classes are a great chance to network with sellers in your area.

Even if you don't have the time to devote to a whole class right away, check out eBay's "Seller Central" pages, which can be accessed right from the home page (see the "Helpful Links" box center right on home page).

The "Seller Central" pages are categorized using these headers: "Getting Started," "Best Practices," "Advanced Selling," "Category Tips," "What's Hot," "News & Updates," and "Resources." I can't stress enough how much information there is just in these pages and the links that they direct you to. There's simply no way that we could cover the full spectrum of all eBay has to offer sellers (in the way of knowledge) in this short book.

For the benefit of your business, make it a priority to review each of these sections. Schedule time to read, if you have to, and consider it a cost of doing business every bit as much as paying your PayPal fees. The more knowledge you have, the better seller you'll be.

Just a few of the don't-miss places you'll access through the seller central:

- EBay Solutions Directory—A pretty thorough listing of third-party software (not made by or provided by eBay) and tools to help you in your eBay business.

- Square Trade Dispute Resolution Program—For when you and your customer just can't see eye to eye.

- EBay's Top Seller Webinar—You can replay the Web-seminar right on your PC.

- Buyer Behavior Report—Climb into the psyche of your buyers and learn how to give them what they want.

- What's Hot—A category-by-category breakdown of what's selling best on eBay at the moment.

- Merchandising Calendar—Heads-up on promotions eBay will be running.

Joining the eBay Community

EBay isn't just a bunch of people selling things on a Web site. It's a bunch of people. The fact that they're buying and selling is just one common factor among them. EBay members have been the backbone of this vibrant online community in a way that is unlike any other on the Internet. Here, it doesn't matter who you are; if you have a question, someone on the message boards will answer it.

And it's always been that way. Right from the early days, eBayers have been chatting regularly with cyber-friends on the site's message boards. They are happy to share their stories, triumphs, frustrations, and thoughts about life. These communities are comprised of people who know each other only by their eBay usernames, and often not much else. But don't you dare tell them that these people aren't really their comrades, their friends! You'll be shunned and scoffed at if you do.

The Internet has created a phenomenon unlike any other in history. It takes the concept of pen pals to the ultimate level. And eBay has seen its share of online friendships grow throughout the years.

eBay has created a community that fosters communication and friendship.

Take, for example, Pamela in Ohio (eBay user "Pamelas_Timeless_Treasures"). This stay-at-home mom began selling on eBay because of the encouragement of another eBay seller named Julie, who she'd met on a message board. Her online friendship with Julie has continued to this day, resulting in the co-authoring of an e-book about eBay, even though they've yet to meet in person! Her story is included in Chapter 11 in more detail.

When Pierre Omidyar started his online auction site, one of the first things he did was to establish a set of community values that every member would operate with. To this day, these values are upheld and touted by all at eBay. They may seem Pollyanna-ish to some, but they are very important to the vast majority of eBay users who uphold them and expect the same of others.

These values are simple and brief:

- We believe people are basically good.

- We believe everyone has something to contribute.

- We believe that an honest, open environment can bring out the best in people.

- We recognize and respect everyone as a unique individual.

- We encourage you to treat others the way you want to be treated.

If you explore the "Community" link (on the top toolbar), you'll find about as many different **message boards and groups** as there are categories on eBay. This is a great resource, especially if you don't understand something or can't find a "Help" topic for something you need to know.

There are four basic discussion formats available:

- Discussion boards: Sorted by topic, these are for discussing eBay auctions, questions, and information.

- Groups: Some are public, some are private (you have to ask to be included), but these tend to be more close-knit than the discussion boards. Groups are listed by state, by collector types, or by other interests.

- Answer Center: These boards are staffed by devoted eBay volunteers helping others with eBay problems of a more technical nature, such as checkout troubles, photo questions, etc.

- Chat rooms: Casual, real-time groups where the topic may or may not be about eBay specifically, but still must maintain a sense of dignity and decency.

This page is also a good place to find out what's going on with the "Calendar of Events." Join in a town hall-style meeting in cyberspace or listen to archived programs. Find out when and where the next eBay University sessions will be held or when the next online workshop will be and what the topic is.

EBay is committed to their sellers' success (as it directly affects their success), and by providing you with tools and assistance in every way possible, they have made eBay's sellers the huge success that they are!

Educating members isn't all that eBay strives to do; they also give recognition where it is due. Their annual listing of Hall of Fame members can be viewed from the "Community" page, including a brief description of the members' contributions to the eBay community.

EBay also has a featured member every month (and you can nominate yourself to be in this spot once you have a feedback rating of at least 100 with 98 percent or better feedback score). The profiles are interesting and in an easy-to-read Q&A format.

In the next chapter, we'll walk through the steps of creating and posting an auction. We'll follow the process of selling an item the "traditional" way including pre-planning and strategy as well as a step-by-step setup of the auction on eBay.

Checklist of Tasks:
Becoming an eBay Seller

❏ I have made my eBay account a seller's account by using:

> My credit card and business checking account information.

> The ID Verified system (a good idea even if you do the other route).

❏ I have started a PayPal account that will be dedicated to my business transactions.

❏ I have reviewed my "Preferences" section of my "My eBay" page to be sure they accurately reflect my status as a seller.

❏ I have read and completely understand all my obligations to eBay as laid out in the User Agreement including:

> The nature and scope of my relationship with eBay.

> My obligations to honestly and properly list items for sale.

> My obligations to my bidders/customers.

❏ I understand at least the basics of copyright law and how not to infringe upon the copyright, trademark, or intellectual property rights of others.

❏ I understand that I may have copyright, trademark, or intellectual rights to protect, and I will become a member of eBay's VeRO network to protect my rights.

❏ I have spent some time learning how to search current and past listings with ease so that I can use this information to help me sell my products more efficiently.

❏ I have spent some time learning my way around my "My eBay" pages so that I can best utilize all that eBay offers me in options and assistance.

❑ I have located and read or printed out these reference materials:

EBay's list of banned/prohibited items.

EBay's acronym list.

EBay's glossary of terms.

❑ I will sell with eBay's community values in mind:

We believe people are basically good.

We believe everyone has something to contribute.

We believe that an honest, open environment can bring out the best in people.

We recognize and respect everyone as a unique individual.

We encourage you to treat others the way you want to be treated.

If you have never set up an auction, you'll probably benefit from doing some pre-planning on paper first.

Think Before You Click

Planning Your Auctions

You have your business structure in place, you have a reliable stream of merchandise (or a supply of items to start with), and your accounting software, spreadsheets, ledgers, or blank tables are ready to accept the data that your auctions will produce.

Now you just need to log in and... wait a second.

If you haven't ever set up an auction, you'll probably benefit from doing some pre-planning on paper first. Let's follow Willy's neighbor Suzy who has decided to start an eBay business. Suzy has written her business plan, set herself up as a sole proprietor, and obtained her reseller's license. She also registered with her state and local authorities, received permission from her local zoning board to run a business out of her home, and had Willy help her set up a basic recordkeeping system similar to his.

Suzy has decided she doesn't want to sell the same products over and over again like Willy does, so she's spent the past month attending every estate auction and garage sale she can to accumulate some inventory. She has some very nice items, some antiques, and a lot of miscellaneous items that she got for next to nothing or in boxes of items for one low price. She feels that this will help her learn what the demand and resale value of many items are; as she learns which merchandise sells best or has the most demand, she can then start to specialize and search for only certain types of items to resell.

For her first auction, Suzy is going to sell a Wagner Ware waffle iron made in 1910. She obtained this item at an estate sale. She assigns it an inventory number, sits down to work out the details on paper, and signs into her eBay account to do some preliminary searches for other auctions of this item.

One of the first things she wants to determine is what type of pricing strategy she should take with this item. She searches using the words "Wagner" and "waffle" to locate all waffle irons made by this same company. If it's an extremely rare specimen in perfect or like-new condition, she may find others in the current or completed listings that have sold for considerable amounts of money.

In that case, she may want to consider a starting bid price that would be a reasonable amount for her to accept but still be a good deal for the bidder. Or she may wish to consider a reserve auction, where she sets a minimum price that isn't disclosed to her bidders. If the reserve price isn't met by the bidding, she isn't required to sell the product.

However, Suzy has heard that the reserve price feature actually turns away some bidders, and since this waffle iron is a bit rusty, the heat ring has a small piece missing from it, and there is some wood missing from the end of one of the handles, she doesn't believe it's a prime specimen of Wagner waffle irons.

By searching on eBay, Suzy has been able to determine that similar waffle irons with similar defects have sold for $6.50 to $20, depending on the year, how well one can see the details (the date made, patent number), and how rusty the item is. This also takes into consideration how many buyers are utilizing eBay during the listings; there may be many buyers wanting that item on any given day, or only a few.

Suzy searched both active and completed listings. When she takes these factors into account and compares the prices for other similar items made by the same company in the same time frame, she aims for a closing bid of $9.99 or more.

Try an Advanced Search

To search completed listings, go to "Advanced Search" (the link under the search box that's at the top right of every eBay page) and click the box that states "Search Completed Listings Only." The results will show you all completed auctions in the past fifteen days matching your search criteria.

Even though Suzy was very excited when she got this waffle iron at the estate sale for $2, she realizes now that while it seemed to be a valuable item to her at that moment, there actually are a fair number of these items available, thus driving down the prices as supply has met the demand. This is all part of the learning curve for Suzy, and she takes it in stride. Next time she sees an antique waffle iron, she'll have some idea of their value and rarity and only buy one in mint condition if the price is right.

Or she may turn this product into one of her specialties, continue to buy them in average condition and be content to make a few dollar net profit on each. But for now, since she has just this one waffle iron, she'll just use this auction to feel out the market and learn a little bit, even if she doesn't make more than a few dollars after expenses.

Now that Suzy has determined what her approximate value is, she begins to think about how to price her item. There are numerous options, and even different twists on ways to save a few pennies on a fee: by using a starting bid of $0.99 rather than $1, you'll save $0.10 in listing fees!

One fee-saving strategy that you might see used by other sellers can lead to serious trouble with eBay. Read this PowerSeller's story of an innocent mistake that could have been disastrous:

Brooke in Virginia (eBay user "bbaysellers") recently was the possessor of a very hot item: a children's Old Navy monkey costume for Halloween. These are no longer available at Old Navy stores, and they were very much in demand this past fall. Brooke did a search to see how many of these were available and what their pricing and other options were. She found one seller who sold the identical costume for just $5! She couldn't believe it, so she read the listing and discovered that while the seller did indeed sell the item for only $5, she also charged $35 for shipping it within the United States!

Brooke was aghast, or maybe intrigued. She knew that the costume should bring in about $40, but was surprised at the method this seller used to get that amount. She noted (from looking at the counter) that the low "Buy It Now" price had indeed attracted many lookers to the auction, but only one had been willing to pay that shipping fee. But since getting a buyer is the whole point, she thought maybe she'd try this pricing strategy this one time.

She discussed it with her husband Kurt, who didn't think the other seller's method was very good business practice. To him, it seemed like trickery to advertise such a low price, when indeed the price technically was much higher. Brooke decided to list the costume anyway, just to see what happened, and did so for a "Buy It Now" price of $2.99. She was very clear in the auction listing that the shipping would be $35, so there would be no confusion or risk of a non-paying bidder to deal with.

She had plenty of lookers, but that wasn't all. Within days, she had received two rather unpleasant e-mails from potential buyers, blasting her methods. One person even noted that "eBay wouldn't be happy with what you're doing" but didn't elaborate further.

Kurt clucked his tongue, *I told you so!* Fearing any more negative e-mails and criticism, Brooke decided to revise the auction, raise the asking price and lower the shipping to reflect the actual postage plus her standard $1.50 handling fee.

Unbelievably, when she went to make the change, she found the auction had indeed sold—and had already been paid for as well! There was nothing to do but to complete the transaction and ship the item.

Shortly after this, she learned what one of her angry e-mailers had been hinting at: fee circumvention.

What Brooke didn't know when she posted her listing is that it's against eBay's policy to price your item extremely low (such as the desirable costume for $2.99) and then charge an exorbitant amount of shipping (such as the $35 Brooke was charging). Even if the item is worth every penny of the $37.99 total paid, that isn't the point.

The point is that Brooke's final value fee (the commission she paid to eBay based on the amount of the winning bid) amounted to only $0.16 because it's based on the winning bid amount (5.25 percent of the $2.99). Yet Brooke collected $37.99 for the item. If she had priced the auction competitively, she may have had a final bid of $35, and her final value fee would have been $1.59.

That's a big difference; if you were to do this on all your auctions, your profit margin would definitely go up. But it's strictly prohibited by eBay's policies to utilize this type of pricing strategy, for obvious reason: it robs eBay of fees that are rightly theirs. Most people have seen auctions like this; even Brooke had seen the one that gave her the idea to do an auction that way.

But despite years as an eBay seller, she had never heard of fee circumvention. Being an honest person, it would never occur to her to try something like this for that reason. She thought of it more as a slick marketing technique: a way to entice lookers into checking out her auction as opposed to someone else's.

Once she learned that her auction had been a violation of eBay policy, she was quick to swear off that method of pricing. Not only does it cheat eBay of their well-earned fees, but she feels that it doesn't lend itself well to her focus on good customer service. If you're getting nasty e-mails from lookers, you're probably doing something wrong!

She learned her lesson and was grateful that the e-mailer didn't notify eBay of her violation. It was an honest mistake on her part, but the embarrassment of having eBay yank her listing or suspend her account could have been a costly blot on her otherwise clean and polished sales record.

Luckily, even though Suzy is new to selling on eBay, she has the benefit of knowing about this policy and she will be careful to always price her items properly. She now turns her thoughts to some of the acceptable pricing strategies she might choose in conjunction with a reasonable shipping fee policy. She might choose to:

- Start the auction at $0.01, as this can spark mere curiosity on the lookers' part and qualifies her for the cheapest listing fee of $0.25.

- Start the bidding at $0.99, as that, too, seems to attract buyers and lookers who think, *Gee, maybe I can get that item for less than a buck!* This starting price also qualifies for the $0.25 listing fee.

- Start the auction for a minimum price she feels she needs to cover her outlay, which includes her $2 acquisition fee, the listing fees, final value fees, and PayPal fees that she may encounter. A starting bid of $3.99 would let her break even, even if the bids didn't go higher.

- Try a Buy It Now in addition to a minimum starting bid. She might offer a Buy It Now for $9.99 or more, since her research indicates that sometimes these items do go for up to $20. Someone who "wants it now" may be willing to pay a bit more than the bidder who's not as anxious.

- Consider a Reserve Auction, but since Suzy has already determined that there's nothing spectacular or rare about this waffle iron, she's not going to choose that option this time.

 **Using the "Buy It Now" Service**

When you are a new seller, you can't offer Buy It Now until you have a feedback score of 10 or greater or unless you are ID Verified (see page 83 on becoming ID Verified).

When deciding on a pricing strategy for your auctions, you'll find there are as many ways to price an item as there are people with different opinions. Sellers who have a gambling spirit might start all their auctions with an opening bid of $0.01 to $0.99. Some believe this is the only way to go. They swear by it, and even if they do occasionally have to lose money on an item by selling for $0.99 or less, it's more than balanced out by the auctions that earn them a tidy profit. Some PowerSellers of the highest echelon utilize this strategy.

On the opposite end of the spectrum are the sellers who are aghast at the thought of losing money on an auction or only breaking even. They absolutely won't sell any item unless they can get a comfortable profit from it, and preferably the maximum profit. They won't spend an extra penny on their listing that isn't completely necessary (no frills here), and they set their minimum prices to give them a reasonable profit so they are assured of at least that amount. They don't feel the need to pique a looker's interest; their attitude is: If the looker wants it for this price, fine; if not, fine.

While this may be something we'd all love—to get the maximum profit for every single item—it's not very realistic when you're talking about auctions. Items in your eBay store are fixed-price and have a 30-day listing period for a small fee. Those are the items you can aim to get maximum profit from, but an auction format is geared toward the highest bid at the time your auction is running. The sellers who don't understand this can become bitter and give up on their business if they find they are constantly re-listing items because they don't sell (more on re-listing in Chapter 10).

Somewhere in the middle are the sellers who try a combination of all acceptable tactics. They may have some items that they feel they can afford to just break even on, or maybe even lose a small amount on, because that gives them the opportunity to cross-promote their other items or their eBay store. For that exposure, they are willing to risk doing the penny auctions on certain items, and they consider it almost as an advertising cost. If they make money, great; if not, that's okay too.

However, there are some items that they simply can't afford to lose money on, so they employ minimum starting bids that will allow them to break even if the price doesn't go higher than that. They can add a Buy It Now for maximum profit, but this gives lookers the chance to try to get the item at rock-bottom pricing.

And for the items that they don't want to settle for breaking even on, they can either set a higher minimum starting bid (or a reserve price, if appropriate) or do a fixed-price auction (no negotiations or bidding). If they have a store, they could also choose to add it to their store inventory utilizing Buy It Now only.

There are a couple of other things to consider when planning a pricing strategy:

- You can always revise your listing to lower or raise your price if you feel that you're not attracting enough lookers. You must do so before at least 12 hours before the listing is set to end and there must not be any bids on it yet. Lookers who have your item on their watch lists may be enticed to take the next step when they see a price reduction.

- You can opt to have a link on your listing that says "Submit a Best Offer." If buyers want to purchase the item outright, they can make their best offer instead of waiting for the bidding to get that high. Sellers can accept or decline any offers. Be sure to read about up on this topic by searching that term on eBay's "Help" pages before offering this option.

- If you see that there are plenty of items identical, or similar, to yours available for auction, you can hold off on your particular item (as long as it's not seasonally in demand) and consider listing it again in a week or two. Perhaps there won't be as much competition at that time.

- If you have several items that "go together," such as a group of collectible figurines, consider selling together for one price (this is called a "lot") rather than trying to sell them individually. This will save on listing fees and, for the buyer, save on shipping as opposed to paying several shipping charges.

Joining some of eBay's discussion boards is a good way to learn about different pricing philosophies and strategies from those who have been doing this a while. You may get some good ideas or learn what truly doesn't work for different merchandise types.

The **Buy It Now (BIN)** feature also is looked upon differently by various sellers. Some believe that if you list a BIN price, you're stating the maximum value of the item, which can translate into bidders not going above that point. Others feel that it's an excellent tool for speeding up transactions for those who don't want to bid it out and are willing to pay the asked price. And since that option disappears once the first bid is made, future bidders may not even know what the BIN price had been.

Fixed-price auctions are basically a Buy It Now with the bidding, so the stated price is the only price the buyer must accept. This gives some sellers a better sense of security over their listings. Some buyers like this option, for the same reasons they like the Buy It Now. All listings in your eBay store inventory are fixed-price listings, but many people don't realize this because your current auctions are also displayed in your store.

Buyers may or may not warm up to a fixed-price auction, since that goes against their desire to "get a good deal" by shopping on eBay. Remember, they pay shipping and handling as well, so if they can get it for the same price locally, they might. Always keep in mind what even the largest retailers in the nation advertise: lowest prices.

Dutch Auctions are probably not something the new eBay seller is going to jump into right away unless they are purchasing bulk wholesale lots for resale. When you sell items at a Dutch Auction, every single bidder ultimately pays the same price: the amount of the lowest bid. Yes, the lowest bid.

For example, Willy decides to list ten of his gidgets at a Dutch Auction. When someone places a bid, they specify how many of those ten gidgets they want to purchase and a price they are willing to pay for each.

At the end of the auction, here are the bids that have come in:

Bidder Number	Quantity Desired	Price Willing to Pay for Each
1	1	$1.99
2	1	$5.99
3	2	$6.24
4	1	$6.59
5	3	$6.99
6	1	$7.49
7	2	$7.99
8	1	$8.24
9	1	$8.55
10	4	$9.01
11	1	$9.40
12	3	$9.89
13	1	$10.09
14	3	$10.50
15	1	$10.99

By the end of the auction, Willy has fifteen bidders wanting 26 gidgets. However, the auction was for only ten of them. So here's how it's decided who gets them and who doesn't. The highest bidders get them, of course. Bidder Number 15 will get a quantity of one. Bidder 14 will get three of them. Number 13 will get one, number 12 will get three and number 11 will get one. That leaves bidder Number 10. He wanted four, but there is only one left. So he gets only one, or he can choose to pass on the offer and then the last one would be offered to bidder number 9. And the price they will all pay is $9.01 each: the same as the lowest bidder who is going to get a gidget. If bidder Number 10 passes on the offer to purchase only one, then bidder Number 9 will be offered the final one for his bid price of $8.55.

Like with other auction styles, opinions vary on the effectiveness of Dutch Auctions. Some believe that by having a Dutch Auction, the seller is admitting to having an overstock of the item, and that can drive down the price. Or it may appear that there is a large market for the item, since so many people are bidding on it. This may invite competition in its own way.

If you're considering a Dutch Auction because you'll be able to list it with just one listing fee, think again. The fee for these auctions is based on the quantity you fill in during the listing process (covered in the next chapter) and your opening bid price (the same way an ordinary auction would be charged), so doing a Dutch Auction isn't a big money saver.

There are other rules involved in Dutch Auctions that you need to be aware of. For one, proxy bidding is not allowed, and you can only place your auction in one category. If you have a large enough quantity, you can split it into two groups and place each group in a separate category for more exposure.

Dutch Auctions can be good for the right seller with the right merchandise, but do some investigating and research about them before considering them to market your product.

Generally, no pricing strategy is always right every time, and there is always a risk that your auction won't sell. In fact, statistics show that only approximately 41 percent of auctions sell the first time around. Your best strategy is a combination of knowing the appropriate asking price, knowing when to take a bit of a gamble, and knowing how best to utilize all the options and tools available to you on eBay.

If the waffle iron that Suzy is now preparing to sell had been in her family for three generations, she may have had an emotional attachment to it that, in her own opinion, elevated its worth. It's very important that you don't over-estimate the true value of the items you sell, especially if they originated as your own possessions.

The reality is that people come to eBay, among other reasons, for bargains. If they can spend a few dollars more and get a brand new equivalent of what you're selling by driving to their nearest mall, they might very well do that. Just because you paid $50 for an item new doesn't mean that you'll get anywhere near $50 for it used, even if it is in like-new condition.

What you get at auction is based on the amount that the current lookers are willing to pay. You never know if the current lookers will be experienced buyers who are willing to wait it out for a better deal or new eBay members who may overpay during the thrill of the auction. You may get lucky and, while your auction is running, someone who desperately wants just what you have will go hog-wild bidding on it.

Or, the auction gods may not smile on you and your item will go unsold despite your attractive starting price and other good auction qualities. While that can be one frustrating thing about selling on eBay, it also is one of the most thrilling things: You never know just how much money you might make!

This brings up something that sellers may not understand unless they also have some buying experience on eBay: **how bidders bid**. Suzy may watch her auction like a hawk the first few days, checking it frequently to see how many times her auction has been viewed (we've all done it, even if we don't want to admit it sometimes) and agonizing over the fees she'll have to pay even if her waffle iron doesn't sell.

If Suzy has done any bidding herself, she may well recall that when buyers search on eBay, the listings that are ending first are the ones that are shown first by default. Lookers can change the order to show items newly listed, items with the current lowest or highest prices, or other options. However, that choice can't be made until after the default view pops up. So she may not get a lot of lookers or bids on her listing until the final days or hours.

Lookers also put things that they are interested in on their "Items I'm Watching" lists and wait till the last minutes to place a bid, hoping to be the first or only bidder to nab the item at the opening bid price. But anyone who has been outbid in the final seconds knows that isn't a surefire technique for winning the item. Many buyers have been bested by other unseen lookers who had the exact same thing in mind!

Bidders can place bids on items hours or days before the auction ends through eBay's proxy bidding system. When they place an initial bid, they must do so at the current price (if they're the first bidder) or raise the current bid by a small amount. They also enter an amount that will be kept secret from the seller and other bidders: what their maximum bid amount is.

When the next looker comes along and thinks "I'd be willing to pay a dollar more than that guy bid." and puts in his bid, he may be outbid instantly by the proxy bid that had been previously set by the previous bidder. The computer will keep raising the bid up to the previous bidder's maximum.

Once any bidder has been outbid, he must either enter a larger maximum bid, watch the auction himself and try to sneak in a bid at the end, or give up.

It can be a dizzying spectacle keeping track of who's winning and who's losing when the bidding gets fierce; it's a seller's dream to have an auction that ends in a bidding war. The bidder who's just been bested keeps upping his or her bid amount a little bit more, hoping to get in the final bid. Sometimes it works out in his favor, sometimes in the other seller's favor. And sometimes there are multiple sellers upping the bid, entering higher bids and proxy amounts, furiously hoping to be the highest bidder when the seconds tick down.

Bidding in the final seconds to win the auction is known as sniping. While it may seem unfair to the bidder who lost out on a great deal in the final ten seconds, it's completely allowed in eBay's rules. Many a seller has been pleasantly surprised to see an auction's final bid go up higher than they were anticipating because of sniping.

If you are really interested in getting the best deal but don't want to stay up all night trying to snipe, there are online sniping services available. You may be able to get a free trial, but after that time frame, you'll have to determine if the fees will be worth the deals you'll get.

Many people have studied another aspect of bidding: **when bidders bid**. EBay has done a lot of research to determine the buying patterns of the public, which could be translated into the **best time to start (and end) your listings**. If you can time your auctions to end at the same time as a lot of buyers are online, then you may have an advantage over the seller whose listing is ending at 3 a.m. on a slow day of the week.

According to eBay's Seller Central Report: How Buyers Use eBay (located at **http://pages.ebay.com/sellercentral/buyers.pdf**), "just over one-third of all Internet users in the United States visit eBay each month." The majority of visitors to eBay surf during the weekdays, while Sundays and Mondays are the traffic-jam days.

You might also want to consider other factors, such as time zones across the country, people who work second shift, or parents of small children who may not be able to access eBay except at naptimes and after the kids are in bed for the night.

One thought about listing ending times: Try not to compete with major events such as the President's "State of the Union" speech or the Super Bowl. They may or may not play a part in how many people are online, but if you can avoid them, you might as well.

When she sets her auction, Suzy will be given a choice to schedule the listing to start at a specific time. If she were putting her listing on at 1:44 a.m., she knows that her listing will end at 1:44 a.m. as well. That might not entice the bidders who like to snipe, so in that case she could have scheduled the listing to start the next evening, for an additional fee. When she downloads and uses Turbo Lister, Suzy can plan out her auction completely and then simply not upload it until a better time of day. This, and other aspects of Turbo Lister, will be covered in Appendix B.

Once Suzy has decided on when to start her auction (based on when she wishes to have it end), she also needs to consider how long to run the auction. She can choose to do a one-, three-, five-, seven- or ten-day listing. There is no difference in the fees for any of these listings (except for an additional $0.40 fee for a ten-day listing), so the choice between a five-day and seven-day listing is purely for strategy.

One thing that may help Suzy decide on a duration is this: She has noticed that someone has already posted a seven-day listing of a nearly identical waffle iron. She also sees that this competitor has a starting price of $12.99 and a Buy It Now of $24.99. Sally feels that, based on her research, this seller is expecting too much, and isn't surprised that after two days the listing has only been viewed twice (yes, she peeked at her competitor's counter!).

If Suzy chooses to run a five-day listing starting immediately, her item will be ending at approximately the same time as the competitor's item. At the very least, when lookers search, both of their listings will come up in very close proximity to each other.

So Suzy decides, based purely on strategy, to do a five-day listing this time. And since it's currently a Wednesday, she won't miss out on any of the weekend viewing, as the auction will run until Monday evening.

Sometimes it may not be a good idea to time your auctions to end close to your competitor's listings. If you're a new seller, bidders might be wary of buying from you when they could just as easily buy from someone with experience. There are a lot of unknowns about new sellers, and bidders may be worried that you won't provide timely shipping or have any customer-service skills.

Entice a hesitant bidder with a better deal on shipping, by comparing your competitor's costs and yours. If you can offer cheaper shipping with no handling fee, you may be able to beat out your competitor on overall price. If your shipping is cheaper than others, try to work that into your title (Low Ship, Free Ship, Cheap Ship, etc.). Comparing shipping rates is one way that bidders save money.

Other reasons for choosing the listing durations might be if you have fifteen identical items to sell, you might not want them all ending at the same exact time because bidders will soon clue in that if they didn't win the first one for the minimum bid, they can wait five minutes for the second one and try again. To avoid this, you might list one or two at a time, a day or more apart.

Or if you want to list them all at once, then you'd do some three-, five- and seven-day listings. In this case, notify the non-winning bidders in the first auctions that there are others available so they can bid on the next group.

Just before a holiday you might want to offer shorter auction times with speedy shipping (even if you have to take special trips to the post office twice a day). Buyers will appreciate your efforts during rush times.

A one-day listing also might be necessary for items that are tied to an upcoming event, like tickets or during a special one-day-only sale on special items.

A three-day listing that starts on a Friday evening will run all the way through Monday evening. Since the prime time is commonly believed to be during this time frame, you might want to consider a three-day listing.

If your item is steadily a good seller and you know this from research, then five days might be enough time to attract the attention it needs. Remember, these auctions will get to the top of the list (when listings ending first are shown by default in search results) two whole days faster than the same items on a seven-day listing.

However, since you can't control who is online at any give time or day, you will get the most exposure out of a seven-day listing. It might be considered the most bang-for-your-buck duration, but the drawback is that it takes six and a half days (or longer) to reach that all-important first page of search results.

Ten-day listings have their place too. If you want to start an auction on a Thursday and want it to be active through two complete weekends, then you can do that with the ten-day listing. The downside of this is that for the extra $0.40 you'll spend, you could have done a 7-day listing and (if it didn't sell in seven days) re-listed it immediately for 14-day exposure. If it sold the second time around, you'll even get some credit of the second listing fee from eBay.

After Suzy has worked out her pricing strategy and decided on her five-day auction, she begins to hammer out a title and a description for her waffle iron. After numerous auctions, she may find that titles and descriptions come easier to her. She will find what works and what doesn't, and she will develop a flow in the way she words her auctions. She'll begin to write auctions in a similar tone of voice, just as if she were giving the same sales pitch over and over again. While the product might change from auction to auction, she'll utilize the same techniques or pattern and flow repeatedly.

Writing an effective title has become its own art form. Here are some tips to think about while you contemplate every one of your 55 available characters (including spaces and punctuation).

The point of the title isn't just to entice the looker to click on your auction and view the description. The title is how sellers (for the most part) find your auction. The title points the search engine to your item through proper phrasing and use of keywords. While it is possible to search the title and the description for keywords and specific information, sellers often type their search criteria in the box and hit the enter key. In order to search the description as well, they have to move a hand over to the mouse and click on the box indicating they want to search title and description.

Not to imply that lookers are lazy, but the title should contain the words they're looking for, unless they're not searching properly. And many lookers are confident enough in eBay's search results that they don't go out of their way to search both title and description unless they're looking for a rare or unusual item.

So think of your title as how you are going to locate the lookers and buyers. Think in terms of "what words will they be using to look for my item" and act accordingly. Here are some tips about what to put in your titles:

- Use keywords, not full sentences. It doesn't have to be grammatical to be useful to the search engine. No one ever searched for "look at this cute sweater," but they will search for a "Ralph Lauren blue wool cardigan ladies size 8."

- Add the size, color, fabric/material used (tin, wood, resin), model number, and other important features.

- Specify if it's new or used, if you have room and it's not obvious by other items (such as acronyms).

- Use appropriate acronyms to save space, such as NIP (New In Package) and NWT (New With Tags), but consider typing these phrases out in the actual description.

- Your title must make it clear what your item is and can't be misleading.

- Avoid gimmicks and catch phrases such as "L@@K" and "Must See" and words that are subjective: "very pretty," "cute," "desirable," "awesome."

- Just as in chat rooms or message boards, using ALL CAPS is considered screaming. Choose just one word to scream, perhaps, and leave it at that.

- Go easy on terms that can seem faddish such as "Vintage," "Rare," or "Hard to Find," unless you have enough experience with the item type to say that definitively.

- Avoid punctuation in titles as it can sometimes confuse the search engine. Even if you have a few characters to spare, leave them blank, as too much punctuation can be !!**annoying**!!).

- No Web addresses, phone numbers, e-mail addresses, etc., are allowed in titles.

- Don't use words that suggest an item is contraband, even if it isn't (for example, "banned," "illegal").

The entire 55 characters may make or break an auction, and that added pressure to help lookers find it can make new sellers anxious to create the perfect title. Suzy paid close attention to the titles in the current and completed auctions she searched when determining her pricing strategy. She found numerous words that were very common, such as "Wagner" or "Wagner Ware," the name of the company that made this waffle iron. She decides that her title will also feature the company's name, to distinguish her waffle iron from those made by another common company at that time, Griswold.

Since the item more than qualifies for "antique" status (it's clearly marked with the patent date 1910), she will likely use that word as well as the year marked on the item, although some might call that redundant. Some of the waffle irons she saw didn't come with the heat ring, which kept the iron from sitting directly onto the stove. Hers has that feature, so she may mention that.

Another phrase she saw in many of the auctions she looked at was "cast iron." Her own personal experience tells her that this is cast iron too, so she adds that to her list of possible words to go in the title. It has other markings such as the word "Sidney," -0-, and "9," and while she doesn't know the significance of these things, she may use them if she has space.

Suzy works out a few possibilities for her waffle iron; she'll make the final decision when she's posting the auction online. Here are her possibilities:

- Antique Wagner Ware cast iron waffle maker 1910 NR

- 1910 Wagner Ware stove top waffle iron heat ring Sidney

TIP ★ Avoid Keyword Spamming

Warning: eBay has a very strong policy against keyword spamming, which is using keywords in your title or item description that don't specifically relate to your item. Read eBay's policy on this at
http://pages.ebay.com/help/policies/keyword-spam.html

With a couple of titles in hand, Suzy now turns her attention to drafting a description.

Writing good descriptions is also important; just because you got the looker to click on your listing and read (at least some of) your description, doesn't mean you'll make the sale. Your own writing talent, attention to detail, and enthusiasm for your product all need to be utilized in order to sell an item. You may only get a looker to read your description once before he or she decides whether to become a watcher or bidder, or move on to the next search result.

Here are some suggestions to consider when writing your description. Much more help and information can be found in the "Seller Central" section of eBay, so don't hesitate to look there for good tips too!

A nice descriptive tone is good for some items, but others will be better served by a bulleted list of features. You might want to consider what type of person is likely to be buying your item. If you're selling office supplies, you may be dealing with busy secretaries and businesspeople who don't have time to read a long, rambling tale of how you want to sell these items to them.

But if you're selling children's clothing, you'll want to appeal to the mothers and grandmothers who can't resist hearing how sweet and special their angels are. I'm not suggesting that you gush, but you can get a little more descriptive and flowery with a satin and lace baby dress than you can with a printer cartridge.

Write a simple and clear description of the item, adding sufficient detail for the bidder to have a full understanding but not overloading the bidder with needless information or details. This can be a tough balance to find. While you should always offer to answer questions about the item or furnish additional photos, some buyers won't bother to take that extra step, or perhaps there isn't time to do so (at the end of the auction), so make sure you're thorough.

Keep your opinions objective. Otherwise it might seem as if you are guaranteeing that the buyer will be just as thrilled with the item as you are, and if they aren't, you may have an unhappy buyer.

Be sure to check your spelling; the buyer will think you're not knowledgeable about your product if you spell the manufacturer's name wrong. Use spell-check in eBay when you fill out your description online.

Include all relevant details: size, color, materials, year made, manufacturer/brand name, condition. If an item is used, realize that what you might call "good" used condition will be called "fair" by another person. Rather than give it a personal rating, describe the qualities that make it "good" (no rips, tears, worn spots, or fading).

TIP Check Out eBay's Help Files

*Search eBay's "Help" files for information about grading and
authentication services. If you're new to selling any type of
collectible, get help determining the difference between
"Mint Condition" and "Excellent Condition" before you
put it up for auction.*

Suggest new uses for your item, or point out cross-sell items that are part
of a matching set. Suggest they buy a second of the same item (if you
have additional quantities for auction) to give to a friend, to keep as a
spare, etc. Word your description as if you were selling them the item face
to face. If you're selling curtains, tell them how nicely they drape and
that they'll look stunning in the buyer's living room or den. Don't lie, but
word things so that the buyer takes that leap from looking at your item to
imagining themselves owning and using it.

Always include an invitation to view your other items (use eBay's built-in
link, if you're not writing HTML code—more in Appendix B).

End your listing description with a motivator: "Place a Bid Today!" as
well as a "Thank You for Looking" message and a brief statement about
combined shipping (if you offer it, which you'd be almost foolish not to
offer) such as "Happy to combine shipping on all auctions won within a
five-day period!" Maybe top it off with one more invitation to check out
your other items, since you just pitched your combined shipping offer.

And finally, back up all claims about faults and condition with plenty
of photos taken by you. Don't use stock photos from the manufacturer
unless your items are new in the factory-sealed packaging.

After reading the other descriptions of waffle irons, Suzy feels she wants
to be brief and to the point. There's no sense in trying to make this waffle
iron out to be some rare treasure, as anyone who searches will know
better, and she doesn't want to sound like she's clueless. But she thinks
she has an angle that might lure in just the right buyer. Here is her rough
draft:

Take a look at this 1910-model Wagner Ware waffle iron. This item has served many a family in the past century and shows wear and tear that would be expected. The heat ring has a chip in it and the wood handles have no cracks but are missing a small piece at the end. See photos for close-ups of these noted items.

Wagner Ware waffle irons were made of heavy cast iron for years of faithful use. This one has rusted somewhat after years of non-use after it was likely replaced by an electric model.

The fine details of early 20th century cast iron pieces can be seen in the name and other markings on the top and bottom. Even the patent date is easily read.

With a good cleaning and some preservation, it will make a nice display piece in your country kitchen.

Bring this lovely piece into your home and give it the place of honor it deserves, just like all the hard-working cooks and parents who used it to feed their families in generations past.

Suzy may decide to change a word here or there, but she is satisfied with the approach that she took: appealing to the lookers' appreciation of old items and their sense of nostalgia. Notice how she invited the lookers to imagine the item displayed in their kitchens, giving them a use for the old rusted item and how she tied such a display to a sense of honoring family values.

There's no guarantee that Suzy's description will make her waffle iron sell, because lookers are a fickle lot. They could enjoy her description but bid on a similar item with a smaller price instead, and still envision the same end result with a different item. But hopefully Suzy's description will entice them enough to hook them into bidding.

In addition to writing your title and description, you should decide what **policies** you'll put in your auction listings every time. These can include your shipping policy, your return policy, or a listing of what payment types you accept.

Since these policies will likely be the same for every auction she posts, Suzy is going to type them up in a word-processing document such as Notepad or Microsoft Word—later she will save them in a template in

Turbo Lister, and then she can copy and paste it into her auctions without having to re-type it.

But first she has to spend some time reviewing all the items she may want to cover in her policies and decide what she will require of, and guarantee to, her customers.

The two most important policies for bidders to know up front are your payment policy and your shipping policy, although all should be clearly laid out in every auction.

Your **payment policy** simply states what payment types you accept. Remember that if you have the PayPal logo in your listing and you state that you accept PayPal, then you cannot also state that you can't accept debit and credit card payments through PayPal (see Chapter 5).

List what payments you will accept and any conditions that go along with any payment type (such as "personal check accepted but merchandise held for ten days while check clears" or "cash at your own risk"). If you receive payments via PayPal, eBay will automatically direct the buyer to your PayPal username, but some sellers state it in the payment policy.

Also make sure you specify the time frame in which you expect payment to be received and any consequences for not following the policy; "payment expected within ten days of auction closing or buyer will be reported and negative feedback will be given to buyer" is one example. Some buyers take exception to the implied threat, so you may want to craft a warmer and fuzzier way to say the same thing.

Your **shipping policy** will generally be the same for all auctions and sales. You might revise this as time goes on and you learn how to balance serving your customers with not overloading yourself. For instance, you might start out saying this: I ship the same day as your payment—five days a week.

You'll soon find out that even if the PayPal payment comes in at 4 p.m., your buyers may expect you to still ship that same day. And even if they are paying for media mail, they might expect the same speediness as if they were paying express.

Over time, you'll determine what you are truly capable of. Your revised shipping policy might state: If your PayPal payment for Priority Mail arrives by 9 a.m. (Central time zone M-F), your item will ship the same day. After 9 a.m., shipping the next business day. For Parcel Post, Media Mail, First Class mail, UPS or FedEx, shipping within two business days.

Your shipping policy should also touch on your **combined shipping** policy. If you are willing to combine shipping costs and mail multiple auctions in one package, then say so up front and give a timeline (all auctions won in a three-day period) and any other restrictions (items must be paid for at one time to qualify for the discount). More about this topic will be discussed in Chapter 10.

Notify Buyers of Shipping

Most buyers are happy with their item being shipped in any reasonable time frame, so long as they know when it is going to be shipped. Consider sending a follow-up e-mail to your customer the same day the item ships to let them know that it's on its way!

Give some thought to making a **policy on optional services,** such as delivery confirmation and insurance. Some sellers have made these items a requirement because they have lost money on packages that never arrived (or they could never prove they arrived) or that arrived damaged, and the buyer demanded a refund. The differing opinions about how to handle a situation like this will be covered in Chapter 10.

Your policy should be clearly stated as to what you require and what services are optional. Delivery confirmation is not expensive, and, as explained in Chapter 5, when you purchase Priority Mail postage online, delivery confirmation is automatically included on all packages regardless of their class. There is no additional cost for Priority packages, but there is a $0.13 charge for other mail classes.

Because of the free delivery confirmation and the fact that they get Priority shipping supplies for free, some sellers have chosen to only ship via Priority Mail. However, don't necessarily limit yourself to one shipping provider or one class of shipping. Customers appreciate flexibility and cheaper shipping options if they're not in a hurry.

You will also need to develop a **merchandise-return policy**. Whether or not you accept returns is entirely up to you. Return policies come in all shapes and sizes, from the extreme, "All merchandise is as-is, no returns, no exceptions," to the less demanding, "Returns only accepted if I made a gross error in listing the item or misrepresented it in some way." Some merchants (especially those who list brand-new items) state that they will "accept returns only if the item is returned in the same condition as when shipped" unless it was damaged in transit.

The one thing that a seller doesn't want to have happen a lot is to have buyers return items just because they've changed their mind or aren't as thrilled with it as they thought they would be. Impulse shoppers often have these second thoughts and can actually dislike an item they bought impetuously, even though it's exactly what they wanted at that moment.

Shipping fees are generally one item that sellers don't refund. Make sure you specify the conditions under which you will accept a return, such as:

1. Buyer pays to ship it back to the seller.

2. Buyer must return it via the same shipping service and class of shipment as sent.

3. Item must be in an acceptable shipping container with appropriate protection, preferably the same box and packing material that you used.

4. The refund amount will be less any shipping and handling originally paid.

Sometimes having a policy such as this will deter the buyer who wants to return an item for the wrong reasons.

International buyers will want to know right away if you have a **policy about international shipping**. Be sure to state your willingness (or not) to deal with international bidders after examining all the issues and particulars (covered in Chapter 3).

You may also need to specify a **policy on local pickups**. If your buyer lives within reasonable driving distance, they may want to come get their item rather than have it shipped. The choice is up to you, but it's nice to state up front if this is an acceptable option to you. If you work from home, you may consider this a security risk, in which case you may choose to drop the item off or meet in a public location.

Make sure you specify if the item must be paid in full prior to the pickup (or meeting) or if it can be paid for at the time of the pickup/meeting. Expecting payment prior to arranging a date will assure you that the buyer won't try to pay with an unacceptable payment type (such as a personal check) at the last moment.

Another possible speed bump with local pickup is the lack of any delivery confirmation. If you frequently have local pickups, make a generic "Pickup Receipt" in your word-processing software with spaces to fill in all the pertinent information: auction date, title, item description, date paid, payment type, and pickup information. Then, have buyers sign and date the receipt for your records, verifying that they did receive the package.

A word of caution: You need to present a clear picture to your buyers of all the aspects of the transaction so that they can make an informed decision on whether or not to do business with you. Some sellers who have had bad experiences or been "burned" in the past use their list of policies to express their anger and frustration. This is an actual example of a policy I saw on an item recently:

> I will NEVER! ship anywhere that requires a customs form. So if you require a customs form, DO NOT BID!

This statement was in red bold lettering (much larger than the font of the item description), and even though I'm not an international buyer, I was taken aback by the emotions exuding from this statement. I didn't give this auction a second thought; this seller is obviously someone I'm not interested in doing business with.

There is a fine line between laying out all your terms in full and appearing to be a cold-hearted seller with no customer-service skills. What will make the difference is your wording. Keep your policies brief and polite, and let customers know that you care about their experience and satisfaction as well.

After researching these topics in eBay's "Help" pages, Suzy has developed an initial policy statement that she is comfortable with. She decides to insert this statement after the item description (in case lookers aren't seriously interested, they don't have to be bothered with this information), in a font one size smaller than the item's description (so as not to appear as if she's more interested in her policy than in the item she's selling).

> I want every customer to be happy, and have worded my descriptions and supplied photos with the intent that you will have a clear and full understanding of the item you're purchasing. If you'd like additional photos or details, feel free to contact me; I'm happy to help!

> Please review these policies for conducting business together:

> Payment: I accept PayPal, money orders, or cashier's checks. Please pay within ten days, or communicate with me if there's a problem in doing so.

> Shipping: I ship USPS (unless you have a special request) ASAP after payment is received—two business days or less. All shipping quotes include delivery confirmation. Insurance is at your option (unless otherwise noted in listing) but strongly suggested.

> Returns: If you feel the item was significantly misrepresented by me (per eBay's policies), I will offer a return/refund, minus shipping costs. Return shipping is at your expense. Please contact me immediately if there is a concern, as I strive for 100% customer satisfaction.

> International Bidders: At this time, I am not offering international shipping, but thank you for looking.

> Local Pickup: If you live within 25 miles of my town, I will arrange to meet you halfway for a fee equal to half of the shipping cost. This fee must be paid, via mail or PayPal, prior to arranging a meeting.

One last thing that Suzy needs to attend to before she begins the auction setup: taking and preparing photos of the item.

It's almost hard to overdo it when it comes to posting photos on your auction. They can pose downloading-time issues with Internet users who have a dial-up connection, but high-speed Internet access is becoming so common and affordable that this shouldn't be a problem for many.

Photos are an integral part of every auction. Very few people will purchase an item without a photo displayed, and most people won't even look at an auction with no photo. There's simply no excuse for not having photos with today's technology.

TIP — Use Photos to Your Advantage

If you're really slick and have the software to do it, you can superimpose your company's name onto each of your photos! Not only does this put your company name into the mind of every looker, it will also help prevent other sellers from using your photos as their own.

The quickest way to get photos of your items is by using a digital camera. The price of digital cameras has come down significantly in the past few years; now you can get a camera for under $200 that would have cost double that amount previously. Digital cameras are fairly easy to use, and you can take as many shots as necessary to get just the right angle and lighting without wasting film, processing costs, or time.

Photo Tips

- You should always have one straight-on shot of the entire item; preferably this would be the first photo that lookers see when they click on your title. To be sure this is the case, use this photo for your "free" first photo from eBay (more about this in next chapter) or as the first photo you place in Turbo Lister (more about this in Appendix B).

- Use a contrasting background for your item. If your item is dark in color, set it on a tabletop or couch with a white sheet draped over it.

- Set your camera on a fixed object, such as a stool or a tripod, at the same height as your item.

- To avoid light coming in from windows, try laying your item on the floor, holding the camera directly above it.

- If your item gets a bright spot on it because of your flash, try turning your flash off and using other indirect lighting to diffuse the light.

- Get several different angles or close-ups of defects and special features such as serial numbers.

- Don't get too close and have the item blur (use your camera's built-in zoom if it's available). Remember, you can always crop the photo and cut out everything but your item, making it appear closer.

- Reference the size of item by laying a yardstick, ruler, pencil, coin, or other common object next to it.

- A craft store can sell you a display stand used to hold a plate or photo frame at an angle. Drape a black cloth over a piece of wood in the stand and lay jewelry on the cloth. Drape the cloth over a piece of wood dowel (or a pen, even) to hold a ring for photographing.

You can purchase camera accessories to assist you in getting the best lighting situations. Depending on what you sell (if you sell brand-new items and can utilize stock photos from your supplier, this isn't an issue) you may want to put these items on your business's "wish list."

- Cloud dome: A white bowl or cone-shaped device that spreads out the light from your camera's flash, reducing the white spot on your item and evening out other light in the room. These are good for smaller items and close-ups.

- Lighting tents: These are nylon or other white fabric tents with an opening in the front for you to insert your item. You then take your photo through the front opening. Some kits come with fabric backdrops for contrasting colors.

- Stands and other portable platforms that have a solid-colored background: This gives you a consistent background color for easier cropping.

- Reflectors (like special umbrellas) to spread the light from your flash evenly around your object.

Much like other items that cost money up front, having the nicest photo equipment right away isn't a true necessity. Use your "wish list" to purchase items for your business that can be used as a tax deduction (thereby reducing your business's income). Your accountant will let you know when you have excess income that would be better used by making a needed purchase than paying taxes on it.

Hopefully you've got a computer dedicated to your business, but if not, consider making a unique folder where you'll store your eBay item photos. Pre-crop and rotate photos, as you can probably do this right in your photo editing software quicker than you can do it online, especially if you have dial-up Internet service. Consider renaming your photo to something easily identifiable, or better yet, give it the same name or number as the inventory number of the item it represents.

If you're selling a book, you can often get a "stock photo" of the book right through eBay, but you also may want to take a photo of the actual book and include it in the listing so that people can see any damage, worn cover, dog-eared pages, or other things. Sometimes people are disappointed in books that aren't as new looking as the stock photo the seller used. Stock photos are nice to have in the photo preview, as they may be crisper and have better lighting conditions than your photo. However, whether or not you add your own photo, be sure to make it clear that the preview photo is a stock photo.

If you haven't yet located an online hosting site for your photos, there are many from which to choose. Set up an account and upload your photos for your first batch of auctions. You can easily find these online hosting sites by searching the Internet for "image hosting" or "free image hosting" (there are some good free services to use). Registration is generally quick and simple. With the free services, you might have to tolerate banner ads, pop-ups, and other marketing, but to start with, at least try the free services if your business budget is tight. Note: How to insert the photos into the auction will be covered step by step in the next chapter.

Suzy took several photos of her waffle iron, showing all the flaws and defects, both sides (since there are details on both sides), the inside, and one overall photo of the product. Due to the overhead fluorescent lighting in her den/office, she found that laying the item on the floor worked out best.

Here is the overall photo of the entire item. This is the photo that she'll submit for the "preview" picture that will appear on the search results page, and the photo that will be "free."

Suzy will upload the other photos to her image hosting service online and later insert them into her listing information using HTML tags. This will save her fees because she won't be using eBay's services to host them.

These photos are close-up views of both sides of the iron, one side obviously has more rust than the other. It's important for Suzy to show all defects, even rust that would be anticipated with an item like this.

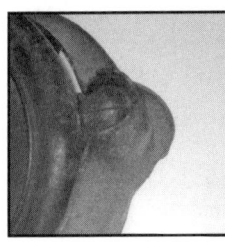
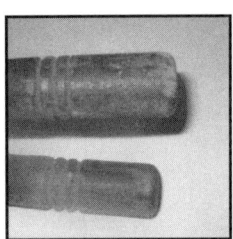

These photos show the other defects that Suzy will note in her description; the chip out of the heat ring and the gouge out of the wood handle.

It is important for Suzy to also show the inside, because of rust, and to show that all the other parts are intact.

Suzy's title, description, and photos are all ready to go; she has boxed up the waffle iron (but not taped the box, in case a bidder wants some other information) and weighed it so she can fill out the online postage calculator during the auction setup process. She has made decisions about duration and her pricing strategy. She's got as many details written down or decided as she possibly can at this point. In the next chapter, we'll follow Suzy as she sets up her first auction on eBay!

Checklist of Tasks: Planning Auctions

❑ I have researched current and previous listings for comparison.

❑ I have chosen an appropriate pricing strategy and understand the pros, cons, and right time to use each one:

Auction without a Buy It Now.

Fixed Price (Buy It Now without an auction).

Auction with Buy It Now.

Reserve Priced auctions.

❑ I understand eBay's policy against fee circumvention (low price/high shipping to avoid paying final value fees) and agree not to use that technique.

❑ I have chosen a good time to start my auction, knowing I can schedule it to start at another time for an additional fee. Otherwise it ends at the same time of day that I posted it.

❑ I have chosen a duration for my listing, based on strategy or to get exposure:

1-day listing

3-day listing

5-day listing

7-day listing

10-day listing (for additional fee)

❑ I have worked out an effective title of 55 characters or less.

❑ I understand eBay's policy against keyword spamming in the title or description and agree not to use that technique.

❑ I have written up a rough draft of a description, including information about any defects. I have checked my copy for spelling and grammatical errors.

❑ I have drafted a simple statement that covers my policy on these issues:

Payments: What I accept and time frame.

Shipping: How and when I generally ship.

Optional Services: Whether I make delivery confirmation, insurance, etc., optional or not.

Returns: Whether or not I'll accept a return and under what conditions.

International bidders: Whether or not I'm open to international bidders.

Local pickups: If I'll arrange a local pickup, and under what conditions.

❑ I have a digital camera and know how to use it for taking photos of my items, or I have access to adequate stock photos (if selling new merchandise) from my supplier.

❑ I have my photos prepared for inserting in the auction listing:

Downloaded from computer.

Named them appropriately for ease of locating.

Cropped away any unnecessary background and reduced the image size to a manageable level (400x600 pixels or 600x400 pixels or smaller is best).

Have several angles or close-ups ready and uploaded to my image hosting service.

One photo designated to be the "preview" photo which I will upload directly to eBay (free photo) Note: If you use Turbo Lister, it's better to have them all uploaded.

❑ I have done these shipping tasks:

Boxed up the item (but not taped in case bidders want more info).

Weighed it on an accurate scale (purchased digital postal scale is best) after packed.

Added a couple of ounces to the weight, which I'll use for the shipping calculator in my listings.

Decided if I'll add a "handling" fee to my listings, which covers my cost for shipping supplies including tape, packing peanuts, or other stuffing materials.

On Your Mark... Get Set... Auction

Finally! After what seems like months of setting up shop, planning, scouring for merchandise, and finalizing a dizzying array of details, Suzy is ready to log in to her eBay account, which she has already set up as a seller's account and had ID Verified, and click the "Sell" button on her top toolbar for the very first time. It's an exciting moment and will be the start of what she hopes will be a long-term business for her.

The step-by-step "Sell" pages (referred to as the "SYI," or "Sell Your Item," form) are almost a no-brainer; you must complete all the required information before you can move to the next step. However, all that planning will make the process quicker and smoother for Suzy. She won't have to make hasty decisions on things that she'll have to revise later, such as misinformation in her description, or things that she'll regret later, such as putting in the wrong shipping weight and having her shipping quotes be all wrong.

The first page of the "Sell" form will prompt Suzy to choose from these three types of listings: online auction, fixed-price auction, or real estate (which is a completely different auction type; this is not applicable unless you truly are selling real estate).

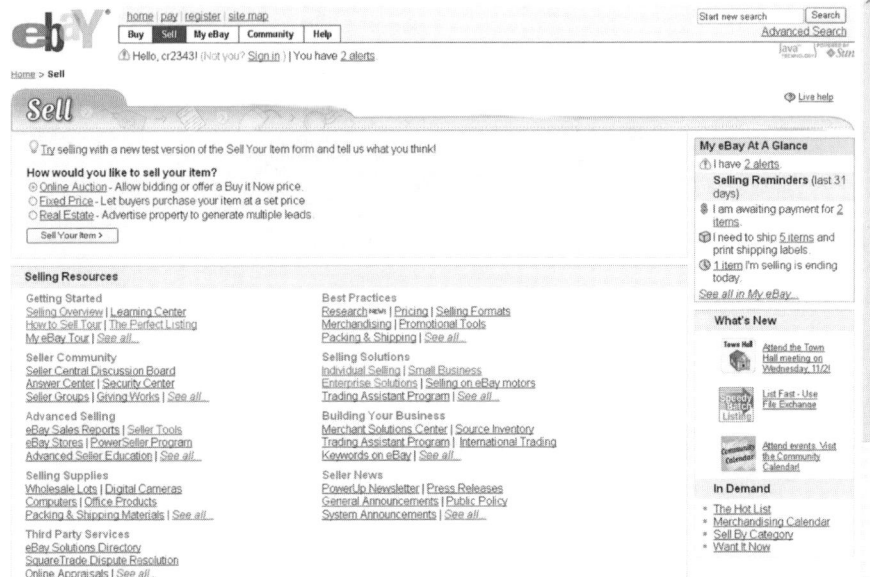

She chooses online auction rather than fixed price, because she can always offer the Buy It Now feature along with the auction. She takes note of the other parts of the page that, while maybe not applicable to selling her waffle iron, are still good things to know. To the left is the "My eBay At A Glance" box that gives her a quick snapshot of what's going on with her auctions. The list of "Selling Resources" is also someplace that she can quickly reference for answers to questions as they come up.

Step 1: Category

The first official step in setting up her auction is to **choose a category** for the waffle iron. This can be a confusing task—there are so many categories to choose from! This is something that can be done before starting your auction process online, but the search and browse features built in at this point in the setup are as good a way to locate a category as any.

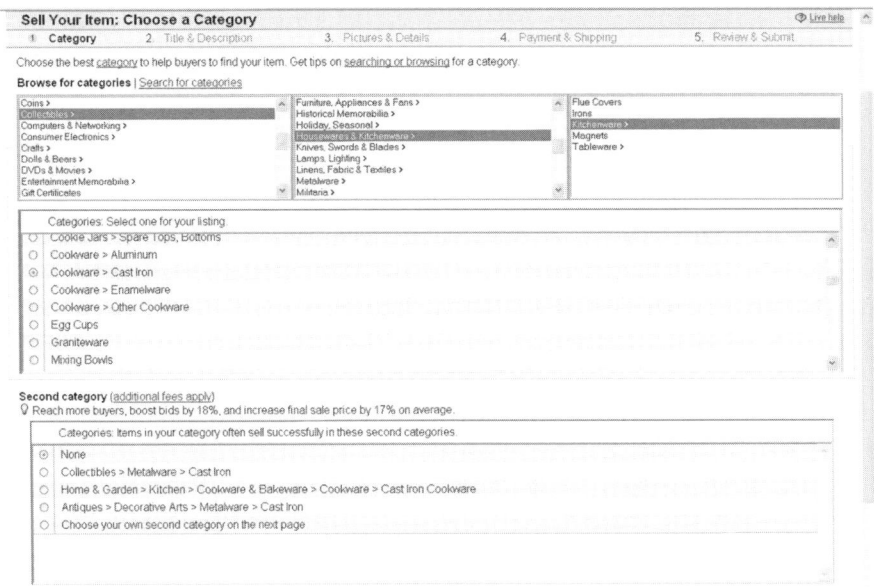

Suzy has some ideas already, as she made note of what categories the other waffle irons were listed in. She wants to be sure she's in the same place as the competition. While she knows that she can list her item in two categories, that also doubles all the fees, so Suzy isn't going to utilize that option this time. There are some times when this really is a very good marketing technique.

Following the same path that her competitors took, Suzy begins by choosing the category of "Collectibles," since this item isn't likely to be put to actual use; its primary purpose is for collecting and displaying. Once she highlights her choice in the box on the left, the middle box opens up a list of subcategories. Suzy chooses "Housewares & Kitchenware" since that is the most applicable from that box. Again, the next box provides her with yet another sub-category, from which she chooses "Kitchenware." This is one of the categories that has up to four levels of choices in it, and so the box below the first three presents Suzy with her final choice of subcategories. She chooses "Cookware>Cast Iron."

This is not the only choice she could have made, and in the next box down, the computer has compiled a list of possible choices for her if she wishes to list in a second category as well. Knowing that this will double her listing fees, Suzy passes on the option, but takes a moment to review the suggested choices in case the computer located a series of categories that made more sense than her choices. There are a few good suggestions, but Suzy feels confident in her choice and clicks the "Continue" button to move ahead.

There are a couple of other things to mention about categories that Suzy may find useful for future auctions. If you are not certain what category to use by browsing (the default category choosing method is called "Browse for Categories"), and you haven't been able to locate any similar merchandise to get suggestions from those listings, try clicking the link near the top of the page that says "Search for Categories."

In the search mode, type in the main keywords from your title and let the computer locate a category for you. EBay will also give each of the computer's choices a percentage based on how closely to your keywords the category comes. More often than not I've found that the search comes up with very good category suggestions. This can also help familiarize you with category options you didn't know were out there; because there are numerous ways to list most items, it can take a while before you become familiar with them all.

 **Choosing the Right Category**

It's not just important for you to choose the right category, it's imperative that you do so. It's against eBay's policy to place items in a category that they obviously don't belong in, just hoping that they will be noticed and purchased by someone browsing in that category.

Step 2: Title, Description, Extra Photos, and Preview

Now that Suzy's category choices are in place, the next page begins with the **title**. Having already worked this out ahead of time, Suzy makes a final decision between her two suggested titles and types it in: Antique Wagner Ware cast iron waffle maker 1910 NR.

Suzy considers putting a hyphen between "cast" and "iron," as she's seen the word hyphenated, but then recalls that the purpose of the keywords is to assist the search engine in locating her item. If a potential buyer were to type in "cast iron" in the search field as two separate words, and she had put "cast-iron" in her title, her listing probably would not come up in the search results. So she resists the urge to be grammatical and technical in these matters.

Like the second category, Suzy is not choosing to use a subtitle at this time. She feels that she covered the keywords sufficiently enough in the title that most lookers will have ample information to decide if they'll read further or not.

The item description is also worked out already and typed into a simple word-processing program such as Notepad, which comes standard on nearly all Windows-based computers. Suzy opens her saved Notepad file, highlights and copies the text, and then comes back to her browser window.

Using the mouse, she right-clicks in the description box and then clicks "paste" to insert her text into eBay's description box. It's as simple as that.

Now, however, she needs to spiffy up the text a little. She chooses a few items that she'd like the lookers to zoom in on, such as the date, 1910.

Highlighting those characters, she uses the drop-down menu just right of the font size menu and chooses from among the colors available. She chooses to make the date red.

Next, she decides that she'd like the font to look less rigid, so she highlights the entire text and makes it italic by clicking the box with the capital "I" on it. Suzy is pleased to see that most of these items are familiar to her because they utilize the same icons as her word processor and other software programs.

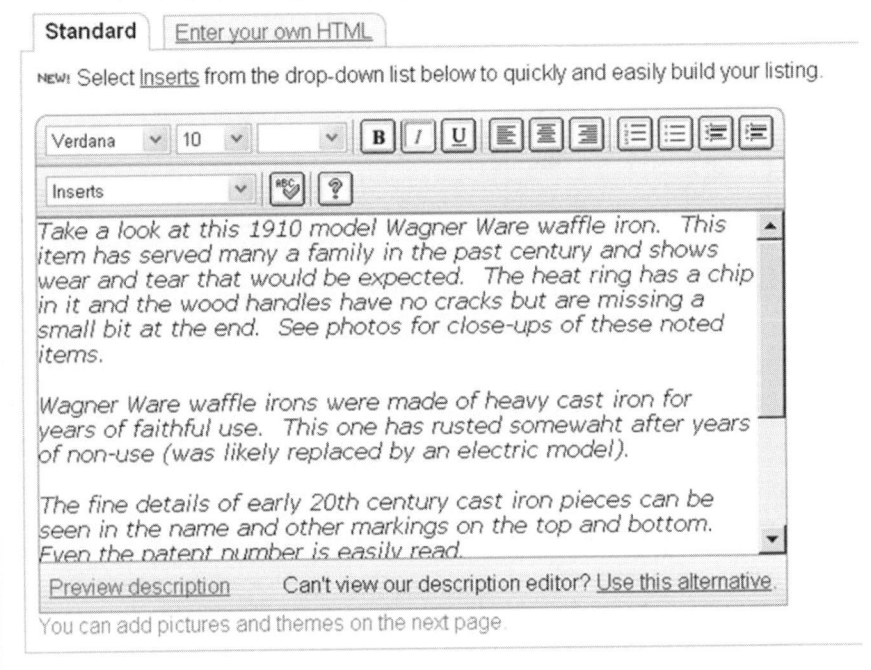

At the end of the description, she starts a new paragraph and clicks on the drop-down menu called "Inserts." Here, she highlights the "Seller's Other Items" phrase and instantly a link that says "Check Out My Other Items" is inserted. When customers see this, they can view her other auctions by using this link. After that, she types in a little message "Happy to combine shipping when possible!"

Starting yet another new paragraph, Suzy minimizes her browser and opens up the Notepad file that she's stored her statement about policies in. After copying and pasting that item in at the end of the auction, she highlights the text, sets the font to one size lower than the description, and makes it italic.

To wrap up the entire description, she sets the font back to the original size and types in a brief closing message, "Thank you again for looking at my auction; please..." and again inserts the "Check Out My Other Items" link.

Now Suzy must minimize her browser yet again and open up a new browser and log in to her online image hosting service where she's already uploaded the additional photos of the waffle iron that she took. The photo that she's planning to use as the "preview" photo isn't on the online site, as there's no cost to upload it directly from her own computer.

Different image hosting sites will do things somewhat differently, but ultimately they will all tell you the URL (address) of where your item is stored. Some hosting sites will give you this information in up to three formats, and you need to know which one to copy and paste into your item's description.

The one you need for eBay will be similar to this:
<img src="http://www.yourdomain.com/images/yourpicture.jpg">

Copy and paste the entire string of information right into your description at whatever point you'd like that photo to appear.

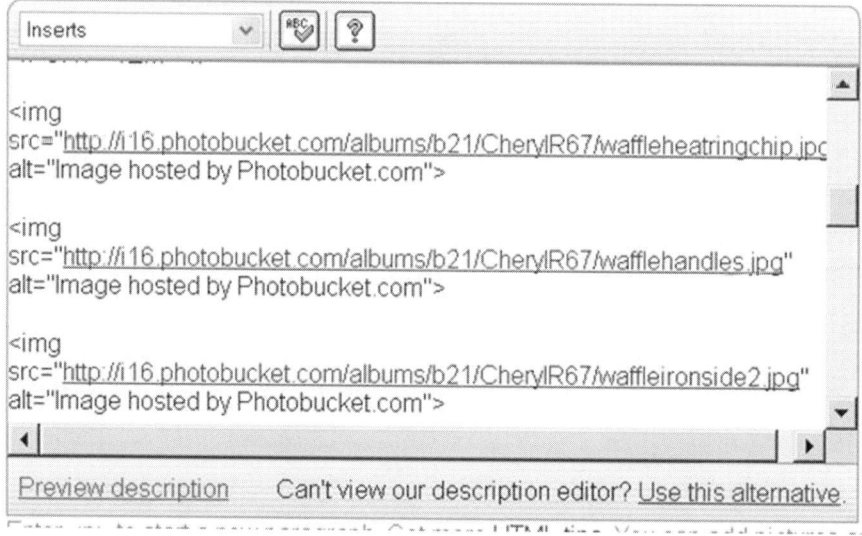

Suzy puts all five of her extra photos, which were pre-cropped and reduced in size, into the description, above her list of policies. She then clicks the link (at the bottom of the description box) that says "Preview Description" and is able to see her auction for the first time. This is fun and exciting, especially when you are able to see the extra photos that you've added using the HTML coding!

You can also click the tab that says "Enter Your Own HTML," just to see what HTML coding looks like. EBay will automatically translate all the formatting you've done into HTML. It's quite interesting to look at, and if you're interested in learning how to do this from scratch, then check out Appendix B, which is a primer on basic HTML programming.

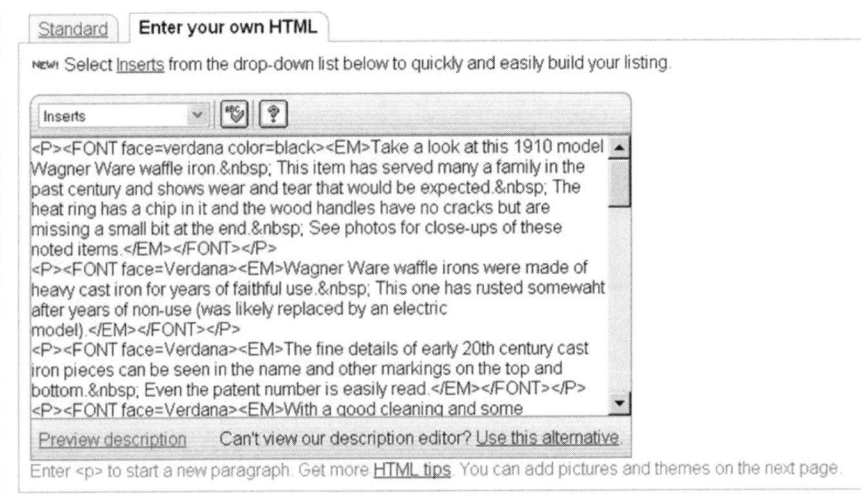

There are some instances when you're wise to do your own HTML writing, such as when you're inserting things like tables and other graphics that aren't able to be saved as a JPEG format, but most beginners will be pretty pleased with the choices that are available to them at this point.

 **You Can Revise Your Auction**

If you're like me, you have been using computers for most of your adult life and don't work as well writing things out by hand. You may think better at the computer and prefer to write descriptions on the fly once you get to this page. That's fine too, just remember that anything you put in your listing is able to be revised so long as there are no bids yet and the auction has at least 12 hours left.

Step 3: Price, Preview Picture, Duration, and Extras

Satisfied with her efforts so far, Suzy clicks "Continue" and moves to the next step: "Enter Pictures & Item Details." This third step is where you'll name your price, set up the duration, schedule a start time (if desired, for an extra fee), add your preview photo, and choose from numerous other options to bring attention or beauty to your auction.

Setting your price and duration are as simple as filling in the blanks and choosing from a drop-down menu. Suzy has decided that she'll start her auction at $4.99, which is a good deal for anybody and allows Suzy to make nearly double what she paid for the item after eBay expenses (listing fee and final value fee). If she has a buyer who pays with PayPal, she'll incur expenses there as well, which will eat away some of her profit, but she has decided that a higher opening bid price might push away potential bidders in favor of other items, so she's willing to take the chance and hope she'll sell for higher than the opening bid.

She's also chosen to set up a Buy It Now for $14.99. In this case, she'll sell to the first bidder who is willing to meet her BIN price. This option, however, will disappear once someone places an opening bid on the item. Because this happens, many bidders who are certain they would be willing to pay up to the Buy It Now price and definitely want that item will opt to purchase using the BIN. Suzy would really like to see this happen, as would any seller. Not only does the transaction close quicker, but you make a profit that is pleasing to you, rather than acceptable or merely palatable.

Sell Your Item: Enter Pictures & Item Details

1. Category 2. Title & Description 3 **Pictures & Details** 4. Payment & Shipping 5. Review & Submit

Title
Antique Wagner Ware cast iron waffle maker 1910 NR

Pricing and duration

Price your item competitively to increase your chance of a successful sale.

NEW! Get ideas about pricing by searching completed items...

Starting price *Required   **Reserve price** (fee varies)
$ 4.99   No reserve price. Add
A lower starting price can encourage more bids.

Buy It Now price (Fee Varies)
$ 14.99
Sell to the first buyer who meets your Buy It Now price.

NEW! **Donate percentage of sale**
No nonprofit selected ⌄   Select % ⌄ Remove
If you choose to participate in this program and your item sells, a $10 minimum donation is required (does not apply to nc
eBay Giving Works.

Of course, Suzy realizes that in order to turn this into a full-time business, she's going to have to do better than turning two dollars profit every auction, or sell hundreds of items every week. But she has set up her business so that she can work at this during evenings and weekends for at least six months while she learns, hones her technique, and zeroes in on a strategy for obtaining merchandise and selling it in the most efficient manner possible.

She has already determined to do a five-day listing to place her listing in proximity to the competitor's listing of a similar item for a higher price. Take note of the "Start Time" option: If you wish to schedule your listing to start at a different time, this is the place to make that choice.

Next we turn to adding your free preview photo and other options you can choose. Adding your free photo is as easy as entering the location of the photo that's stored on your computer. If you don't know that file path from memory, simply click on the "Browse" button and locate it in the same manner you'd locate any file or item on your computer. Having technology that's similar or identical to what's used in all modern computers is part of what makes eBay so simple and user friendly.

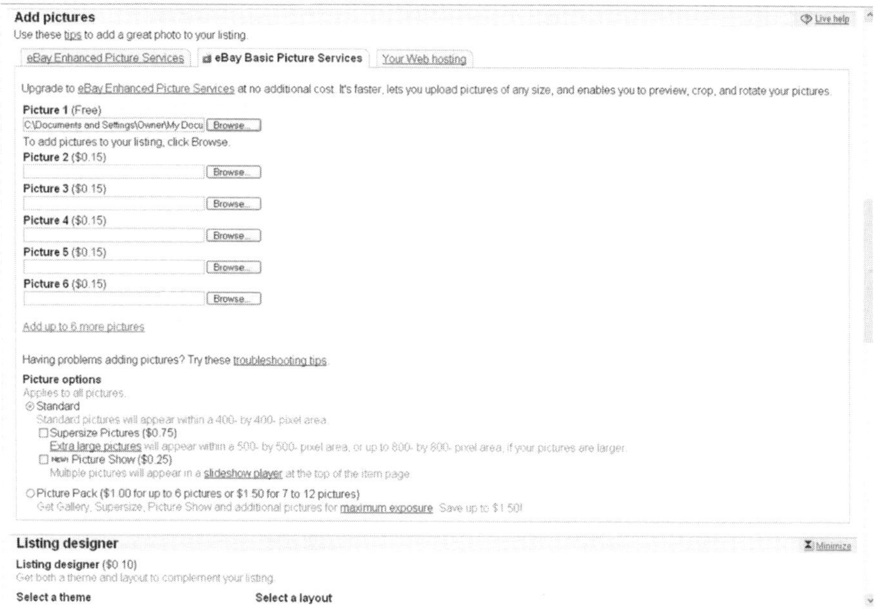

Add pictures
Use these tips to add a great photo to your listing.

| eBay Enhanced Picture Services | eBay Basic Picture Services | Your Web hosting |

Upgrade to eBay Enhanced Picture Services at no additional cost. It's faster, lets you upload pictures of any size, and enables you to preview, crop, and rotate your pictures.

Picture 1 (Free)
[C:\Documents and Settings\Owner\My Docu] [Browse...]
To add pictures to your listing, click Browse.
Picture 2 ($0.15)
[Browse...]
Picture 3 ($0.15)
[Browse...]
Picture 4 ($0.15)
[Browse...]
Picture 5 ($0.15)
[Browse...]
Picture 6 ($0.15)
[Browse...]

Add up to 6 more pictures

Having problems adding pictures? Try these troubleshooting tips.

Picture options
Applies to all pictures.
⊙ Standard
   Standard pictures will appear within a 400- by 400- pixel area.
   ☐ Supersize Pictures ($0.75)
      Extra large pictures will appear within a 500- by 500- pixel area, or up to 800- by 800- pixel area, if your pictures are larger.
   ☐ NEW Picture Show ($0.25)
      Multiple pictures will appear in a slideshow player at the top of the item page.
○ Picture Pack ($1.00 for up to 6 pictures or $1.50 for 7 to 12 pictures)
   Get Gallery, Supersize, Picture Show and additional pictures for maximum exposure. Save up to $1.50!

Listing designer
Listing designer ($0.10)
Get both a theme and layout to complement your listing.
Select a theme   **Select a layout**

TIP
Using Photos

Do not re-add the photos that you've already uploaded when entering your item's description. If you do so, not only will you be charged fees, but you'll display all your photos twice, which will look silly and annoy buyers.

Here eBay offers a plethora of options for extra fees. Photos are no exception. You can supersize your photos or have them placed in a slideshow format that will scroll at the top of your page. Want all the options? Get the "Picture Pack," which includes "Gallery," "Supersize," "Picture Show," and additional pictures, all for one low price.

These options are all nice, and they do have their time and place, but you have to take into account the total cost for your listing. If Suzy were to spend $2 on all these features, would she be guaranteed at least $2 more in her final price? On a common antique like the waffle iron? Probably not. Instead, she'd be left with no profit if her listing sells for the opening price. You'll need to determine if your items will merit these additional options.

Of all the extras available on eBay, the "Listing Designer" is one of the more affordable ones that is also a lot of fun to use. Hundreds of backgrounds or borders are available for a mere thin dime. Again, only you will know if it is worth it for your item.

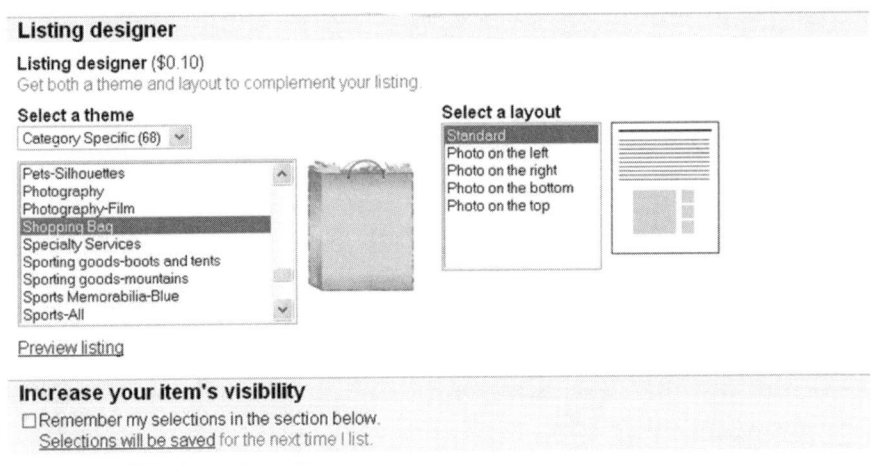

But we're not done with extras yet. The next section shows you what your current listing will look like in a sample search result. This is an interactive display that will change with each feature you click on to show you how your listing will stand out more with the various features. It doesn't cost anything to click on the boxes to see the results, but just make very sure you un-click them all if you don't wish to utilize these features at this time.

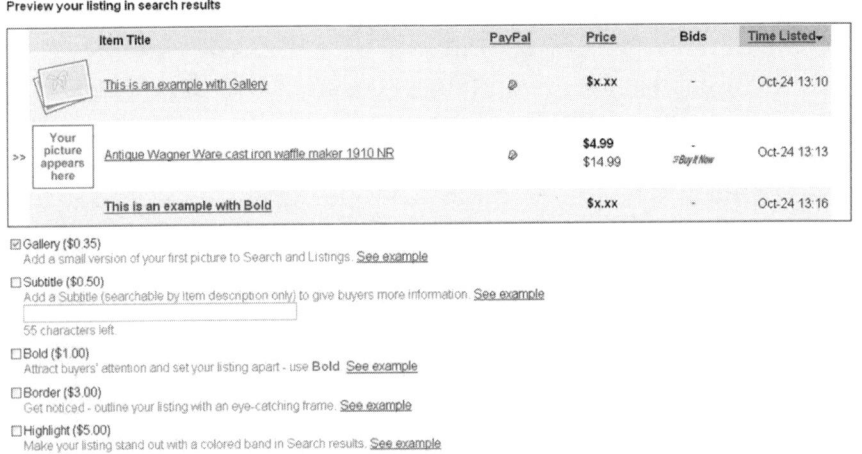

If you choose to utilize one of these options on a regular basis, you can click a box at the bottom of the list and eBay will save your settings for you so you don't have to check the box each time. The Gallery photo option is highly utilized. When I first started using eBay as a buyer, I often found so many auctions that met my search criteria that I didn't even have to bother with listings that didn't display a photo on the search results page, which is what the Gallery option gets you.

Once I started selling, I didn't choose the Gallery photo, because I didn't want to pay the fee. I had been selling for more than a year before I realized that all I was showing was the little green camera icon; all that time I'd thought that uploading my free photo to eBay gave me the photo in the search results as well. Because I frequently did not look at items without a Gallery photo, I was aghast by this information.

I don't mean to imply that forgoing on the Gallery photo is a mistake, because the camera icon does let others know there are pictures in the auction. But now when I sell, I give the photo a second thought and see if I can work it into my budget of extra features.

Every person is different, and they might want to look at every auction, even if they can't initially see a photo. One way I've found to compensate is to make the title catchy enough to entice the browser to look closer. If I can build shipping costs into my actual item price, I advertise "FREE SHIP" in the title; that seems to generate some numbers on the counter!

Next comes a section of extra features that aren't likely to be utilized by a new seller, unless your merchandise is of the pricey sort. However, if you are selling a high end product that you want maximum visibility for, check into the Featured Plus (for $19.95), Gallery Featured ($19.95), and Home Page Featured ($39.95+) promotions. If you click on the links that say "See Example" after the brief description, you can see your listing in these settings.

Have you ever noticed what appeared to be a graphic of a small gift in a search-results page? That little gift icon means that the seller has paid an extra $0.25 to label this item as being "good for gift giving." If you utilize this icon, make sure you talk about it in your item's description, noting what extra services you'll perform so that the item is ready for giving when it's received. That can include pre-wrapping the item, including a gift card, or shipping directly to the recipient. Sign up for this feature on this page.

Just make sure none of the extra-fee features are checked when you click "Continue"; otherwise you'll have to go back and revise it before you submit your listing or you'll be charged.

Finally, stuck way at the bottom is the final feature you need to choose, and this one won't cost you a penny! You get your choice of two styles of free counters, or the option to not display your counter publicly, on each of your listings. The counter shows how many times your listing has been viewed. The first time you set up an auction, eBay may prompt you to sign up for the Andale counter.

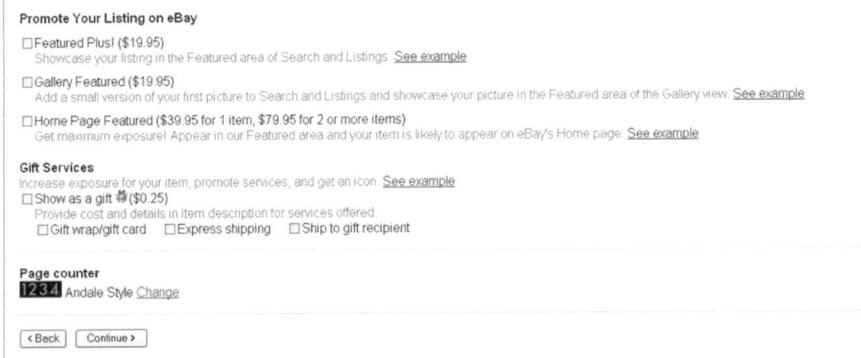

Step 4: Payment and Shipping Details

If you've already set up a PayPal Premiere account so you can readily accept all payment types, then the box for PayPal should already be checked with your e-mail address (the same business e-mail address that your eBay account should be linked to) filled in.

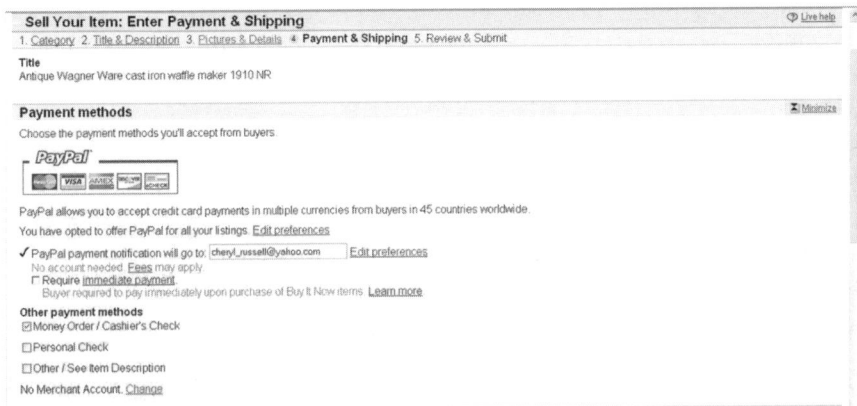

Notice that there is a check-box that says "Require Immediate Payment." If you check this box, then people who wish to buy a Buy It Now of yours will be notified that they'll be required to pay immediately upon bidding for the BIN price. This may or not be a good thing to have.

Sure, it's nice to seal the deal quickly, but what if your buyer wants to be sure they get your item, but it's Wednesday and they don't get paid until Friday? If your payment policy states that they need to pay within a certain number of days, go back and revise it to state that the Buy It Now must pay immediately, if you utilize this option, to avoid confusion.

Below, check the other payment types that you'll accept. Even though you specified all these things in your "policies" statement that you put in your listing descriptions, you should have all acceptable payment types showing as checked here.

In the next section, you can specify which foreign countries you will ship to, or worldwide, by simply checking the boxes. Make sure that this, too, also matches the information in your "policies" statement in the description.

Next, you will specify your shipping prices, or set up the shipping calculator to let prospective buyers know what the cost will be based on their zip code.

First, let's talk about flat shipping rates. This tab will let you set a flat fee for all buyers, regardless of their zip code (within the continental United States; Alaska and Hawaii may be higher due to the sheer distances the item must travel to get there).

Suzy hasn't decided if she'll use a flat rate or calculated rate, so she's going to figure it both ways. To decide on a flat shipping rate, she must have the exact weight of her box and, if the box is irregular or very large, the dimensions. She needs to go to the Web site of the shipper she plans to use, **www.usps.com**, the U.S. Postal Service.

She uses the USPS's Web site's Postage Rate Calculator to determine that Priority shipping for the waffle iron would be $18.80 and Parcel Post would be $15.62 if she sent it a long distance (across country). She does this using the zip codes trick discussed in Chapter 5.

Then Suzy must decide if she'll charge a handling fee. She has re-used a box and packing peanuts she had on hand, so tape and labor are her only shipping investments so far. She decides to add a handling fee of $1. This would give a total flat-rate shipping charge of $19.80 for Priority Mail or $16.62 for Parcel Post.

 **PayPal and Postage**

When you purchase postage through PayPal (if the buyer pays via PayPal), then you will get delivery confirmation free for a Priority Mail package or for only $0.13 for the Parcel Post. But you can't assume your buyer will pay with PayPal, so plan accordingly when using flat-fee shipping.

There is one other thing Suzy must consider before choosing a flat fee. What if a potential bidder lives only two counties away from her? The shipping wouldn't be anywhere near that much, and Suzy's high shipping charge (based on being sent a long distance) might scare away closer buyers.

Suzy re-enters the information into the Postage Rate Calculator using a zip code near her and discovers that there is a rather large difference. To avoid scaring off any potential customers, Suzy decides to let potential buyers calculate their own postage based on their zip codes.

There are times when a flat fee is appropriate, but that would be on items that are going to cost approximately the same postage regardless of where they are mailed. This would include all items under one pound that are being sent Priority Mail. The cost is the same for any item 16 ounces and under for Priority Mail.

Most people know that postal service rates are based on zones, and the longer the distance between the "TO" zone and the "FROM" zone, the greater the postage, so buyers appreciate getting a little break on shipping if they are closer to the seller than someone on the other coast would be. EBay has made their calculated shipping tool very simple to use, and the buyers can even calculate their shipping right from the search results page now! This is a very good reason to use the **calculated shipping** method when setting up your auction.

Buyers like to know the shipping up front. Years ago, it wasn't uncommon for buyers to not get a shipping quote until they had won the auction. You had to contact the seller (or vice versa) and give them your zip code or shipping information. The seller would then take the package to the post office and get a quote for you, then come back and e-mail you, and so on.

It took forever to get a package sent from sellers who weren't large companies with shipping departments. But that was the norm; there was no other way for the average home-based eBay seller to do it. Another thing that happened more frequently was that buyers backed out of the transaction if they found (after they'd won the auction) that shipping was either more than they thought it would be or more than they were willing to pay. Shipping costs became a very big thing for buyers to know up front. With technology being what it is today, there's no reason why buyers can't know that even before they bid!

Buyers also want to be on the lookout for sellers who are trying to make extra profit disguised as "shipping and handling charges." This can be part of the fee circumvention policy discussed in the previous chapter.

If a buyer thinks the shipping and handling is too pricey, they can keep looking without having to actually open your auction and read your wonderful description and see all your wonderful extra photos. With an outrageously high shipping fee listed right in the search results column (or the calculation link that they can use without opening your listing), you can turn away good buyers who may feel you are being greedy or dishonest.

This is a good warning, then, to sellers who often think that padding their shipping charges won't be noticed. It is noticed, especially when buyers know firsthand that the item they're looking at doesn't even weigh one pound, but your listing tells them that Priority Mail shipping and handling is going to be $8.70.

You're not fooling anybody that way; buyers can do the math themselves. It's costing you $4.05. Where is that extra $4.65 going? Even if your handling fee isn't excessive enough to get you into trouble with eBay (even if you don't incite their suspicion as someone trying to avoid fees), you'll probably run afoul with potential buyers who don't like to pay excessively for your "handling" fees.

Because Suzy realizes that the weight of her package may make some shipping quotes large (even though potential buyers should realize that cast iron is heavy, some may not realize how heavy), she revised her description to put in this information:

> This item weighs nearly 12 pounds packaged up! The shipping quotes from the calculator reflect only actual shipping costs — only $1.45 handling fees are being charged.

To set up the calculated shipping tab, simply enter the weight of your package by using the drop-down menu on the left. If the item is heavier than the highest weight on the list, use the custom-weight option, which will bring up boxes for you to enter the exact number of pounds and ounces.

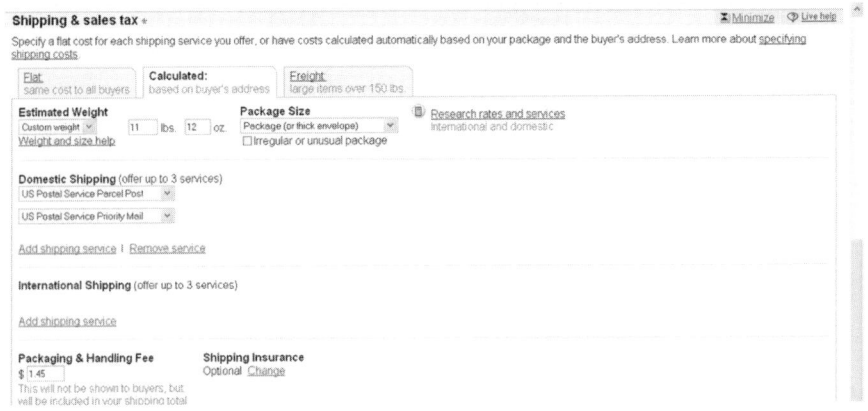

Suzy's packaged waffle iron weighs 11 pounds 9 ounces with no tape or receipt or thank-you note in it, so Suzy has guessed a little high and entered a weight of 11 pounds 12 ounces into the calculator.

She chooses to offer two shipping services: Parcel Post and Priority Mail, as buyers who live farther away might want the cheapest option available if they're not in a hurry for the item. If a buyer requests a third service, such as Express Mail, she can calculate it and revise the information in an invoice after the auction closes.

On the calculated shipping page, you'll see that there is a box where you can enter your handling fee, which will then be added to every quote that a looker requests, without the looker knowing how much it is (although, as noted, if your item is not heavy, experienced lookers will be able to spot a heavily padded shipping charge any day).

 **Shipping Discounts**

If you haven't yet set up a shipping discount program but want to set up parameters for shipping discounts, click on the link that says "My Preferences" and you will be taken to the page to set these up. Buyers like to have shipping discounts, such as paying full price for the first item and a small flat fee (such as $1 or $1.95) for each additional item, as long as they can go in the same box. More about this topic in Chapter 10.

Further down the page, Suzy's sales tax information is displayed. She has set up her PayPal account to automatically charge sales tax to customers living in her own state. If the eBay page isn't updated with that same information automatically, she can do so here.

Next on the page is a box devoted to Suzy's return policy. Since she stated it in her auction description, she can merely put "See item description" in the page provided, or repeat the information. The same holds true for the "Payment Instructions" box; she can repeat or refer the buyer to the auction description.

The "Buyer Requirements" section is a way for you to prevent certain classes of buyers from bidding on your auctions, such as those with little or no feedback, those with a high percentage of negative feedback, or those who have been reported as non-paying bidders. This is the same list as the "blocked bidders list" discussed in Chapter 7.

Whew, this was a long step! But Suzy is almost done setting up her first auction. She's ready for the last step.

Step 5: Review and Submit

If Suzy has thoughtfully prepared her title, description, and all the details, she should be able to get through this step quickly. However, this is a good opportunity to re-read the title and description, checking for typos or incorrect information. Anything that needs revising at this point is easily done by clicking the "Edit" link at the right-hand side of that section.

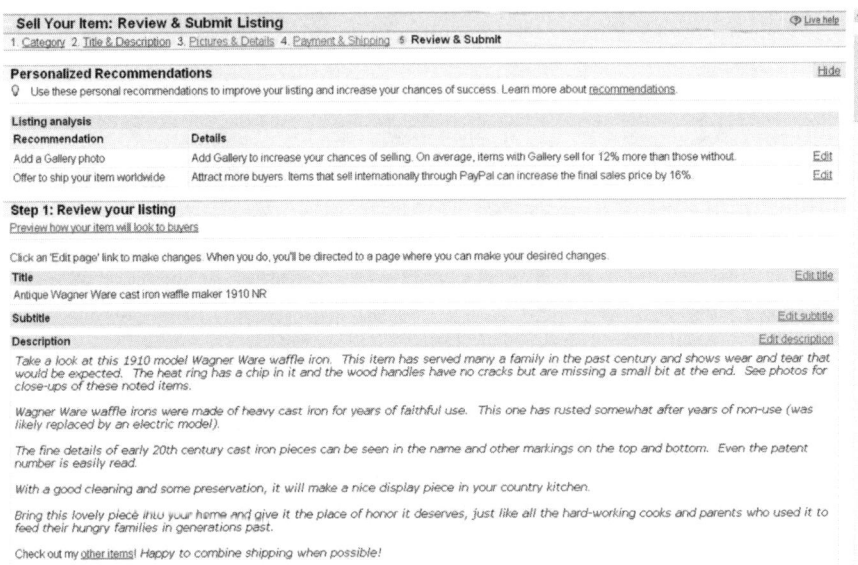

At the top of the page, eBay thoughtfully provides recommendations on things that may or may not increase your listing's viewing and price. It doesn't hurt to read these things, in case you've missed something you actually did intend to do or offer.

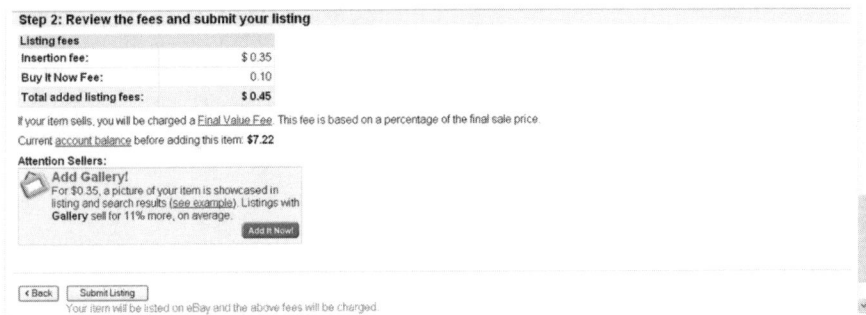

If everything appears as you wished it to, then you need to make sure to double-check the box at the bottom of the page that says "Review the fees and submit your listing." Do just that; make sure that all the fees are what you anticipated and that you're not paying for an extra feature that you may have accidentally clicked on. If so, go back and revise everything necessary. Your auction will not appear if you don't click the "Submit

Listing" button at the very bottom of the page, so you can revise and not have to worry about paying fees for services you didn't wish to utilize.

When everything is acceptable, just do it: Click the button and join the ranks of millions out there—become an eBay seller!

When your listing is submitted and accepted by eBay's servers, your computer screen will show a congratulatory message and your item number. It's a good idea to have a column (either in your spreadsheet or log sheets) to track these numbers. This provides a reference point so you don't accidentally ship the wrong item to the wrong customer, per chance they're both named John Smith. Your eBay invoices will also reference this number as well as the title, but if you're selling several of the same item, titles aren't much help. Having an individual number for each auction is helpful for inventory reasons.

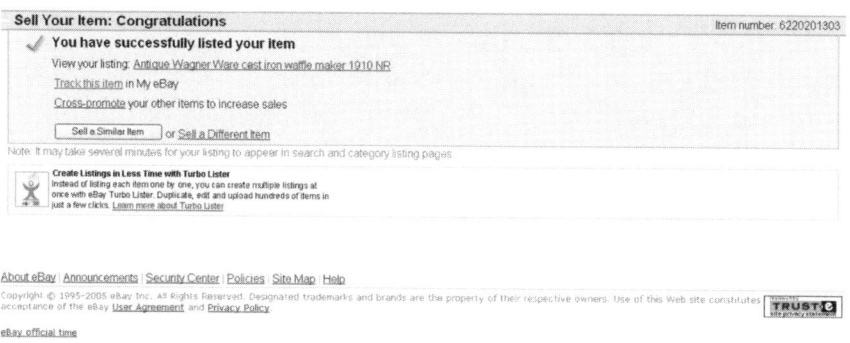

If you forget to write down the auction number at this point, you can find it on the "My eBay" page. Click on the auction title and locate it on the auction page, or better yet, click "Customize Display" on the "My eBay" page and add "Item ID" to your list of columns displayed. See Chapter 7 for information on customizing your "My eBay" pages.

It is exciting to post your first auction, and while you've done a lot of work to get to this point, it's not necessarily all downhill from here. There are some things you'll have to do while your auction is running.

Even though you have been thorough in your description and list of policies, it's not uncommon to have potential customers contact you to ask a question about something they aren't clear about or simply want more information about.

Don't look at this as a failure on your part; it isn't. There's just no way you can think of every possible angle that others will. Try to think of it as an opportunity to provide some excellent customer service by replying with a helpful, polite, and professional e-mail. Be sure to thank the customer for their questions and give as much detailed and correct information as you can, even if it means doing a little research or legwork. And, of course, be speedy in your reply.

When you reply to inquiries, you have a few options, such as sending a copy of your reply to your e-mail in case you need to refer to it later, hiding your e-mail address from the sender, and posting the question and your response in the listing for other lookers to refer to. This last option is a good idea to utilize, especially if the question is one that others might ask as well, or in case there are bids on your item and you can't revise something that the question pertained to.

If you do your eBay business on nights and weekends, you may not receive a question until after an auction has ended (if it was sent during the day). Even in these cases, reply to the sender and apologize for not having received their question beforehand. You just never know who will be your customer tomorrow or who this person might refer to your merchandise because of your quality communication with them.

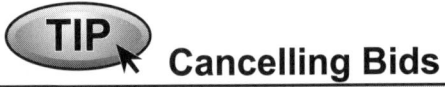 **Cancelling Bids**

If you find that an international buyer has bid on your item despite your stated policies, you can cancel the bid (note: make very sure he or she is an international buyer first). Fill out a brief form with your auction number, the ID of the person whose bid you wish to cancel, and a very brief statement as to why you wish to cancel the bid. Information on this can be found at
http://pages.ebay.com/help/policies/unwelcome-buying.html

You may also get questions from international members who wish to bid or buy your item. If you've already specified that you are not willing or able to ship internationally (in your policies, and by not checking any international boxes during the auction setup), you still should reply to international requests in a professional and polite manner. Someday you might want to consider international shipping, and you don't wish to offend your future customer base by being rude now.

During the time your auction is running, you also can **make revisions** to your listing. EBay allows you to revise your listing as long there are no bids placed on the item and there are at least 12 hours left before it expires. There are a number of reasons why you might make a revision, including the following:

- To change your price. Perhaps you've done additional research and now feel your opening bid is too high.

- To change your pricing strategy. You didn't offer Buy It Now at first, but now wish you had.

- To add information to your description, fix a typo, or clear up something that seems confusing.

- To place your item in a second category for more exposure.

When you make revisions such as adding Buy It Now or placing it in an additional category, you will incur fees for those things. At the very bottom of the review page, before you click the "Submit Changes" button, there is a statement of what new fees you will be charged or a statement stating that your changes do not require any additional fees.

Your listing will state that it has been revised, for lookers who may have looked at it previously.

Other than those two tasks, you're off the hook until your listing is complete. We'll discuss what the next steps are in Chapter 10.

It's an exciting moment to have your first auction end, and yet it is just one more step toward a completed transaction leading to feedback. It's the beginning of building your reputation on eBay.

Congratulations... Now What?

You've sold an item! It's an exciting moment to have your first auction end, and yet it is just one more step toward a completed transaction leading to feedback. It's the beginning of building your reputation on eBay.

Let's follow Suzy as she completes her first auction for the antique waffle iron.

After a few days of anxiously checking to see how often her waffle iron had been viewed, Suzy got her first bid! The opening bid was, naturally, her starting price of $4.99. This will comfortably allow Suzy to "break even" and she's thankful that at least her fees won't be wasted. She continues to monitor her item, and about a day later, she's got a second bidder. The automatic bidding system doesn't allow Suzy to see how the bids climbed exactly, but she's now got a bid of $6.05 on the waffle iron. Considering that there are numerous other similar items currently available with no bids, she's pleased that hers has bids.

The auction ends a couple of days later with many more lookers but no more bids. Though Suzy had hoped to have a final sale price closer to $9.99, she accepts the reality of auctioning: The bidders who are currently looking are the ones who determine the final sale price. This doesn't sour her attitude, but she does decide that she'll be more particular about antique waffle irons in the future. In reviewing the other auctions, both current and past, she has seen some photos of beautiful and ornate waffle irons that are apparently what's capturing the attention of collectors. If she can snag one of those at a future auction, she'll definitely have a better idea of its value.

Although eBay sends winning bidders an e-mail notifying them of their auction won, Suzy will also create an invoice to send to the buyer. The invoice outlines all the details of the transaction, including the exact shipping cost. It also reviews your payment policies based on what you have entered into eBay's template.

 **Create Customized E-mails**

You can create customized e-mails to your winning buyers. Just go to your "Preferences" link on the "My eBay" page (left-hand column under "My Account") and click on the link to "Edit" under "Logos and Branding." Use the form provided to give the default message some of your personality. Be sure to click the box at the top that says "Include my custom message in this e-mail" or it will still send the default message. (Note: This is the same as the PayPal customized end-of-auction e-mail, so if you've done it in one place, you don't need to redo it in the other.)

To create an invoice, Suzy must first go to her "My eBay" page. Under the header "Items I've Sold" will be the auction for the waffle iron. EBay's system automatically moves items from your "Items I'm Selling" section to the appropriate section, "Unsold Items" or "Items I've Sold," once the auction is complete.

Sending an invoice is as simple as clicking on the blue link in the drop-down menu of options on the right-hand side of the screen. Doing so will open a new page where Suzy can double-check the information such as the shipping information, which the system will fill in based on the information from the shipping calculator that Suzy used when she listed her item.

At the top of the invoice form that eBay creates, notice also that the buyer's address may or may not be listed. Sometimes you'll get just a zip code but not the full address. Don't worry; you will get the full address once the transaction is complete. If there was a reason why you had not filled out the shipping calculator when listing your item, you will be able to use the zip code now to determine what your actual shipping costs will be. You can then fill in the shipping options and prices to the right, so the buyer can choose which they wish to utilize and pay the appropriate amount. Chances are that, if you've been buying on eBay already, you've received these invoices yourself and are familiar with them.

Double-check the payment information in the box on the bottom left, and consider typing in a brief "thank you for your purchase" message. You can also encourage the buyer to pay promptly by reminding them of how fast you ship once payment is received. This lets them know that if they are willing to put in a little effort (paying quickly), you'll reward them by making an effort to get it shipped just as quickly. Buyers appreciate little gestures like that and often it's mentioned in their feedback.

A copy of the invoice will be sent to your e-mail, although you can un-check a box if you don't want a copy. If you've logged the various items during the transaction (listing fees, sold price, final value fees, etc.) in your spreadsheet or ledger, then there isn't really any reason why you'd need to have a copy of the invoice. The amount of e-mail generated by each transaction can be overwhelming, so you'll soon decide what you really do want to keep. If you want to keep a hard copy of the invoice, then click the link toward the bottom that says "Preview the Invoice" and print that screen.

Once Suzy has sent the invoice to her buyer, she can finish boxing up her item, taping it securely. Now she must do what sellers dislike most: wait for the payment to arrive. At this point in the game, sellers want to be paid for their hard work, clear out that inventory, and get on with the next auction. Waiting for payment can be frustrating, but unless you institute only fixed-price listings with an "immediate payment required" feature, you'll just have to wait it out.

Most eBay sellers have developed a payment policy that is displayed in their auction description, and it is reiterated in their invoices. However, you'll have to come to grips with the fact that some buyers simply do not read the details, no matter how many times they are presented with them. Here are some common payment issues you may encounter with your customers:

Payment Must Be Received In...

Most sellers have set a timeline by which they expect payment to be received. And most buyers respect those timelines. Be prepared, however, for the inevitable: a buyer who drags his feet.

Perhaps the buyer has received an unexpected bill in the mail or had a sick pet that needed vet care. Stuff happens to everybody at one time or another. Be sure to communicate with your buyer if the deadline is near and no payment has been received. Let the buyer know you're concerned and ask if there's been a delay in paying so that you can work out other arrangements. A buyer who's truly had something unexpected happen will be grateful for your consideration and do what he or she can to make the payment as soon as possible.

If, however, you have a buyer who's having second thoughts or decided he or she doesn't really want your item after all, anything could happen. The buyer could try to back out of the sale, lie to you about a payment in the mail (that really isn't), and, in a worst-case scenario, could try to turn the tables by claiming that you must have received a mailed payment by now and that you are the one dragging your feet or refusing to ship the item.

Encountering buyers like this can be a real headache, and it can make sellers bitter and negative. There doesn't seem to be any way to predict which buyers will be like this, either. A buyer can have perfect feedback, then suddenly you're the unfortunate seller who's having an issue with him or her.

If this buyer continues to avoid payment, he or she turns from a slow payer to a non-paying bidder. We'll discuss what your options are in this case shortly.

Happy to Combine Shipping...

If you have stated a shipping discount policy on eBay, then you may have to wait for payment up to the number of days you allowed in your policy (see Chapter 8) per chance the same buyer wins another auction.

Combining shipping can also bring about some issues of its own, especially for buyers who wish to pay via PayPal. If they win one auction and you send them an invoice, they may pay it, then two days later they'll win a different auction and expect you to give them a combined shipping discount. In the meantime, you've paid two transaction fees to PayPal. This also says nothing of the fact that you may have already shipped the first item!

It's ideal if the bidder lets you know that they are bidding on other items so you can wait and send them one invoice for all items won, with one shipping charge. You'll also incur only one PayPal fee this way. But you must also do your part to let buyers know not to pay an invoice if they are planning to bid on multiple items. Good communication is probably the best way to avoid this potential fee-gobbling issue.

What if a buyer doesn't inform you of this and sends multiple PayPal payments but still expects a shipping discount? If your policy is clear that they must pay for all items at the same time, then you are in the right not to give them a shipping discount.

But is this the best thing to do, in terms of customer service or for your reputation? You'll have to weigh the costs and determine if the possibility of a negative feedback from the buyer is worth it. Whatever you do, you should always communicate clearly and calmly with the customer, even letting the buyer know that you have paid multiple fees because of their multiple payments, rather than just one fee. Suggest an alternative: a shipping discount, but not quite as large a one, so you can recoup some of your excess fees.

Many buyers will be willing to work something out, and may even apologize for their lack of attention to the details. Upon learning that they messed up, some buyers will retract their request for a shipping discount. And then there will always be the small percentage who will demand the largest possible discount regardless of any fault on their part.

Money Orders Are Accepted Only If...

One problem that I seem to experience frequently is that buyers who wish to pay via money order will wait the entire ten days that I allow for receipt of payment. Then on the tenth day, they will mail the money order. Depending on where each party lives, that means I have to wait 14 or more days for payment.

I have recently revised my payment policy to state that if you are paying via money order, please mail it within three days so that I receive it within the ten days allowed. Not surprisingly, this hasn't really changed the behavior of buyers who don't wish to pay any sooner than absolutely necessary.

Unfortunately, this is just one those things out of your control. Like with any other payment type, communicate with the buyer and express concern that the payment may be lost in the mail. Ask for a specific date the money order was mailed, and the serial number of the money order from the receipt. Hopefully the buyer will communicate back with the details. If the buyer knowingly mailed it after the deadline (or hasn't yet purchased it) they may avoid communicating with you until the time frame that they expect the payment to arrive.

You'll have to decide what to do in the case that a money order arrives after the date required. Do you send the money order back, file a complaint with eBay against the buyer for not following your policies, and re-list the item? Honestly, that's probably more trouble than it's worth, since the buyer can always fall back on "But I did pay for the item!" He or she may come out of just such an exchange looking like a petty person who cares more for rules than your customers.

Items Will Be Shipped Within...

If you state in your auction listing that you will ship an item within two business days of receiving payment, make sure that you have noted any exceptions to this rule. EChecks through PayPal can take up to six days to clear, and buyers often don't realize this. So they think they paid on one date, and in your view, they haven't really paid until the funds become available in your PayPal account, several days later. You could end up with an unhappy buyer who feels you were slow to ship. Be sure to communicate with a buyer who has used an eCheck. Tell him or her that you will send an e-mail the day that you receive the actual funds (the date the eCheck clears) and that you will honor your shipping policy based on that date.

One recent experience taught me not to neglect stating all the particulars when promising shipping dates. I listed a number of NWT infant snowsuits and sold one to the first bidder. The item ended late in the evening. By 9 a.m. the next morning, I sent the buyer an invoice. Since it was early in the day, I thought I'd encourage a speedy payment and inserted this statement in the invoice: "If you have the opportunity to pay via PayPal by 11 a.m. Central time today, I will be able to get it mailed out yet today!"

Sure enough, about a half hour later, I had a message from PayPal about this item. I logged into my PayPal account and saw that the status of the payment said "uncleared." The "Details" link gave me the following information:

> Payment Type: eCheck
>
> The eCheck payment you have received will show an Uncleared status until the funds have cleared from the buyer's account—usually three to four business days. Please do not ship any merchandise to the buyer until this payment clears.

When I read that, my heart sank into my stomach. I had promised shipment that same day if the buyer paid via PayPal. The buyer did utilize PayPal. Would she still demand I ship that same day? I knew there was nothing to do but communicate the issue with the buyer and see what we could work out.

Feeling like an idiot (I should have known to specify the exception of an eCheck), I immediately sent an e-mail to the buyer, thanking her for her speedy response to the invoice and also letting her know that if I shipped this item before her eCheck cleared, neither she nor I would qualify for PayPal's Buyer or Seller protection program.

Fearing that she was an expectant mother about to give birth who would need this item to bundle her newborn and bring it home from the hospital, I inquired if there was an urgent need for the item that would make it impossible to wait for shipping until the eCheck cleared.

I also apologized for not pointing out this specific exception, as I do not get payment via eCheck very often. I sent the e-mail, hoping for the best.

Within minutes, I received a reply. The buyer was unaware that her PayPal account was set up to do eChecks, and thanked me for pointing that out so she could change her settings (maybe she was getting a lot of slow shipments?). She noted that while the item was needed for a baby shower, the date was more than two weeks away, so she saw no reason why the shipping couldn't wait until the eCheck cleared.

She didn't express any anger at me for being unwilling to ship the item as promised that day, and she even assured me that the payment would be cleared without any problem. I sent a reply, promising to notify her as soon as her payment had cleared and get the item in the mail that same day, if at all possible.

Another exception that you might wish to note is that personal checks need time to clear the bank as well. If you accept personal checks, give your bank a call and ask them for a reasonable time frame to expect items to clear.

This Looks Fishy to Me...

You should never mail an item without making sure a personal check has cleared, but I often mail items before depositing a money order. With the sophisticated computer software and printers available to anybody, counterfeit money orders are a definite possibility. There are so many companies that issue money orders that you can't very easily keep up with the intricacies of each company's product.

Some sellers have stated that they prefer (or only accept) money orders from the U.S. Postal Service, as nearly everybody lives near a post office to purchase one. However, the USPS's fees are a bit higher than other places, such as convenience stores and gas stations, so buyers may not like being forced to go to the post office for a money order at your demand.

Money orders that are authentic have security features built into them. Some have a specific spot on them that will change colors when heat (such as from a finger) is applied. Some have specific watermarks that can only be seen from a certain angle with the light shining behind it. Read any money order carefully for instructions on how to verify its authenticity. If you have any questions, do not mail the item until you have taken the money order to your bank for verification.

Counterfeit cashier's checks are also a potential issue. Treat them like suspicious money orders, and don't mail anything out until your bank has verified their authenticity.

Even payment troubles often pale in comparison to the headache of dealing with a non-paying bidder. The good news is that most eBay sellers will tell you that these people are few and far between. But that still doesn't make it any easier to deal with them when you find that your communications are being ignored.

EBay has a setup procedure for dealing with non-paying bidders. The first step is to file an unpaid item dispute form within 45 days of the transaction, but generally you must wait seven days. There are a couple of exceptions, such as if the buyer is no longer a registered user or if the buyer is from a country you do not ship to.

To begin the process, click the link to the "Dispute Console" on the left-hand side of the "My eBay" page. Then click the "Unpaid Items" link. You can also read up on the unpaid items policy and process by using the links in the box below this. It's a good idea to thoroughly read and understand the process before beginning.

Once the form has been filled out, eBay will contact the buyer. Depending on whether or not, or how, the buyer responds to this form, the dispute may or may not be resolved quickly. For buyers who are merely dragging their feet a little, the friendly reminder directly from eBay seems to get buyers in the mood to pay sooner than later. If, however, this person is downright determined not to pay for the item, the process gets a little hairier.

At any point in the process, the buyer and seller can mutually agree to just forget the whole transaction. If so, the buyer doesn't get any "Unpaid Item Strikes" and the seller can get a final value fee refund. At all times during the process, eBay tries to maintain their position as the vehicle by which the buyer and seller can communicate and work together.

At some point in time, the dispute must be closed. Whether or not there is any satisfaction between the parties, the dispute will only remain active for 60 days. If you open a dispute, it's in your best interest to remain involved in the process and close the dispute within this time frame. If you don't do this and eBay must close the dispute for you, you cannot claim a final value fee credit, and even if the buyer was in the wrong, the buyer doesn't get a strike against him or her.

Leaving feedback in the event of an unpaid item is tricky. Sometimes emotions can get the better of us and you might leave feedback (or a response to the buyer's negative feedback) that later you might wish wasn't available for all your other customers to read. Even if you must say something negative, you can do so calmly and without compromising your integrity. Feedback will be discussed later in the chapter.

Despite the occasional blip on the eBay radar, the majority of transactions completed on eBay are smooth and hassle-free. You will receive your payments in a timely manner, some of them within 24 hours of the auction's end and occasionally even one immediately upon the close of the auction, and in return, you ship in a timely manner.

When Suzy receives her PayPal payment from the winning bidder of her waffle iron, she immediately proceeds to the next step: **shipping the item**. Since her item was pre-boxed and weighed to utilize eBay's shipping calculator during the auction, all she has to do is get it in the mail.

Suzy has already decided to utilize the services of the United States Postal Service (unless the buyer has a special request or the item is too large for the USPS to handle) and print shipping labels and pay for shipping on all her auctions through PayPal. Here are more than a dozen good reasons why you should do the same:

1. You don't have to leave home to ship items; leave them right in/near your mailbox, protected from weather, of course! This makes it very easy to ship every business day and even Saturdays, for the truly dedicated sellers.

2. You can e-mail a message to your local post office letting them know that you have packages to be picked up.

3. You can prepare packages for mailing in the evenings or over a weekend; it's easy to specify the next business date for your label.

4. You don't have to spend your own money to ship items from your post office if the money is still in your PayPal account because the postage is paid from PayPal funds! You definitely should not wait until transferred funds from PayPal arrive at your bank; this will leave you branded as a "slow shipper."

5. You can even ship items that were paid via other means (money order, etc.). Just use the drop-down menu on the item's line on My eBay and click print shipping label. You have to have sufficient funds in your PayPal account, so it's a good idea to leave some if you transfer to your business bank account.

6. You get delivery confirmation free with Priority Mail, and other mail classes (First Class, Parcel Post, Media Mail) for a mere $0.13. That's actually cheaper than your post office, without leaving home or waiting in line!

7. You don't have to hand-write a shipping label. You will print a nice label right from your computer, complete with both addresses and delivery confirmation number, plus a receipt for your own records, on one sheet of paper!

8. You can have the label print without the postage amount displayed, so your buyers cannot easily determine what your handling charge was.

9. Your buyer is notified via e-mail that you have created the shipping label and is given the delivery confirmation number, without you ever lifting a finger.

10. You can include a personal message to buyers (sent with the delivery confirmation number) stating the ship date or thanking them for the purchase.

11. You can determine when your item has been delivered, right from My eBay or PayPal, although it doesn't display full "tracking" like UPS or FedEx.

12. An upgrade to the system late in 2005 now allows you to create and print international customs forms and shipping labels in the same simple manner.

13. You can upgrade to a special printer for the self-stick labels.

14. You will be charged no extra fees by PayPal or the USPS for this service!

With all these great benefits and features, this should be one of the easiest decisions to make. When you open accounts with FedEx or UPS, you can also create shipping labels right from your computer. UPS also works with PayPal, and you can create both domestic and international shipping labels right on PayPal's site and pay through PayPal. This gives UPS an edge over FedEx for those sellers who need to utilize carriers other than the USPS (for larger items, etc.). Other shipping companies might utilize PayPal or you can get a PayPal credit card to use with other shipping companies. Contact the individual carriers to determine who will let you pay with PayPal funds and who will not.

Once Suzy has her label printed and attached firmly to her package, she can place it outside in time for her mail carrier to pick it up. To finalize her end of the transaction, she lets the buyer know that the package is on its way and leaves positive feedback for the buyer.

 **Utilize Online Carrier Pickup**

Even if your mail carrier comes daily to deliver mail, utilize the online scheduling system so that he or she knows to look for your items the next day.

If you choose to take your packages to a shipping location such as the post office, a UPS store, or a FedEx location, then you'll have to determine a shipping schedule. Unless you have a lot of free time, driving to a shipping station every day isn't very practical. In this case, set a schedule of days that you ship, such as "every Monday and Thursday" or "every Monday, Wednesday, and Friday." Make sure that this is stated clearly in the text of every auction, preferably in your policies that you will copy/paste into every auction.

Some other shipping companies will also schedule pickups of your packages, but be sure to ask about any fees for doing so before actually scheduling these.

What exactly constitutes proper packaging is a subjective matter. While you might think that your packaging skills are adequate, a buyer might be aghast at how the item was sloshing around in the box. The best rule for packing is to use the smallest box or envelope that you have that will hold the item with just enough room for adequate cushioning: no more than three inches around is usually sufficient for all but the most fragile items. Nobody wants to receive a huge box with 90 percent newspapers and 10 percent of the space used by the item. Not only does that leave buyers with a lot of waste to dispose of, it can make them feel like they paid postage for a lot of unnecessary shipping materials.

Patrick Walden (eBay user "waldo53") admittedly wasn't the best packer when he first began selling on eBay. To explain, he recalls the time he once sold some pilsner glasses to a customer. These tall, heavy glasses used for beer were well packed. Almost too well, he now concludes.

When the customer was unpacking the box, she set aside a large bunch of paper that she mistook for packing materials. As she was carrying it to the trash, the glass that had been wrapped inside the wad of paper fell out and broke. She notified Patrick of the broken glass, but did not blame him for the incident.

When he heard how it had happened, however, he concluded that his packing may have left a little to be desired and sent a partial refund to the buyer. She was surprised by the refund but also appreciative, resulting in positive feedback for Patrick.

Patrick now wraps bright-colored tape around items so they are easily distinguished from the packing materials. Although insurance is at the option of the buyer and his policy states that he isn't responsible for broken items, Patrick does try to be as fair as possible. He states that he will "almost always refund money to people if I remotely believe I had something to do with the issue." That sets him a bit higher than many sellers who will simply stick by their policy even if they had something to do with the resulting problems.

When you print your shipping labels with PayPal Shipping, the address will always be correct—human error is factored out. That's a good thing! If you write or type out labels, be sure that you double-check the address. If the item was paid through PayPal, be sure to use only the confirmed address that is on file with PayPal, in order to qualify for their buyer and seller protection programs.

This can pose a problem when your buyer, due to a time constraint or to save postage in re-shipping, asks you to ship the item directly to his sister in Albuquerque, instead of his own address in Cincinnati. What do you do then? Sometimes you'll have to choose between the seller protection program and customer service.

One way to handle the situation is to not print the shipping label through PayPal but to physically take the package to your shipper's location. Make sure you purchase delivery confirmation and even perhaps signature confirmation (if your buyer has communicated this wish before you invoiced him you can add these costs to the postage). While you still won't qualify for any assistance from PayPal if the buyer claims the item never arrived, you will at least be able to prove that you sent it and that it did indeed arrive.

This is something you may want to cover in your policies as well. Some sellers have noted in their listings that they will not ever ship an item to any place other than a confirmed address. You'll have to decide if this the same route you'll take when dealing with the occasional customer who needs something done out of the ordinary.

Combining shipping can cause a payment delay, as noted above, but it also can cause other confusion. Most buyers think that combining shipping is always going to save them a lot of money, but it may not be the case. For instance, if you sold two items that, when packaged in small bubble envelopes, each weighed seven ounces, you'd be able to send them each for about $1.75 via First Class Mail, or approximately $3.50 for both. When you put both of those items into the same envelope, they now weigh 13.5 ounces, and no longer qualify for First Class Mail. Your only option now is Priority Mail, which is a minimum cost of $3.85. The buyer actually pays more this way. Where this can make a difference, however, is if you do not charge any handling charge for items in a multiple purchase.

If you were to charge $2.50 for each of those seven-ounce items ($1.75 postage plus $0.75 handling), then the buyer would be charged $5 in total shipping and handling if you mailed them separately. If, however, you charge a combined postage of $3.85 for Priority Mail and only charge one handling charge of $0.75, then the buyer would pay $4.35 for shipping and handling. In this case, combining shipping is cheaper for the buyer.

When you decide on a combined shipping policy, you can fill in eBay's shipping discount calculator which will then create combined shipping quotes for buyers on invoices with more than one auction item.

You can choose from two basic methods of combining shipping: the flat-fee method or the combined-weight method.

The Flat-Fee Method

On combined purchases, the calculator will automatically use the highest shipping amount from any of the items, and then add a flat fee for every additional items. If the buyer purchased three items and the individual shipping quotes (this only works if you've set up the shipping calculator when you listed the item) are:

Item	Shipping Quote
#1	$2.60
#2	$3.85
#3	$6.95

The calculator will start with the highest shipping cost, $6.95, and then add your flat fee ($1 in this case) for each additional item. So this buyer would pay a combined shipping fee of $8.95 for all three items, as opposed to $13.40. You can also set the calculator to use the highest shipping price and have additional items sent free.

The Combined-Weight Method

On combined purchases where you have entered each item's individual weight into the shipping calculator when you listed each item, eBay will add together all the weights and, using the buyer's zip code, calculate a combined shipping quote. The combined items will need fewer boxes or envelopes, but you will also likely be using a larger box or envelope, so the total weight may very well differ somewhat from what the calculator determines. However, you can re-package all the items in a different container and revise the shipping cost on an invoice before sending it. If you need to do this, be sure to communicate with the buyer why he or she may not be getting an invoice quite as quickly. Most buyers are willing to be a bit more patient in order to get a lower shipping cost.

Local pickups are utilized for larger items that would be impossible or very expensive to ship, such as automobiles and furniture. You should have formulated a local pickup policy along with your other policies, but when it comes to these very large items, it may not be logical to expect the buyer to meet you halfway. In the case that the buyer must really come to your home, take precautions to keep your home, valuables, and family safe.

All shipping companies have rules about what can be shipped (no flammable materials) and in what type of container (no FedEx boxes sent through USPS unless the FedEx logo is covered by labels or inked out). These rules can usually be found on your shipper's Web site or by asking a representative at your shipping location.

One set of regulations that needs to be covered briefly is the **different classes of USPS mail** and what is allowed in each type. Gone are the days of Second Class and Third Class mail for super-cheap rates. The USPS revamped its classifications several years ago and now features different choices.

Media Mail

Media Mail is the cheapest rate of mail. However, it is restricted to these items:

- Books

- Film

- Manuscripts

- Sound recordings

- Video tapes

- Computer media (CD/DVD-ROMs and floppy disks)

The package can't include advertising, which is why most magazines are excluded, unless they are not current magazines purchased as collectibles. This class of mail takes two to nine days on average to reach its destination, depending on distance. Media Mail packages can weigh a maximum of 70 pounds.

Media Mail has been heavily abused in the past by persons who wish to mail items at its economical rates regardless of what they are mailing. In the past, if you marked a package as "Media Mail" the USPS staff might have not even questioned you as to its contents. Recently a change in rules (which you should find posted at post offices) states that Media Mail packages are now subject to opening and inspection at the discretion of the USPS, to cut down on this fraud.

EBay sellers should promote a high standard of integrity and not even offer to ship items via Media Mail when they don't qualify. Recently I was interested in a set of collectible coffee mugs that match a set I've had for twenty-five years. I really wanted this item, but the seller listed his only shipping option as Media Mail for $8.

This annoyed me on two levels. First, I know that there is no way that item weighed enough to merit an eight-dollar charge on Media Mail. Therefore, it was obvious the seller was very heavily padding the shipping, and I know that Media Mail can be very slow. I didn't object to paying $8 to ship the item, but I objected to paying $8 for the slowest service that would cost the seller far less than half that amount.

Second, I know that coffee mugs don't fit into any of the restricted categories, which led me to suspect deceit of the USPS regulations was planned by the seller. To give the seller the benefit of the doubt, I e-mailed a question about the item. I asked if there had been an error in the listing, and perhaps the shipping quoted was for a different class of mail as the item wasn't really Media Mail. The seller never even bothered to answer my question, so I did not bother to bid.

Being an honest seller also requires all of us to be honest buyers. While that item doesn't come up on eBay every day, and I really wanted it, I simply could not bring myself to deal with that seller.

Parcel Post

Parcel Post is more expensive than Media Mail but often less expensive than Priority Mail. Parcel Post does not have the restrictions of Media Mail, but neither does it offer the same services as Priority Mail, such as mail forwarding. In cases where the package weighs less than two pounds, the difference may be as little as ten cents. Considering the potential for slower delivery (two to nine days), Priority (two to three days) is often a better overall deal. Where Parcel Post becomes more of a bargain is with a heavier package. Parcel Post packages can weigh up to 70 pounds.

First Class

First Class items can be in envelopes or small packages, but there is a maximum weight restriction of 13 ounces. First Class items often can reach their destination in three days or less.

Priority Mail

Priority Mail has a flat rate for anything up to one pound: $3.85. For a package that weighs very close to one pound, that's not much more than Parcel Post for the same item. If the item is 13 ounces or less, consider First Class unless the buyer would like the package to definitely arrive in two to three days.

Priority Mail packages can weigh up to 70 pounds. For items over one pound, the cost is based on a combination of weight and distance. If you mail an item to a town 30 miles away, it would be cheaper than mailing the identical item 3,000 miles away.

Express Mail

Express Mail is the fastest way to get your item delivered. It's also the most expensive option at the USPS. With a weight limit of 70 pounds, you can express packages to anybody in the country with a guaranteed delivery in one to two business days.

Certain items you sell on eBay may merit express delivery, such as time-sensitive items like tickets to an event or last-minute holiday gifts. Express Mail uses a flat fee with a package up to eight ounces costing $13.85, or nine ounces up to two pounds for $17.85. Insurance up to $100 is included free with Express Mail, as is full tracking online.

 **Classes of Mail**

To see a chart with brief descriptions of the mail classes and their restrictions, go to
www.usps.com/customersguide/dmm100.htm

Insurance and delivery confirmation are offered by the USPS for the protection of both buyer and seller. It is important to note that PayPal's buyer and seller protection programs do not replace the USPS's insurance or delivery confirmation services. Be sure to read up on PayPal's programs so that you are clear about what they do offer you as a seller.

We've already noted that when you purchase shipping through PayPal, delivery confirmation is automatically utilized on every package, regardless of mailing class. There is no extra charge for Priority Mail packages to get delivery confirmation, but all other classes are charged $0.13. This makes delivery confirmation affordable for all shipments.

Insurance is not included automatically, but it's very easy to purchase it right along with your label. Just one click of the mouse insures your package for the appropriate fee, which is determined based on the final bid price of the item.

You'll have to determine for which items you'll require your buyers to purchase insurance. If there's any way you can build insurance into your shipping quote, do so; buyers like to feel that they're getting a good deal when "insurance is included in the price."

TIP — Insure Your Packages

PayPal's buyer and seller protection programs are not to be confused with insurance. In order to qualify for assistance through their program, you may have to produce proof that you insured the package to begin with. Read up on all the intricacies of this program so you are aware of its benefits and limitations.

What do you do when an item is damaged in transit and the buyer had not purchased insurance? That's a tricky question, indeed. If your auction policies clearly state that insurance is at the buyer's option but suggested, then technically you are in the clear and the buyer should have no claim against you.

However, what if the buyer's "claim" specifically blames you, the seller, for not properly packaging or padding the item? Could this be merely a way to coerce you into refunding the money, when you really weren't at fault? Or could this be a type of fraud?

When it comes to any item that has a serial number or other specific identifying marks, it's a good idea to keep a record of those per chance you have a buyer who will try to defraud you. One such scam is to purchase an item identical to one that the buyer already owns (but is broken, defective, or damaged in some way) and then when the newly purchased one arrives, the buyer claims that it was damaged, broken, etc. They want to keep the newly purchased one and return the original, broken one for a refund.

Any returns or refunds should always be done after the merchandise is received back from the buyer (with return postage at their expense). If there is any reason to suspect fraud of this sort, contact your shipper and eBay for assistance.

A recent thread on one of the eBay discussion boards focused on a seller's question of a similar nature. He had a buyer who refused insurance, had a damaged item, and demanded that the seller take the item back and refund his money. The seller, while technically not to blame, was seeking advice from other eBay sellers on how they've handled this situation.

The responses were lively, agonizing, and varied. Some sellers said they'd do it just to keep the peace with the buyer. Others said that they'd do it under certain conditions, such as the buyer not having any feedback to indicate he tries to return things frequently. Others stated that they'd stick to their policy and "too bad for the buyer."

As with many other issues, you'll have to determine what's best for your business when it comes to issues of damaged merchandise without the purchase of insurance.

So many of these issues have one common theme to them: **customer service**. With such a simple phrase to describe it, you'd think that customer service should be a no-brainer, but this is a topic that can be anything but simple.

Providing good customer service in some ways is easy:

- Don't misrepresent your product or mislead your customers in any way.

- Provide timely and efficient answers to questions; be helpful.

- When the auction ends, communicate with the buyer (via an invoice) within one day or less.

- Thank the buyer often for the purchase and express wishes for future transactions.

- Don't cheat the buyer or overcharge for things like shipping.

- Keep your word about shipping timelines and ship in a timely manner.

- Communicate with the buyer on the date you shipped the item.

- Follow up with the customer by giving good feedback.

As long as the customer is happy, it seems like good customer service is smooth and simple. But when the customer is not happy, you still must provide good customer service in a calm and professional manner, to the best of your ability.

If you've been honest all along in a transaction, then you have nothing to hide from an angry buyer who merely wants you to be responsible for his lack of purchasing insurance or who wants to scare you into doing more than is reasonable. In short, some people want something for nothing, and they'll prey on an eBay seller, who to them is not a face but just a user ID to get it.

Do what is right in trying to make things right with your buyer, and always remember that while your goal might be to have 100 percent customer satisfaction, it is just that: a goal. It's not the end of your business if you don't make an overly demanding buyer happy. If you ever feel threatened by an angry buyer, do not hesitate to get eBay involved. Sometimes a buyer who thinks nothing of being hostile with you won't have the courage to do so when eBay is involved.

But under all other circumstances, always treat each customer as if you were them. For example, I personally like to know exactly what day an item I ordered has shipped. Often I've received a package and thought to myself, "Gosh, the seller never even notified me that he shipped it."

There's not really any reason I can put my finger on for why I like to know this, but I do. So, per chance my buyers are like me, I make a point of always notifying each buyer when I ship their items (and thanks to PayPal Shipping, that is a much easier task than it used to be!). Buyers love to have their items shipped quickly, and when they know the items have been shipped out, they can anticipate their arrival.

Patrick Walden (eBay user "waldo53") shares a story of a sale where negative feedback seemed almost inevitable. On a recent transaction, the buyer chose the Media Mail rate when he paid for his book purchase. The book was duly packed up and shipped in a timely manner. Walden recalls that "Within a couple of days, [the buyer] e-mailed and said he hadn't got it yet. I politely explained to him that he chose the cheapest method and that it could take one to four weeks."

By the end of the first week, the buyer e-mailed again. This time he was piping mad because he felt that he should have received the item within three days. While that wasn't likely, since the buyer's and seller's zip codes were not within three-day range for Media Mail, Walden again politely reiterated what the first e-mail had said.

Ten days after the transaction's close, he received yet another irate e-mail.

With each new e-mail, Patrick said, it seemed as though the buyer had not read one single word of his previous e-mails because he kept insisting that the item should have arrived within three days! Frustrated that it seemed the buyer wasn't bothering to read his e-mailed replies, Patrick copied and pasted all of his previous e-mails to the buyer and used the "Contact Buyer" link (on his "My eBay" page) to send the entire string of responses to the buyer. He figured that the buyer might be more inclined to open and e-mail from the eBay system.

However, nothing changed. "This went on for weeks," Walden states. "Finally, he e-mailed me and said he got it, but thought it was way too slow in arriving so he wanted to leave me a negative feedback." One thing was different about this e-mail: it was sent from a different e-mail address than the others.

Patrick replied to the new e-mail address, stating that if the buyer wished to leave negative feedback, that was his prerogative, but that he, as a seller, felt that he'd be entitled to leave negative feedback in turn. The reason: the buyer had never responded to a single one of his e-mails with any sense of cooperation or understanding. He'd been, in short, a very demanding and unreasonable buyer. Again, Patrick copied and pasted every e-mail that he'd sent in reply to every e-mail the buyer had sent, the total of which numbered over twenty in that several-week period. Only this time, he sent the entire package to the buyer's different e-mail address.

The buyer, upon receiving this e-mail from Patrick, finally got the full story. And when he e-mailed back, Patrick finally understood the whole scenario. Patrick explained, "He e-mailed out from the other e-mail address but never read any e-mails there because it was full of spam. So he never saw any of my e-mails," and added that he finds this explanation "very strange." However, the seller offered his full apologies and left positive feedback for the transaction, to which Patrick did the same.

Even though his communications were not received by this buyer, Patrick kept communicating in a calm and positive manner all along. He did not lose his cool or write off the buyer. If he had given up on the buyer, he may not have read the e-mail that was sent from a different address, would never have got to the bottom of the mystery, and likely would have received that negative feedback the buyer was threatening to give.

One very important way to have your customer-service skills displayed to future customers is through the eBay feedback forum. When your customers are pleased with your service, most of them will take the time to actually point out what they appreciated about you. Fast shipping, nice-quality products, excellent prices, and value are all things that buyers will point out.

Future customers do look at your feedback, especially when you are newer to selling than a competitor. If they find that of the 25 feedback comments you've received, and 22 people made a point of noting that you shipped very quickly, then a potential buyer who appreciates fast shipping might buy from you as opposed to some big corporation whose shipping department may or not get their item out quickly.

Feedback has its flip side too. You need to give feedback to every buyer who purchases from you. Nothing is more annoying to a buyer who pays in a timely manner than to have to bug the seller to leave feedback. Sellers can become lax about feedback once they have a very high score themselves. Don't let your company become too busy to leave feedback.

Some sellers have policies about when they will leave feedback. Some sellers state bluntly, "I will not leave you positive feedback if you leave me negative feedback." If the buyer did nothing wrong, that is not fair. Others hold the buyer hostage with a do-or-die statement such as, "I only leave feedback after you leave me feedback."

Feedback is intended to reflect how each party to the transaction has performed. One of the best policies I saw recently on a seller's listing was something akin to this: "Once you have performed your duty by paying in a timely manner, then I will leave you feedback. I do not force you to leave me feedback, but I'd appreciate it if you did so when I have completed my duties to you." Interestingly enough, this was a seller who was relatively new to eBay. Perhaps she'd devised this policy because of experiences as a buyer who had to pull teeth to get some sellers to leave her feedback.

Although I'd never thought about it quite that way before, I personally leave feedback for buyers as soon as they pay. They did their part; therefore, I feel they deserve the feedback for doing so.

If the buyer, in turn, is unhappy with your service or product, then he or she rightly can leave you negative feedback, although it's always best to communicate with you before doing so to try to work it out. Your fair policies, quick responses to questions, fast shipping, and good communication all the way through the process will build goodwill with your buyers, so that they may be more inclined to contact you before leaving negative feedback.

However, think of it this way: If the buyer has never had any personal service from you other than a standard invoice with no personal message, what would give them the idea that they should e-mail you when they are unhappy? If you give off the feeling of being a cold stone wall with very negative or harshly stated policies and no personalized communications throughout the sale, buyers might think of you more as a "company" and not a "person" on the other end of the e-mail.

So good customer service all through the process will go a long way to getting you good feedback. It seems almost inevitable that you will eventually get a negative feedback, but you do have the opportunity to post a comment or explanation in your defense.

Always try to think of yourself as the buyer. If you've ever, as a buyer, left negative feedback for a seller, then you'll know that you felt very justified in doing so. While there are buyers who utilize feedback in the wrong manner, try to put yourself into your buyer's shoes and work from there. Even after negative feedback has been given, try to work it out. If you can later come to some agreement and salvage the transaction, you can mutually agree to have the feedback removed by eBay.

If the feedback is truly unfair, eBay may be able to remove it for you. EBay seller waldo53, Patrick, recounts an incident he had with negative feedback. The buyer, says Patrick, "accused me of scamming him after I 'overcharged' him ten cents on postage. I explained that I got the rate off the USPS Web site, but for some reason it was a little different when the box was weighed at the post office."

Patrick even sent the man a refund of the "overcharged" amount after going back and forth with him via e-mail for a week. Did that satisfy the customer? Nope. "After he got his dime in the mail, he left negative feedback." But that wasn't all the customer left. Against eBay policy, the buyer put a link to a Web site in the feedback, as well as a "choice" word or two.

When Patrick saw the link, he clicked it and was surprised at what he saw: "a massive list of sellers he claimed ripped him off." Patrick took the appropriate action, reporting the feedback to eBay, who immediately removed it. The buyer was eventually banned from eBay. "Guess he'll be buying his printer's ink cartridges elsewhere from now on," muses Patrick.

Sometimes the best way to learn what to do is to be shown what not to do. I reviewed literally hundreds of current auctions to find what was done right and what wasn't. Overall, I'd have to say that I found far more good examples than bad ones, but one auction I stumbled across was just too unbelievable not to share. While I could not duplicate the entire auction because the work is the intellectual property of the author, I have extracted just a few of the phrases used. These phrases all came from one actual auction; any identifying information has been removed. This auction was several screens long, with the font size getting larger and larger (3 different sizes) as it went along, finally ending in red, bold, and mostly capitalized wording. I have duplicated the typos and grammatical errors exactly and have put the items in capitals when it was done so in the listing.

Top 10 Things to Say or Do to Drive Customers Away

10. Public Displays of Ignorance

"the 3pc set at the bottom is not included slight picture problem" I could only take this to mean that the seller didn't know how to crop a photo properly. Any sophisticated buyer will be under-impressed by the poor grammar and the lack of techno-savvy displayed by this seller. Not to mention that this "disclaimer" was in a font smaller than, and separated from, the main item description. Very confusing and misleading to the looker who would see two outfits in the photo—if it would have displayed!

"Selling price has nothing to do with quality of item I know how much dresses are costing now." The grammar is awful and the implied "I'm not stupid so don't try to fool me" attitude is far from inviting to the reader.

9. Trying to Redeem Yourself?

"No returns nor refunds. All items as is. Used and detailed unless marked new." And a little later we get, "If I make a mistake I would like the chance to correct it." How are buyers supposed to know which policy is the right one? Does it depend on the seller's mood on any given day, or how quickly you paid, or what?

8. Don't Say What You Don't Mean

"SHIPPING IS NOT FREE! If there is no shipping quote or it's stated as free please e-mail me for a quote." Are you implying that if you tell me it's free, it's really not?

7. Who Needs Technology?

"Shipping costs are estimates for the continental United States only." The reason why eBay has set up their online shipping calculator is so that potential bidders can know up front exactly what the item will cost to ship. If you can't input an accurate weight up front, don't use the calculator or plan to absorb any excess postage yourself. A good digital scale can be had for under $50 and will solve any issues with "guessing" how much an item will weigh.

6. The Flip-Flop Technique

"I DO NOT SHIP INTERNATIONAL OR TO ANY ONE THAT NEEDS SPEICAL FORMS." And then later on it says (in red, no less): "International bidders must e-mail BEFORE BIDDING!" Why, so the seller can refer them back to the first statement?

5. Twist the Knife a Little

"If you pay before the shipping price is quoted to you, I will charge an added $1 fee for additional paypal payments." This policy may actually violate eBay's "Payment Surcharges" policy, which clearly states:

Not permitted:

• Charging an extra fee to use a credit card instead of a check.

• Charging an extra fee to use PayPal.

4. Do Unto Others

(Note: In the largest font of the three sizes used) "IF YOU WAIT TO PAY FOR AN ITEM FOR 3 WEEKS AND EXPECT ME TO SEND IT NEXT DAY DON'T BID." And two sentences later, the seller reiterates, "DON'T PAYPAL ME 3 WEEKS AFTER THE AUCTION ENDS AND E-MAIL ME TWO DAYS LATER WONDERING WHY YOUR ITEM HAS NOT ARRIVED!" Wow! That's really going to encourage people to pay on time! And to think, we got to hear it twice!

3. Feedback Misfortunes?

(Note: In that largest font again) "PLEASE NOTE I NO LONGER LEAVE FB FOR BUYERS UNTIL I RECIVE FEEDBACK. DUE TO MANY WHO LEAVE BAD FEEDBACK FOR THINGS OUT OF MY CONTROL." And a few sentences later: "AND LEAVE ME A NEG I HATE TO BE THAT WAY BUT TO MANY ARE LEAVING ME BAD FEEDBACK..." This seller honestly seems surprised by bad feedback. For the record, this seller's feedback rating was 97.2 percent positive with a feedback score greater than 700. As a side note, the seller's "About Me" page was, in many ways, a continuation of the angry babble in the auction, including this notable sentence: "We tend to have many non paying bidders who get mad when leave a negative for them not paying and leave us sellers with negative feedbacks."

2. Hey Buddy, Can You Spare a Dime?

"PLEASE NOTE IF YOUR FEEDBACK IS LESS THAT 25 DO NOT BID I HAVE THE RIGHT TO CANCEL BIDDING!" Wouldn't you love to know who bought from or sold to these people when their feedback score was less than 25?

And the #1 Thing to Say or Do to Drive Customers Away:

"DO NOT BID UNLESS YOU PLAN TO BUY!!" "IF...DO NOT BID" "Please do not bid if you cannot abide by these conditions" "IF...DON'T BID" "IF YOU THINK MY RULES ARE TO MUCH

TO FOLLOW PLEASE DO NOT BID!" "I AM A HONEST SELLER AND BUYER AND CAN ONLY HOPE TO RECIVE THE SAME FROM OTHERS" In this one auction, I was told "Do Not Bid" at least five times. Five times! This seller's "Business Policies" (so titled in a pretty font) were so offensive that I just had to watch the item to see if anybody would bid on it. Nobody did. Big surprise. I also checked out this seller's other items to see if they all contained this same tirade—they did. As a potential buyer, the seller's fervent words about being an honest seller and someone who's being pelted with "UNCALLED FOR" negative feedback did not fill me with sympathy. I only knew one thing: There was no way I was doing business with this person.

Good customer service and good feedback go hand in hand. One often brings about the other. Giving your customers high-quality, efficient, friendly, and caring service has benefits beyond the positive feedback. It can bring about repeat customers or referrals when your customers send their friends to your eBay store. The positive feedback it generates is a referral, of sorts, as well. And the bottom line is this: It's the right way to do business.

"Re-listing Items" and "Second Chance Offers" are auction features that you'll probably become familiar with, although we all wish that these weren't necessary to utilize. The reality is that not all of your auctions will sell the first time out. In fact, sometimes it takes a number of different attempts to sell the same item.

Doing your research and placing items in the right category, with the proper keywords in the title and with an appropriate price will help you sell your items. But nobody can force the buyers to be looking the week that your item is listed, and nobody can change the fact that twenty other sellers just happened to list the same item around the same time. Those are all unknowns about eBay that can throw a loop in your well-laid plans to meet a certain sales goal for the week or month.

There are times when things seem to go all your way. Some weeks, your auctions seem almost on fire. Those are the times that carry you through the slow times and will keep you coming back to eBay for your selling platform.

And when the slow weeks come, learn quickly to take it all in stride.

Use the time to read up on all the eBay announcements or take an online course that week. Spend some time finding a discussion board that interests you, then join it and get involved in the discussions. When you have really busy weeks and months, there won't be as much time to get involved in the social aspects of eBay, so try to think of your slow times as your time to expand your network and educate yourself to be a better seller. Investigate all those nooks and crannies in eBay that you haven't yet had time to look at. EBay is like an iceberg; there's so much more than meets the eye.

If your items don't sell the first time around, you have the option to re-list them and, if they sell the second time, eBay will refund your insertion fees after the auction ends. The refund does not apply to extras like bold, highlighted listings, or gallery, but just to the actual listing fee. You don't have to do anything to request the credit; it's done automatically by eBay. To see if your credit has been applied, check your "Seller's Account" and view your fees since your last invoice.

In order to receive a re-list refund credit, you must re-list the item within 90 days of the original ending date. Also, the credit is good only if the item sells the second time. If not, you do still have to pay for that second listing fee. You can start a new listing (third listing) for the item, and then if it doesn't sell, the re-list (actually the fourth) will now qualify for a re-list refund credit. It's up to you how many time you choose to re-list an item; eBay doesn't put any limit on that.

Other requirements to note:

- Only listings in auction or fixed-price formats qualify, not store inventory or real estate listings.

- Dutch Auctions and multiple-quantity auctions do not qualify.

- You may lower the starting price or keep it the same as the original listing, but you can't raise it.

- If the original listing did not have a reserve price, then you cannot use reserve on the re-list. If you used reserve both times, the second reserve must not be higher than the first time.

A re-list refund is also given for auctions that were successfully won by a bidder but were never paid for. In order to qualify for this refund, you must have completed the Unpaid Items Process, which includes filing an Unpaid Item Dispute and requesting a Final Value Fee credit for the item.

When you re-list an item that didn't sell the first time, go over every aspect of the listing to see if there are ways you can improve it. It may not have sold due to the roll of the dice, so to speak. Perhaps the buyers simply weren't looking for your item at that time, but perhaps there are things that you can do to make sure your item gets its fair share of lookers the second time around. Be sure to reconsider the following:

- Are your photos adequate? If not, try taking a fresh batch in a different room, with different lighting or angles. I've seen many photos of clothing where the clothes are quite literally tossed in a pile on a bed and photographed. Iron a garment and display it on a hanger. Use a contrasting colored background. Take more close-ups to add, using HTML so as to avoid extra fees.

- Does your title drive traffic to your listing? Do some searches using the keywords in your original title. Are you coming up with other items similar to yours? If not, then find out why. Once you find other items similar to your own, review their keywords to see if some of yours could be changed effectively.

- Also, double-check your title for accuracy. If your title states a "Men's Winter Jacket size XL," is that accurate? If your item description lists it as a size large, then one or the other is wrong. Make sure these two things match. If not, you may be inadvertently driving buyers away.

- While you're cross-checking your title and description for accuracy, review the description for typos and confusing information. Make sure you give enough information so that shoppers can really feel like they fully understand all there is to know about this item.

- Review eBay's list of categories to see if there's a more appropriate category you could place your item in. Or perhaps you'd be better served by listing it in two categories the second time around.

- Was your starting bid, or fixed price, too high? If your auction was current during a week that twenty other similar items were available, the ones with the lowest starting price might get the most action. Even if the auctions ended at a higher price than your starting price, you might want to consider lowering your starting price, perhaps even to the break-even point.

- Were your handling fees causing you problems? If your item is fairly lightweight and potential bidders can probably guess that it weighs less than one pound, your $2.50 handling fee might be glaringly obvious to savvy buyers who know that Priority Mail will cost you only $3.85.

- While there's nothing ethically wrong with a reasonable handling fee, buyers chafe against it, so consider eliminating it or building into your item price. Then, advertise in your description that "Shipping is a low $3.85 for Priority Mail with FREE Delivery Confirmation!" If you purchase your postage through PayPal, you'll get free delivery confirmation, but buyers don't have to know that!

A Second-Chance Offer can also be utilized when a bidder does not pay for an item. Instead of re-listing the item, if you had another bidder who was bidding on the item, you can choose to offer the item to that second bidder for their highest bid.

Or, if you have an identical item to one that sold (and the buyer did pay for), you can offer the second one to the next-highest bidder. This is a useful tool because it saves you from re-listing the item and hoping that the other bidders will see the auction and bid on it. If the next-highest bidder is interested in an identical item, then he or she can purchase it for their highest bid amount. You don't incur any listing fees when you utilize a Second-Chance Offer, but you will pay final value fees.

A third occasion when you can correctly use a Second-Chance Offer is when you have listed an item with a reserve price that wasn't met. If you decide that you are willing to sell the item to the highest bidder, you can offer it to the bidder this way.

In the "Selling Reminders" section of "My eBay," you'll find a link to all your recently sold items that are eligible for a Second-Chance Offer.

Basically, any item that had more than one bidder is eligible. To start the process, use the drop-down menu to the right of the item in your "Items I've Sold" or "Items Not Sold" section of "My eBay."

TIP ↖ Second-Chance Offers

When buyers have chosen not to receive Second-Chance Offers, you will be promptly notified as you proceed through the steps of offering the item. If you have reason to believe that the bidders may actually want the item, you can always contact the members through eBay and politely inform them that the item is available for a Second-Chance Offer but that their settings are blocking you from sending them such an offer. If they wish to receive the offer, instruct them to change their settings and to contact you when they are ready to receive the offer. Bidders may not realize that they are not set up to receive Second-Chance Offers.

When bidders receive a Second-Chance Offer, they'll see a pre-set number of days for which you, the seller, have made the offer available. In order to take advantage of the offer, they must complete the checkout for the item before the offer expires. This is so that you can offer the item to yet another bidder in a timely manner.

Some sellers theorize that giving the bidder more than 24 hours to decide if they want your item is asking for trouble. Since buying often involves the current, urgent desire to possess an item, if you give a buyer too much time to decide, they're as likely to pass on the offer as to choose it. If, however, you've built a sense of urgency into the offer (by giving them only 24 hours to pay or pass) then you may ultimately have more luck selling the item.

You do not have to utilize the Second-Chance Offer system at all, or you may also continue to utilize it (by going down the list of bidders) until you find a buyer. Keep in mind, though, that each bidder is offered the item at his or her highest bid—not the final bid of the item. So you have to decide at what point you might be better off re-listing the item and hoping for a higher bid price, and potentially claiming the re-list refund credit.

Other things you should know about Second-Chance Offers:

- You can only offer them for up to 60 days after the original auction ends. However, unless the item is extremely unusual, rare, or highly desirable, many bidders will have moved on and found something else fairly quickly, so consider utilizing this feature sooner than later.

- If you are using this feature due to a non-paying bidder, be sure that you have done everything you can to complete the first transaction before moving on to the other options.

- You can't use this feature for Dutch, or multiple-quantity, items.

- If you have more than one duplicate item, you can send out offers only for the exact quantity of items you do have. In case all bidders wish to buy, you must be able to provide product for them all.

- If a bidder does not respond within the deadline, the seller can't re-offer the item to that same bidder.

- Be sure to check out special rules for Second-Chance Offers if your item was listed in "eBay Motors" or the "Business & Industrial" categories.

- Only the non-winning bidder to whom you've sent the offer can view and purchase it, even though it will show in your "Items I'm Selling" view.

- You can cancel an offer at any time if the bidder has not yet responded.

One final point that we need to touch on in this chapter is keeping a customer database. Although this was reviewed in Chapter 6, it's worth mentioning again. When you make a sale to a satisfied customer, keep track of the buyer's e-mail address. This can be done in a number of ways, from keeping a simple handwritten list in a notebook to a database set up on your computer. If you have your list on your computer, be sure that you either print it occasionally or that your computer's hard drive is backed up regularly so that in the unfortunate event of a computer crash your data isn't entirely lost.

A computer database or blank table that's filled in by hand could be as simple as this:

Name	E-mail Address	Transaction Date(s)	Purchase Types
Suzy Buyer	suzybuyslots@e-mailprovider.com	1/27/06 5/15/06	1 Widget 2 Gidgets

Don't forget to store e-mail addresses of customers in separate folders in your e-mail program so you don't accidentally forward jokes and other things you might send to your friends. Many e-mail address book programs allow you to add notes as well or classify them in some way, such as by the product type they purchased from you.

When you open your eBay store, you'll receive Selling Manager Basic for free with your monthly fee. This software will assist you in keeping a database that stays on eBay's servers, so it will not be lost in a crash of your hard drive. Although it's hard to imagine eBay's computer system being wiped out, crazier things have happened, so it might be wise to occasionally print or copy that information to another source for safe-keeping.

Protect your customers' information with the same zeal that you expect from sellers who have your e-mail stored. Use your database wisely, and don't bombard your customers with too much e-mail, or you'll be branded as junk mail. Utilize the nice built-in features of your eBay store for sending custom e-mails and newsletters.

In order to build a repeat customer base, you have to keep yourself in your customers' view. Even though I have ordered my pet cockatoo's food from the same Web site for years, they mail me catalogs on a regular basis. That's wise for a number of reasons: it keeps their company name fresh in my mind; it gives me a chance to view products I may not have seen on their Web site and peruse their selection at my convenience; and mostly, it gives me something tangible to pass on to friends and family who have pets and are looking for a reliable company to do business with. It also doubles as a shred-toy for the cockatoo!

While there are numerous Web sites that sell the same specialized pet foods that this company sells, I am a repeat customer at this one because their Web site is never inaccessible, they have always had the product in stock, they e-mail me an order confirmation as well as a shipping confirmation (remember, I love to know when things are on their way), and they have always shipped very quickly. I couldn't say that about the other companies I tried before finding this one.

Find a way to set yourself and your company apart from the competition by offering the best in reasonable prices, friendly and helpful service, honest transactions, and speedy shipping. Buyers who need a steady supply of your product will take notice. Buyers who don't need a steady supply will remember you, and all buyers have the potential to send other customers your way.

These are just some of the ideas and tips that are given by the sellers who are profiled in Chapter 11. From part-time sellers to PowerSellers, each one has a unique story and a bit of advice that will be useful to you as you venture into the world of an eBay seller.

Sellers Clue You In

EBay sellers come from every conceivable walk of life, from every corner of this great planet, and sell just about everything imaginable. Of the millions of sellers out there, I was fortunate to learn the stories of a small, but wonderful, handful of them.

Each one has volunteered a bit of their story with tips, blunders, and encouragement. You've already been introduced to some of them in other parts of the book, others of them will be new to you. If you enjoy their stories, take a moment to check out their auctions and learn from them — and even let them know how you learned about them; it will make their day!

In order to locate any one of these members via their eBay names, use the eBay's "Find a Member" feature. From anywhere on eBay, click the blue link to "Advanced Search" (at the top right corner of every page) and then click "Find Members" in the yellow box on the left side. Type in the member's ID and it will take you to a page where you can view their feedback, go to their items for sale, or go to their store.

And the Two (Accounts) Shall Become One

In retrospect, their wedding vows should have been phrased something like this:

Do you take this man to be your lawfully wedded business partner? Do you promise to set up auctions, handle the bids, and box up the product, on weekends and holidays, with a broken foot or a puppy gnawing at your slippers, for richer or for poorer, for as long as you both shall eBay?

Avery Bernstein probably would have answered "I do" anyway, but on that early morning in April she couldn't have guessed that within three months she'd have a broken foot and be cooped up in the couple's second-story apartment in a new town with few friends. The puppy came later.

Not being one to sit idle and pout, Avery (eBay user "dhb9876") made a proposal of her own to her new hubby. She wanted to sell on eBay full time. Daniel didn't hesitate; he already knew that his bride had been selling sewing and quilting supplies on eBay throughout her college years. She knew how to get merchandise through wholesalers and manufacturers, and she had the education necessary to keep the business's books properly.

She even still had her business structure in place—they were all set. They just needed merchandise to sell. Daniel, a bachelor until he met and married Avery at age 39, had accumulated quite a large collection of sports cards. Over 100,000 cards large. He'd been buying and selling on eBay himself to facilitate the improvement of his own collection, but was willing to do more selling of his collection than adding to it for the moment.

They each had eBay usernames but decided that two would be confusing; they needed to be one. Since they were going to start their full-time venture by selling some of Daniel's sports cards, they decided to use his existing ID, since it was already associated with sports card buying and selling.

So Avery went to work, scanning the cards slated for sale, using descriptions written by Daniel, and sending out the goods, all with her foot propped up at first. It gave her something to think about besides her doctor's bills and set in motion a serious business. Within three months of selling full time, they had qualified as PowerSellers, and the business has been growing ever since. They soon opened an eBay store, Dab's Cards And More, and got a Web site address that redirects visitors to their eBay store: **www.dabscardsandmore.com**.

The first year or so was tough; operating a full-time business with inventory and shipping supplies all over their apartment created the perfect environment for chaos. Things got misplaced a few times, details fell through the cracks. Moving three times that first year was a definite low point. But those trying times also gave them the opportunity to build a reputation of positive customer service. They were humble and apologetic to customers whose merchandise was mixed up or lost. They made amends the best they could and offered refunds if the customer desired it.

And when they finally bought a house of their own, they set to work making it their business headquarters. Their four-bedroom home has been invaded by sports cards, quilting supplies, and other items they've branched into. Their basement has been converted into a packing and receiving warehouse. One bedroom is the office and its closets have been useful in keeping inventory straight.

"If you sell for any length of time, you will ship the wrong thing to the wrong person," Avery notes. That's why she's devised a system in the office's closet for inventory. "You don't have to get fancy," she adds. She has an "It Is Listed" shelf and a "Not Listed" section. Items that can be stored in zippered baggies or clear plastic storage containers are kept from dust and pet odors (from their puppy, which can be seen on the store's page).

Not merely content to set up her house in proper business-operating mode, Avery also schedules her day as if she were going to an office and had a boss looking over her shoulder. Otherwise, she admits, she may just fritter away her day and not accomplish much. "If I treat it like a job, it will be a job," is her motto.

Despite being an accountant, Avery keeps the majority of her records in a simple ledger book. She plans to invest in QuickBooks Pro within a couple of years, preferring to wait and buy the professional version she's accustomed to rather than a less-expensive, fewer-features version.

However, her low-tech approach to accounting doesn't apply to much else. Avery utilizes all the features of Turbo Lister to their fullest potential. She's mastered HTML for posting multiple photos by storing them on a Web site that offers free picture hosting.

Those two items—Turbo Lister and an online photo hosting site—are what she calls the "must haves" of selling on eBay. Her third "must have" is a digital postage scale. Spending time shuffling back and forth to the post office to make shipping quotes for customers is a waste of time. With an accurate scale and the shipping company's Web site, she can accurately determine the shipping costs when setting up an auction.

Their shipping policies are in line with their customer-service philosophy: Treat the customer as you'd like to be treated. They give their best shipping rate to repeat customers who purchase multiple sports cards at one time. They offer international shipping, and they don't charge extra to ship sports cards to Canada, much to the delight of our hockey-loving neighbors. "We would be out of business if we didn't ship internationally," she notes.

Customs forms can be time consuming, Avery admits, but she feels that if you "suck it up" and learn to do them correctly, you will be rewarded. So far, she's encountered no problems with international shipping, but she does her homework first. For instance, she's learned that you cannot ship "cardboard playing cards" to Italy. To avoid any possible confusion or problem with customs, they have a policy of not shipping sports cards to that country, even though sports cards aren't technically "playing cards."

Their policy of treating customers fairly also extends to foreign governments. They refuse to mark items as a "gift" so that the recipient may not have to pay taxes on it, since that practice is illegal. Additionally, they don't under-value the contents of a package for the benefit of the buyer who wants to pay less tax on it. They mark the value as the actual amount paid. Buyers may not always appreciate their policies, but it shows that they are honest sellers, and everybody has to appreciate that.

Even though they haven't always been treated fairly by others on eBay, Avery and Daniel insist on doing the best they can for every one of their customers. It shows, too, with the PowerSellers' feedback rating quickly topping 1700 with a 99.9 percent positive rating. Avery says, "I have total faith in eBay; it was founded on the principle that all people are basically good."

They may not be millionaires yet, but that's their final answer.

Where's Waldo? Wisconsin!

Patrick Walden (eBay user "waldo53") isn't really a geeky-looking kid with round glasses and a red-and-white striped shirt. Neither is this Wisconsin man trying to hide; in fact, he wants users to find him and buy from him!

A longstanding member of eBay (since 1998), Walden started selling for a specific reason: extra income to increase his collection of New York Yankees memorabilia and sports cards. It didn't take much for him to "get hooked" on eBay; his very first auctions were the stuff that makes every new seller foam at the mouth with jealousy! "I bought some toys at an auction cheap one day, brought them home, and made $175 on my first listings," Walden recalls. In the years since, he's gathered a feedback rating over 1500 with over 99 percent customer satisfaction.

"I will sell anything I can make money on," he proclaims, rattling off a list of items that includes new computers, collectible toys, and clothing. Additionally, he'll ship an item wherever it's desired (as long as it's legal) with a customer list from countries like Poland, Russia, Israel, England, Germany, France, Singapore, Australia, and... Pennsylvania!

One memorable item, an empty 55-gallon Amoco Oil Company drum, went all the way to Pennsylvania. "I sold this to a frat house; they used it as their garbage can," he recalls, noting that the shipping charge was "ten times what they paid for the item!" As long as the customer was happy, which they apparently were, Patrick will do his part to help the transaction along.

Selling on eBay is more fun than a garage sale, he notes, and nets him more money in the long run anyway. He's glad that not everybody feels this way, because much of his inventory is gleaned from local garage sales, estate sales, auctions, and thrift stores. He even occasionally lands a good deal from an antique dealer who might not know the true value of an item. As a part-time seller, he averages net earnings of $5,000 a year, though one spectacular year he earned close to $15,000!

To make sure he stays on the good side of Uncle Sam, Walden reports all his income with a federal tax ID number, which then qualifies him to take the appropriate deductions for things like eBay and PayPal fees, mileage, and shipping costs. He uses QuickBooks to track all this information. This makes his tax-time paperwork much easier. His education in accounting also helps a little too, he admits.

Other aspects of selling didn't come so easy, though. "At first I didn't package (items) well enough," he admits. "It took some hard lessons before I started getting the packing down."

Dealing with unreasonable buyers is never easy, either. When he first began selling, he'd leave feedback for the buyers once they paid. Over time, he's revised his methods and now waits until the buyer leaves feedback for him. The reason why, he notes, is because "a couple of times [when I'd already left the buyer positive feedback] I got held hostage for a refund or they would leave me negative. In all those cases, I believe the buyer got the item and lied about it."

Even though sellers can leave a rebuttal to any negative feedback given, he feels that withholding feedback until after it's given provides a better safety net. If a buyer wants to leave an unfair negative, Patrick can simply leave no feedback for the buyer, or leave negative feedback in return if the buyer did not hold up his end of the transaction. This has almost eliminated the incidence of buyers utilizing the "I'll leave you negative feedback if you don't..." type of threats.

Patrick's customer-service policy is based on his own experiences as an eBay buyer. "As a buyer, I don't like [receiving an item and finding it had an] inaccurate or pumped-up description, so as a seller I want to make sure that I don't do the same." Another big beef of his is sellers who don't ship in a timely manner. "I try to ship as soon as I get payment," he explains. He also likes to offer as many shipping options to the customer as possible. He sets up the shipping calculator to offer Priority Mail, Parcel Post, and, if they qualify for these rates, First Class and Media Mail.

He's had pretty good luck with shipping items internationally as well. Since most of his merchandise isn't "high-dollar" stuff, he feels that most international buyers don't have any incentive to try to cheat on things like their import duties.

He shares his hot tip for international shipping: "Many items can go Global Priority Flat-Rate in a large envelope for only $9 to anywhere in the world," he points out. "That's the way to go if the item will fit in the envelope. You would be surprised what you can jam in there. It doesn't have to end up flat, either, as long as it seals!"

Overall, he has one bit of advice for those who are getting into the business: "Make sure you find items you can make money on. Too many people I know have lost money because they didn't do their research. If you are going to buy and resell, then know the value!"

To illustrate this point, he recalls an estate auction he attended with his mother. One item up for grabs was a plastic bag with several small old plastic-type toys in them. Cowboys, Indians, horses, and such. He knew nothing about the toys but was willing to give them a shot. The auctioneer got a bid of $3 out of him. Someone else bid more. Did that other person know something about the real value of these items that he didn't? Although you can't always be knowledgeable about every little thing, he wished he'd known to do some research on this type of product beforehand. He could lose money if he overbid and couldn't resell them on eBay for any profit.

At the urging of his mother, he outbid the other person, and so it went until the little bag of items reached $6. Walden won and hoped to make back his $6 on eBay, maybe even a few bucks more.

That small bag of early plastic horses, cowboys, and Indians turned out to be rare and highly collectible Stuart Toys that were marketed in dime stores in the 1950s and 60s. Patrick listed them and was amazed at the results. "They went like crazy on eBay," he remembers, stating that he "could not believe it!" It's a good thing he listened to his mother (and she reminds him of it to this day) because his $6 investment netted him about $674! Although he wishes he could find such a great deal every day, he realizes that these finds are few and far between.

Still, every penny made on an auction gets him that much closer to his next acquisition of sports cards. Thanks to his eBay income, his collection of 10,000 cards in 1998 now roughly numbers 400,000 cards and is still growing!

"Luv Makes the World Go 'Round"

While her husband Timothy was stationed in Iraq, Tana just needed to keep busy. It eased the worries about his safety, the fears that perhaps he might not come home. What better way to keep busy than to start a home-based business? Tana did just that, though at the time she didn't know that's what she was doing!

Her husband's parents, recently deceased, had fifty years worth of collected and everyday items in their house. It all needed to be sold. By the time she was through that project, Tana (eBay user "amommysluv") was pretty comfortable in her new role as an eBay seller. She decided she'd like to keep at it and, in addition to cleaning out her own unused items, began to sell for other people. Consignments would soon become a large share of her business.

When Timothy came home from Iraq and, after 27 years of service, retired from the military, he went right to work helping Tana in their burgeoning business in the Spokane, Washington, area. They worked together as a team, posting auctions, answering questions from customers, and boxing and shipping the items in an efficient manner.

Soon they had 15 consignment accounts that had helped them branch their selling into many new categories, such as eBay Motors and children's clothing. By this time they were also selling brand-new retail items such as clothing and home décor. Their eBay store, A Mommy's Luv Embroidery, helped set them apart; they could personalize many items with embroidery for the customer.

The large variety displayed on their eBay store changes frequently, and they often have entire collections of items to sell from their consignment clients. Their house has been swallowed up by their business, so they recently took the next step: moving to a retail location. They are proud of being able to get to this level. "We see this business becoming a full-time growth opportunity," notes Tana. "We are adding to our consignment base while also looking at some wholesale opportunities!"

Setting up their business efficiently was easy for Tana, who has more than twenty years worth of experience in the financial services industry.

She's been an income-tax preparer as well, so IRS rules or paperwork didn't frighten or confuse her. While they have managed to keep the business running with just their own manpower, Timothy and Tana's two daughters, Amanda and Sara, are utilized as seasonal employees when things get crazy busy. It gives the entire family a real sense of accomplishment to have their own business together.

While running their business efficiently and profitably is important, Timothy and Tana would also like to give back to the eBay community by helping train others in the art of selling online. With experience in both eBay and Half.com sales, they feel they have much to offer the new seller in way of encouragement and practical advice. To follow is some advice they share with new sellers:

- Organize. "Find one system to do all the customer management for your business. A lot of money can be wasted in trying to piece a system together — we learned the hard way!"

- Purchasing the right items for resale is crucial but unpredictable. "Be willing to purchase items out-of-season and hold inventory until it is back in season."

- Get help. "Learn to rely on the information given to [you] via eBay and other market research companies."

- Put the customer first. "Always try to treat others the way you yourself (as a consumer) would want to be treated!"

Their feedback is a good testament to their customer-service focus. With their feedback steadily climbing towards the 2000 mark with over 99 percent positive responses from their customers, these PowerSellers credit their "underlying character" for propelling them toward this high status. "We want our customers to be happy," Tana states simply.

It's not just a matter of making your customers happy, however. Good customer service starts with the seller's own personal commitment to being an honest seller. "Never lose sight of your ethics," Tana warns. "Don't play into the games that other less-ethical sellers may be playing. Keep your customers' interests at heart and remember to cater to them."

One way to practice honest, ethical selling is in your product descriptions.

"Always list your products with an honest, full description. If questions are asked that you can't answer, let the customer know," she advises.

One final note of advice: Have fun! When you become burnt out to the point that you are no longer enjoying your eBay business, your attitude will carry over into every part of your experience. Customers will pick up on this change and your business will suffer.

Finding support through other eBay sellers helps lessen the stress and frustration that this type of business venture can bring with it. If Timothy and Tana have their way, they will be doing just that type of education and support of sellers, both new and seasoned, for some years to come!

The Border Fiasco

Pamela Vasquez's first auction was the stuff of nightmares—for the buyer!

Pamela (eBay user "pamelas_timeless_treasures") had been searching for a part-time income in all the traditional places, but nothing gave her the flexibility to homeschool three daughters, be home with her husband in the evenings, and be there for the housework, the pets, anything. The weak economy in her area didn't help, either; even during the holidays, seasonal jobs were hard to snag.

In an effort to gather potential ideas for earning money, Pamela posted an inquiry on an online message board (not on eBay) asking other stay-at-home mothers how they located the best jobs. One encouraged her to consider eBay.

This woman had been so successful on eBay that her husband had been able to quit his job in "corporate America" to help her with auctioning. While the story was amazing, eBay wasn't exactly what Pamela had in mind. But having never really considered it, she was willing to post an item and just see what happened.

So that is how the jungle-print wallpaper border came to be up for auction in November of 2003. Like many new sellers, Pamela hawked over her auction, checking to see if there were any bids or even any lookers. Even though she didn't have any use for them anymore, she found it hard to believe that nobody wanted the borders, even for her opening bid amount. She checked the auction on the last day and, discouraged, didn't bother to even look at it again after it had ended.

Taking that as her cue, Pamela decided that eBay wasn't her cup of tea and began to explore other ideas again.

About eight weeks later, she happened to check a rarely used e-mail address and to her shock (and utter embarrassment) found a rather anxious message from someone she'd never even heard of! The message was clear: Where is my wallpaper border?

She did some quick checking on eBay and discovered that in the final hours, her auction had indeed sold! They buyer had even paid via PayPal, and somehow she'd never been notified. That rarely used e-mail address was the culprit; it was the one on file for eBay and was the one she'd used regularly when she first became an eBay member.

Now she was in a serious bind: eight weeks and a buyer who had real cause to be angry with her, all because she failed to realize that her eBay correspondence was going to that e-mail address.

Pamela explains how she handled the situation: "I immediately e-mailed her, apologizing profusely. I explained what happened and told her I would even drive the borders to her home if it would get them there sooner!"

The buyer, who lived approximately one and a half hours away, was very gracious and understanding. She was remodeling a child's bedroom and needed the borders, but was willing to wait a couple more days for the regular mail service. But Pamela's offer to drive the borders to her made an impression. Despite everything, she left positive feedback when the transaction was complete.

"If the buyer had not been so understanding and positive about the entire fiasco, I do not think I would have continued to sell on eBay," notes Pamela. Among other lessons learned through this experience (keep your eBay contact information up to date!), Pamela learned early that if she did "everything possible to remedy the situation," the average customer would be understanding and work with her in return.

When recalling this incident recently, Pamela went to her records and located this buyer's e-mail address. Even though it's been almost two years since the transaction, she again e-mailed this person to thank her for her patience and understanding. "I let her know the impact that her kindness in [that] situation has had on my life—it has been significant!"

Although it took Pamela a little time to really get serious about selling on eBay, she has been at it regularly since March 2004. She sells primarily used books for children and homeschooling families. Great literature is a passion for her children, who love to peruse Mom's pile of eBay inventory to see if it's something they'd rather add to their own collection than let her sell. Pamela tries to foster a great love of learning in her girls, and literature plays a big part in that effort.

Pamela finds her merchandise at a variety of places: library book sales, rummage sales, and thrift stores to name just a few. Recently she's started taking in consignment merchandise for people who don't have the time or interest in learning how to work on eBay themselves.

When she started selling regularly online, Pamela felt that if she could contribute $400 to her family's income every month, she would be happy. It took a couple of months to meet that goal, but once she did, she's been steadily padding the family budget ever since.

There are things that she wishes she'd done differently, of course. She initially didn't do enough research to determine what the proper price for her items should be. She lost plenty of money by not knowing how to price items and by not utilizing proper keywords so that buyers could locate her items easily. "Had I done my research differently, I would have used different keywords and not had to pay for that very expensive lesson," she notes.

Pamela also had to learn about off-eBay resources that offer her options to increase sales, such as storing photos online and utilizing HTML to offer multiple photos in a listing.

But even though there's been a learning curve to eBay and mistakes made along the way, Pamela did have one big advantage that many eBay sellers don't: a community of other eBay sellers who offered advice, tips, and encouragement! The woman who initially encouraged Pamela to sell on eBay, Julie Anna Schultz, also hooked her up with a large group of sellers who have their own group discussion board on the Yahoo! Groups site.

Having other people learn her name and give personalized advice was a great benefit to Pamela: she knew she wasn't alone in this venture. Now that she's got nearly four hundred auctions under her belt with a greater than 99 percent positive feedback score, she still credits much of her success to the members of that group. In fact, she's so convinced that having a group of people like this to support you is so beneficial that it's the first thing she'd suggest to anybody who's considering eBay as a job.

And even though they've never yet met in person, Pamela and Julie Anna have teamed up to write an e-book called *The Cyber-Mom's Guide to Creating Income with Online Auctions*. This e-book shares a wealth of tips and stories from the members of their Yahoo! Groups board and their own personal experiences with auctioning. To learn more about their e-book, check out their Web site **http://cybermomshomeincome.com** or contact Pamela through her eBay store: Pamelas-Treasure-Chest.

From Hobby-Sellers to PowerSellers

Brooke and Kurt from Virginia are PowerSellers with a feedback rating of nearly 3,000 and rising, with 99.7 percent of their customers being delighted and satisfied with their experiences. After registering with eBay in 2000, both used the site for purchases but didn't really consider selling until at least a year later.

The selling bug was planted in Brooke when Kurt got caught up in the frenzy of an auction for an out-of-print music CD that he really wanted. He won—to the tune of nearly $40! Brooke was shocked that her husband had paid so much, the rarity of the CD notwithstanding. However, when he told her about the excitement of the bidding and how he got "sucked into" the desire to win the auction, it made her wonder if she could sell items and get others excited about buying them. Shortly after that, she began "dabbling" in selling, mostly outgrown but still-nice clothing from her children and other quality used clothing she found at rummage sales and thrift stores.

Brooke laughs, recalling that her desire to resell her children's clothing was so great that the children became almost "neurotic" about staining or damaging their clothing in any way! Her hobby also gave her the ability to spend a bit more on her children's clothing; buying good-quality items may cost a bit more to begin with, but when you resell it, you make back the difference on what you would have spent on lesser-quality goods. It's a system that works for Brooke!

As they sold more clothing, Kurt and Brooke began to get a feel for the market and trends. At some point, both Brooke and Kurt began picking up new clothing from clearance racks and other discount locations with the intent to resell them next time those items were in season. What followed was a flood of items in the next couple of years: up to one thousand items would be stored in their home in clean plastic storage bins, awaiting the following spring, summer, or winter. Huge closets were built and a home office set up to accommodate what had somehow become a serious selling endeavor.

They are a familiar site at department stores and outlet malls and are looking for one thing: the "deepest markdowns of the season," notes Brooke, who says that she rarely buys anything that isn't marked down at least 80 percent off the original price. To get these great buys, she keeps a fairly constant watch on the prices and even has a few inside contacts at some of the stores. But it's mostly persistence and patience that gets her the best bargains. Waiting for that rock-bottom price isn't always easy, but if you want to sell the item for a nice profit and still give the buyer a good deal, you must wait it out.

As their business evolved, so did their realization that they, too, must evolve along with it. A few costly errors — shipping the wrong merchandise to the wrong buyer — prompted a simple but effective inventory system. Every item that comes into their home is assigned a number that is then recorded in a handwritten log. Identical items are all given the same inventory number, but the log will note how many and the specific sizes. The log is translated into a Microsoft Excel spreadsheet created by Kurt, who then enters all the other data from the sale. It's not a fancy system, notes Brooke, but it works out well for them.

In addition to keeping a proper inventory, Brooke and Kurt have also moved closer to all the aspects of setting up an official business in their state. Their continued success has over and again shown them that they are a business, not just hobby-sellers anymore. With their good recordkeeping thus far, setting up shop should be a breeze.

A little technology has made setting up auctions a breeze as well. Kurt made a few basic templates with HTML coding so they can add just item-specific information and copy/paste the works right into eBay. HTML has saved them loads of money on picture fees as well. They are fortunate to have an Internet service provider who allows them a certain amount of free Web storage space with their account. This lets them store the photos online and use HTML programming to insert the photos into the auction, thus bypassing eBay's fees for multiple photos.

Not everything has been as easy to figure out, however. Along the way, Kurt and Brooke have encountered a few roadblocks that they quickly maneuvered around. They had a few sales where the buyer did not receive the item. Either it was lost or, perhaps, there was a dishonest buyer. Since they did not initially make delivery confirmation a requirement (in an effort to save on shipping costs), there was no way to track the package and they were left with no choice but to refund the buyers' money. This led to a firm policy of delivery confirmation being required on every sale.

What do you do for sales where no delivery confirmation is available, though? That is a dilemma they face every time they ship to a foreign country. Many shippers have no way to track a package once it's left the United States. Many carriers also do not sell insurance for international shipping. It's a risky business, for sure, but Kurt and Brooke's customer base is growing internationally, so for the time being, offering shipping overseas is still an option for them.

International shipments can be tricky for other reasons too. One of their few negative feedback comments centered on a package that had been opened by customs. Even though the sellers have zero control over what happens to a package when it's going through customs, the buyer saw fit to take his ire out on them.

Another problem with customs, Brooke notes, is that the buyer often has to pay a duty on the item bought overseas. How all this works, she isn't sure, but she says that their overseas customers generally ask them to remove all the price tags on the items before shipping them. On the customs papers she must attach to all shipments internationally, she declares the amount of the winning bid as the actual value of the item.

This is the value that the duty on the buyer's end is based on. However, if customs chooses to open the package (and they randomly do so) and sees a price tag for a much higher price (even though the winning bidder did not pay the price on the tag), the buyer may be charged duties on the amount of the price tag.

It's a zany system and one that they are glad they don't have to deal with on a daily basis at the moment.

For shipping within the United States, their fee structure is simple. Using the weight of the package, they use the shipping calculator in the auction setup to allow potential buyers to enter their zip code and determine the shipping cost. When setting up the auction, they allow a $1.50 shipping and handling fee, which the calculator automatically adds into the quote given to potential buyers.

Brooke feels that charging "actual" shipping plus a small fee to cover the cost of shipping supplies and paperwork is reasonable, and she feels that most buyers would agree.

Good customer service is important to Kurt and Brooke, but Brooke admits that she's the stingier of the two. She has always had a disclaimer on their auctions that all sales are final unless a gross misrepresentation has been made on the seller's part. However, she felt that this was more to prevent buyers from asking for a refund just because the item didn't fit them well or they didn't like it as much once they saw it. Having to take returns and attempt to re-list the item was more hassle than she wanted.

That policy ended up backfiring on them once, but it taught a good lesson. A buyer purchased a pair of girl's pants that were used but in good condition. Brooke wasn't aware that a few decorative rhinestones on the pants were missing, and thus didn't note that information in the listing. Upon receiving the item, the buyer noticed the missing rhinestones and was dissatisfied but didn't ask for a refund because of the no-return policy. Who's to say if a few missing rhinestones constitute "gross misrepresentation"?

When Brooke saw the negative feedback, she e-mailed the buyer and asked why the feedback was given before contacting the seller about a refund. The buyer stated that the policy led her to believe that no refund would be forthcoming regardless of the circumstances.

Because of that incident, Brooke now notes in her auctions that any dissatisfaction with the item should be brought to the seller's attention immediately so that something can be done to make the transaction successful. This more "warm and fuzzy" refund policy is better for customers, which ultimately is better for business. "It's really important for customers to feel that customer service is there," she says.

Consignments Are Like a Box of Chocolates

The loss of loved ones is never easy to bear, and when Linda (eBay user "LindaCatNH") lost both of her parents at the same time, it was a dark hour in her family's history. But this woman from the Northeast found a way to use this tragedy to motivate her into a new business venture: selling on eBay.

Her parents had left behind a house full of things that needed to be sold for the estate. Linda had some time to devote to the project and volunteered. Rather than tying up her weekends holding garage sales or paying commission to an estate auction service, she chose to start auctioning items on eBay.

"I loved selling those cherished items to another person who was willing to pay good money for them—I did not want to just throw all those memories in the trash. It's nice to know that they went to another home where someone else will appreciate them," she says.

Linda had been an occasional buyer and had even sold a few personal items on eBay, but this event really catapulted her into a whole new line of work. She found that she enjoyed the online marketplace and decided to take on consignment merchandise from others when she was finished with the estate items. While "you never know what you're gonna get" is the tricky part of consignments, Linda plunged ahead with her plan and opened an eBay store, Auctions in NH.

Nearly two years and three hundred auctions later, Linda is still selling on eBay, and very few are her own. Her offerings include everything from replacement automobile parts for a Fiat to used baby clothes, which she catalogs, photographs, sells, and ships. She then sends the profits (minus eBay and PayPal fees and her commission) to the owners on a monthly basis. It's a system that works well for her, because she doesn't have to invest in inventory, as well as for her clients who are too busy or not computer-savvy enough to set up auctions themselves.

Selling consignment brings Linda satisfaction as well. She is enthusiastic about "helping people de-clutter their lives by selling their items and getting more money for them than they would [get] at a yard sale. Many people just want the stuff gone and out of their life; I can do that for them!"

If she weren't selling mostly consignments, Linda says, "I'd be selling jewelry and home décor, but doing consignment gives me a much broader background." In order to learn about her client's items, such as auto parts, she does research online so that she is knowledgeable about the product. She also has the owners fill her in or write a brief description of the items themselves, which she can then base her auction description on.

Linda has made some common mistakes, such as accidentally posting the wrong photo to an auction. Those types of things are going to happen, she notes, and if you don't catch it yourself, a potential buyer often will e-mail you to clue you in. Many common mistakes are avoidable by setting up an organized system and automating as much as possible. Linda uses Turbo Lister; although, she notes that if you use templates, it will save the weight of an item from one auction to the other, so you must always double-check the weight it fills in automatically. Otherwise, when your buyers get shipping quotes, they will be inaccurate. That could end up causing grief or costing money if you have to make up the difference.

Other suggestions that she makes to new sellers are to find a mentor, read a lot of books about eBay, and study other auctions to determine what has made their products sell. Was it a good description, a good title, or a lower starting price? Emulating other auctions that are successful can help you learn what entices lookers to become buyers.

The people who hand over their items, both new and used, have been very trusting of Linda. In order to provide the best information to eBay members, she prefers to have the items in her possession so she can provide additional photographs or answer questions from potential buyers. A quick glance at her feedback, however, will assure you that her clients have put their trust in the right person. Even her eBay customers have remarked about how trustworthy she is or how she refunded extra shipping fees that turned out to be unnecessary. With her feedback currently at 100 percent positive, Linda has a goal to keep it that way.

In addition to selling consignment for people in her own area, Linda has recently become an eBay trading assistant. A trading assistant is someone who does consignment auctions for a fee, but all business is generally done online unless the two parties live near each other. "I'm hoping to catch the eye of a wholesaler, warehouse, or small business that wants to sell their inventory on eBay and use me as their assistant," she says.

When she accepts merchandise to sell, she first photographs it and then boxes it up to determine the shipping weight. Since she doesn't tape the box shut (so she can access the item for further photos or questions from lookers) she adds a couple of ounces to her shipping weight. Merely adding a thank-you note and taping up the box can push the weight up to the next pound, as she found out the hard way a couple of times.

Linda has found that her source of free USPS Priority tape is as close as her local post office. No point in spending your own money on box tape if you're going to ship it via USPS Priority. You can also get free supplies online from the post office's Web site, she notes.

The local post office is also a good source for information about shipping internationally. When she first began shipping items to foreign countries, Linda went to her post office to learn about the customs forms. They even sent home blank forms for her so she can fill them out as much as possible before coming in with her package.

Linda has had "pretty good luck" shipping internationally so far. Most of her international customers have been from Canada, Japan, and Sweden. She always states in her auction description to contact the seller before bidding if you are an international buyer. This is because some items simply can't be shipped overseas or will not easily clear customs. Different countries have differing rules regarding imports, so she checks these out beforehand.

While consignment selling has brought Linda a nice small business and a broad knowledge of products she wasn't otherwise familiar with, she does contemplate having a specific product line in the future, or perhaps a brick-and-mortar store where she takes in consignments to sell on eBay and in a traditional manner. It's hard to say what the future will hold for Linda, but you can probably guess that eBay will be in there, somewhere.

Sugar and Spice So Your Store Will Look Nice!

For four years, Amber (eBay user "sweet-peas-and-bumblebees") was an eBay hobby-seller who used the online marketplace to resell her children's used clothing and other things around her house that were no longer in use. Because her family's finances didn't depend on her making money on eBay, she didn't get serious about selling until 2005.

What prompted Amber to start an eBay store and populate it with very cute and creative merchandise? She's not really sure anymore, but she tried to sell her custom-made product online before and not really had any luck. This time, however, her stick-with-it attitude has prevailed and she's running a swinging little business now!

As Amber puts it, she "loves baby clothes and shoes," so even though her main product is neither, she couldn't help but get into that line, even if just a little bit. In addition to the new children's clothing and infant shoes displayed on her store, Sweet Peas And Bumblebees, Amber creates custom graphics and storefront packages for eBay stores.

Some of her design packages include the Sugar Cookie, Forever Funky, Ladybug Lane, and Ric Rac Pink & Black themes. Various designs feature a scrolling marquee, a logo, up to twenty category buttons, a button for users to click "Add Me To Your Favorite Sellers," buttons to redirect the looker to your feedback or your "About Me" page or to "Contact Seller."

For a low price that's well within reach of every new eBay store owner, Amber sends you the complete HTML code. All you do is copy and paste into eBay's page for designing your store. Oh, and the best part: it's generally available in less than a week!

You can add additional graphics for a small fee and even move things around somewhat from the template. And if you have something a little different in mind, for a little more dough you can have a storefront that's custom designed for you.

With nearly a dozen storefront package deals available at any time and new ones being designed regularly, new store owners are sure to find something useful.

Amber also designs auction templates and store logos. All of her products come with free unlimited technical support offered by this one-woman storefront show!

Coming up with new designs isn't difficult for Amber, who has no formal education in graphics. She uses Paint Shop Pro to make her products, which seem to come naturally to her. About five years ago, she started teaching herself, and through trial and error and a lot of practice, she's come a long way.

This isn't the first time that Amber has marketed her graphics ability, and she's never had this much success. She saw that there was a need for her product. "There aren't a zillion people out there selling graphics," she notes. About selling children's clothing, she says "everybody and their brother sells clothes." But in graphics, she feels she has a unique product at a good price.

One mistake she feels was in pricing her product almost too low to start with. There's only so much a mother can do in one day, and at $15 per storefront, Amber was swamped when she first began selling them on eBay. It didn't take long for her to raise her price so she actually was getting paid a little wage for her time. However, they've continued to sell even at their new price. "I guess my talent is valuable," Amber notes, seeming just a teeny bit surprised that she's still busy after several months.

There are a number of positive things about selling graphics, one of which is that she doesn't have to have a lot of money tied up in inventory. Children's clothing and shoes, however, can be a very different story. Purchasing initial inventory is expensive, Amber notes, and can even set your business into the red a little at first. She utilizes one method that a lot of sellers use: purchasing items in the off-season and storing them for the next season.

She also does some wholesale purchasing. But either way, you're out the money up front until you recoup it in sales. That can be stressful on a new business's finances. Having her graphics products helps offset that because her only investment is her own personal time and occasional updates to her software.

When she posts her storefront designs for sale, she doesn't have to worry about things like photographing the item properly. That's something that can be tricky with items like clothing. She recommends that sellers do a lot of experimenting to get good photos. Using a good background that won't interfere with the photo is very important. Amber also uses an online photo hosting site so that she can insert multiple photos of her items at no extra charge. If you have a lot of detailed photos that show off the clothing properly, you'll have better luck selling the items.

Setting up an inventory system also isn't really relevant to her custom storefronts, but that has been a challenge for the other products. To keep track of the basics, she utilizes a simple ledger-style system with a blank table made in Microsoft Word. It's not fancy, but it will keep her records straight until she either comes up with a better system or purchases software to help her out.

Oh, and don't forget shipping. Imagine being able to "ship" your product via e-mail! For the HTML portion of Amber's business, that's exactly what she does. For all other items, she generally has a flat-fee system that's very reasonable. Admittedly, she sometimes even loses a little profit because she undercharges on shipping, but she feels that it evens out in the end.

Because she's also been an eBay buyer for more than four years, Amber knows all too well how buyers feel about shipping charges. "Over-charging for shipping is a huge turn-off to buyers," she notes. Apparently, Amber's customer-service skills extend to more than just her shipping-price policies. Her 50-plus feedback score boasts an over 99 percent positive rating.

As long as she has kids, Amber will be selling clothes, and as long as there's a need for her storefronts and auction templates, she'll be making graphics for eBay users. And she may even be coming up with some new graphics surprises in the near future, but she's not giving out any hints... just yet!

Is This What Pavlov Had in Mind?

When people in White Bear Lake, Minnesota, have a garage sale, they only hope that Joe (eBay user "whitebears") is in the neighborhood. Although he says that he's developed "more selective ways to build inventory" for his eBay sales in recent years, Joe will always have a "soft spot for those neon-colored signs that dot the neighborhoods on Thursdays, Fridays, and Saturdays."

It all started in 2000 with some clutter. There wasn't enough to have a real garage sale, not to mention the weather in Minnesota late in the year. Joe had recently heard about a new Web site, Half.com, and thought he'd try to sell a dust-gathering pile of videos that were no longer being watched by anyone in the family. Despite his naturally skeptic nature, he found that they sold well and plunged ahead with clearing the entertainment center of even more dust bunnies. About that time he also listed a few things on eBay, trying his hand at the auction format.

By spring, he'd made a decision to "forge ahead as a small-time entrepreneur" and began spending weekends picking up bargains in books, videos, music CDs, and other interesting items. He was testing the markets and learning what sold well or what didn't. He bombed out on the books, but found he had a knack for the videos and CDs. Some might call it his "light bulb moment" but for Joe, it was more like hearing a bell ring.

His interest in garage sales, moving sales, thrift sale, estate sales, and the like quickly turned into a real buying frenzy. Joe recalls those early years: "I suspect my family thought I had gone wacko, salivating like Pavlov's dog any time I saw a "sale" sign on the side of the road!" At his peak, Joe would hit forty to fifty garage sales a week. Like he said, he's pared down the rummaging, but certainly not eliminated it from the lineup of merchandise sources.

While Joe started by selling VHS videos, the market has taken a serious downturn in recent years because of the DVD format's popularity. He still sells VHS videos and has plans to continue to do so. "There are a lot of eBayers and others out there who say the VHS market is dead," he notes, but he doesn't see it that way. "Selfishly speaking, I don't mind seeing people say that, because it keeps them from taking up space in my niche market. The VHS market is not dead, and probably is not even on life support."

His strength in this market lies in the knowledge of what truly is going to sell and what is not. A typical garage sale with fifty VHS videos might yield only two or three that are worth his investment. Because he's been selling VHS videos for five years now, he knows what five or ten percent of those available are collector's items or have what he calls a "niche viewership." "This is not something that a new seller will know without some prior experience in this market," Joe points out.

While Joe feels that the fixed-price format of Half.com or other similar sites can often yield a higher profit margin, those sites aren't really conducive to selling some of the other items that he picked up here and there as he rummaged throughout the Twin Cities.

"The more sales I went to, the more I would pick up trinkets or novelties or sports memorabilia, another market that I had a modicum of interest and knowledge in, and list those items on eBay and wind up turning a profit," he recalls. Over time, his knowledge base became quite diversified, and he found he was doing as much business in all those other areas as he was in CDs and VHS videos. Nowadays, his CD and VHS inventory account for less than half of his sales.

One of Joe's growing areas of merchandise is in the collectibles: everything from pewter figurines and trinket boxes to Elvis memorabilia. He tries to tap into the nostalgia of the Baby Boomers and looks for things he knows will be of interest to them such as games, dolls, and other items that were popular during their growing-up era.

A personal interest in what Joe calls "old paper" includes things like sheet music, documents, old postcards, and magazines. One of his favorite paper goods is stereoview cards (recall the opening story of this book). He finds these items "interesting from a historical perspective—as well as often highly profitable."

Although every businessperson wants to make profit, Joe feels that it's not just about selling the right things to the right person. Joe's business philosophy is simple: "Any business should have two main goals: first, turn a profit, and second, serve the customer. You absolutely cannot achieve goal number one in the long run without achieving goal number two. And beyond that, customer service is more than good business; it's just plain the right thing to do," he states.

In order to gain satisfied customers, Joe's policies are honest and straightforward:

- Give honest, courteous, prompt, cordial, and professional service—always.

- Respond to e-mails in one day, or less if at all possible.

- Ship quickly and at a reasonable cost to the buyer.

- Fully disclose all defects and other conditions of sale in every listing.

- If a buyer has a problem, work with him or her to come to a solution.

- Offer a no-questions-asked money-back guarantee.

For the rare buyer who is out to "strong-arm" him, Joe relies on his thorough knowledge of eBay policies and uses eBay to his advantage when he is in the right.

His willingness to work with buyers to achieve their satisfaction has been a big hit with international bidders, who often have to hunt far and wide to find sellers who are willing to go that extra mile for them. "I opened my auctions to international sellers two or three years ago, and it was one of the best business decisions I've made," he claims. "There's no question I sell more, and sell at higher closing prices, because I ship internationally."

Joe hasn't had many troubles with international shipping, with an estimated 99 percent of the buyers being polite and appreciative. Payments generally arrive promptly from international buyers as well, he notes. He does make it clear to international buyers that he will not mark their item as a gift as a way for them to avoid paying duties. That doesn't jibe with his overall policy of honesty.

Like every eBay seller, Joe can look back and think of things he wishes now that he hadn't done. That includes a fair amount of "junk" purchased while rummaging that turned out to be nothing more than dime-store-quality goods. However, he does admit that part of his business, buying used items for resale as opposed to new items, involves taking such risks. "If you're any good at all at dealing with the speculative nature of this business, making some really dumb purchases should bother you for all of, oh, about seven seconds," he jokes. Joe has developed a "thick skin" over the years and doesn't let an occasional loss bother him anymore.

Another thing that Joe doesn't let get him down is his lack of savvy with computer databases and spreadsheet programs. Who needs Microsoft Excel when you can pick up a good old-fashioned ledger book at the office supply store? Joe has developed a practical system for tracking his inventory in ledger books. He uses a different book for each type of merchandise (one for VHS tapes, CDs, DVDs, miscellaneous, etc.) and enters the items as he purchases them in the left-hand column. He uses additional columns to list the inventory number assigned to the item, track the selling price, and any other information he has decided to gather.

Using different-colored pens for each new calendar year allows him to flip back through each book and know what was sold in what year. Storing inventory is simple thanks to a Minnesota invention: Post-It notes. Each item gets a number written on a note that stays stuck to the item until it sells. When the item sells, it's easy to locate in the ledger because of the attached number.

Other tidbits of advice from Joe:

- Get involved in the "Community" discussion boards. "They're invaluable!"

- Take some time to randomly read feedback of other sellers. "You can see how people deal with each other, or fail to deal with each other."

- Keep talking to an unhappy customer. "Ninety-nine-plus percent of problems can be worked out just by keeping open the lines of communication."

- Don't be afraid of your items not always selling. "You lose some and you win some, but more often than not, you win."

In the long run, Joe's only regret is that he didn't start his online sales venture sooner. While his business nets him a part-time supplemental income, it has given him full-time joy and satisfaction to know that he's now a PowerSeller with a feedback score exceeding 2,600 and 99.9 percent of his customers reporting their satisfaction. Pavlov might not give a hoot, but it sure makes Joe proud!

Keeping His Finger on the "Pulse"

If you were twenty-four years old and had already bombed on two Internet startup businesses, would you try again? And if you did try again, this time selling on eBay, what would you sell?

If you're Brian S. (eBay user "EZas123"), your answer is as easy as 1, 2, 3. First, you'd sell an empty candy wrapper (read: no candy). Second, you'd sell an empty box. Just a box, and as noted: empty. Third, you'd sell a pancake (note: not for human consumption).

You cannot be serious! No doubt that's a phrase that Brian's heard a lot lately. What kind of person can build a business by selling pancakes and empty containers? And why doesn't eBay kick his young arrogant rump off their site?

If you're Brian, you just chuckle and shake your head. "It's not about pancakes and empty boxes," you reply to the jesters. "If you'd take a closer look, you'll see what it's about."

"Well then, 'EZ' (as Brian is popularly known on eBay), tell me: What is it all about?" the unbelievers retort.

"It's all about pimping your stuff!"

Okay, so maybe that's a bit too much for some people's palates, and maybe it's a bit too, well, graphic for others to digest. For those who prefer a more traditional explanation, here goes: It's all about selling your product.

And selling a product is something that Brian knows. Not that it's always worked, of course. Yeah, yeah, those two failed businesses. But that's okay, as Brian states "I learned a lot and fell forward from the failure." One of his favorite mottos is "Character cannot be developed in ease or quiet. Only through experience of trial and suffering can the soul be strengthened, ambition inspired, and success achieved."

So how did Brian get to be "EZ," an eBay rising star with feedback that can resemble the rabid mania of a pop star's fan site? It all started in 1999. Fresh out of Wayne Valley High School in Wayne, New Jersey, Brian had big dreams for the new millennium: He was headed to Arizona State University where he would major in Economics. This seemed to be a safe bet for Brian, who always had an interest in business and numbers. Who knows, maybe he'd do something stunning in the world of economics! Maybe he'd become a corporate bigwig. Maybe he'd be rich and famous.

Two other events of 1999 helped shape his future. First, he received a digital camera as a gift. Back then, these high-tech devices were a novelty to some, an expensive investment for others. Having his own digital camera gave Brian something the average teenager didn't have: instant photos. Secondly, he joined eBay. This was done for the purpose of making an occasional sale, earning a buck on the side. He remembers when photos on listings weren't nearly as common as they are today.

Back at Arizona State University, a third seemingly common event joined forces with the first two: Brian joined a fraternity. Hoping to network and make some friends, he was as surprised as anybody when he was suddenly voted to be the "historian" for their organization. You know — the guy who takes all the photos (hint, hint, using your fancy new digital camera) and the guy who posts them to the frat's Web site.

Then what? Brian had no clue how to reserve a domain name, much less build a Web site for the fraternity. But a Web site is what they wanted, so he taught himself how to do it. Man, what some guys won't go through for a little acceptance, huh?

The frat's site went up in 1999, and soon Brian was getting compliments from people who'd seen the site. "Dude, why don't you, like, learn how to do some of this stuff for a job?" was something he heard a lot that year.

And that's all it took. Soon after, he changed his major (who needs economics, anyways?) and got serious about "learning the art of the Internet," as Brian calls it. And so it was that his fraternity had the best frat site out there for four years. In 2003, he graduated with a bachelor's degree in Industrial Technology, which is a combination of web/graphic design and marketing.

So now he knew how to design some of the coolest stuff on the Internet and had mastered some techniques of marketing things to people. You know: sell your product (a.k.a. pimp your stuff). Ah, now you're following me.

Fast forward to May 2005. With only a few dozen auctions under his belt, eBay user "asubry" goes bye-bye and is replaced by the new Brian: "EZas123." He isn't an ASU student anymore, and he's ready to update his image with a name that will help market his products. He's ready to be hip; he's ready to take eBay by storm and offer up his genius for the sake of sellers who want more.

For literally pennies, buyers begin receiving his services: Gallery photo designs that stand out, compressed songs that will play when the auction is opened, customized flash text animations, tiled backgrounds, specialized banners, company logos, even label designs for actual products. The list is almost endless, and if he hasn't yet thought of it himself, he'll create it for you!

Some of his early feedback (in the post-"asubry" days) is just a glimpse of what the near-future held:

- Creative, funny, gutsy, talented nice guy. Somebody give him a six-figure job!!!

- Very Creative Seller with lots of VITALITY.

- You are a wonderful person...

- WOW! YOU DO EXCELLENT WORK!

- A++++++ Totally Amazing work!! Highly HIGHLY recommended!!

- Creative and easy to work with.

Coming from the bottom of the barrel in terms of business success, the feedback that was rolling in gave him the confidence to open his own eBay store in June 2005. His eBay name was "EZ" to remember, but he wanted something truly unique for his store's name.

Brian explains that after much brainstorming, he found the perfect name for his store: "My store name, PIMP YOUR STUFF, was strategically developed to accurately reflect my business offer yet not give too much away, and to attract curious lookers. I feel the brand of my username and nickname along with my store name work together seamlessly."

His overall mission for his eBay business is also "EZ." About selling on eBay, he says, "The competition has become fierce, with tens of thousands of new sellers entering the eBay marketplace. I figured coming up with a service to target the ever-increasing number of sellers [that would help] differentiate them from their competition would be an excellent niche market."

About this time, he also was toying with ideas on how to get people to notice his store among the thousands of eBay stores online. He posted some auctions in the "Totally Bizarre" pages that showcased his talent and gained some notice. But it wasn't until he heard about the "eBay Pulse" page that things began to get really interesting.

The "eBay Pulse" page highlights the most-watched auctions on the entire site, as well as the most-watched auctions in every category, although only the biggest ones reach the "main page." There is a growing fervor among sellers to get their auctions "watched" and be recognized for having the most unique, hottest-selling, or most bizarre products.

Another eBay seller had seen Brian's work and had an idea: What if they worked together to post the mother-of-all-auctions? If they made it all the way to the top of the "Pulse" page, the publicity would be unbelievable! So they made a deal: Post an auction for a completely useless product, add in the most amazing graphics, music, and every other Web-design gizmo Brian could come up with. If they earned any money off the deal, they'd split it.

One of the most important aspects of the auction, however, had to be a creative way to invite users to add the auction to their "Items I'm Watching" page. Brian got right to work, and blew the auction world out of the water with the M&M-themed, rap-music blaring auction that had been viewed tens of thousands of times and had over four thousand watchers by its end!

The publicity was amazing. Newspapers picked up the story and by the end, the biggest novelty-buyer on eBay, the Golden Palace Casino, swooped in to snatch the prized candy wrapper! With a mind-blowing final bid, they sealed the deal and proudly displayed their prize in a frame alongside their other memorable auction purchases.

Armed with his newfound fame and a desire to outdo even himself, "EZ" set to work creating other auctions for pretty much nothing.

First came "A Box" with a subtitle mysteriously inviting lookers to "Wait, Watch, and Whisper." People who had never heard of "EZ" (and those with no imagination) actually thought "EZ" was selling an empty box. How ridiculous; who would buy an empty box? Two days later came the next zany auction: "A Pancake" which was rightfully listed as being "not for human consumption." Well, if not to eat, then what is it for?

People who'd already seen what "EZ" could do with graphics, banners, and animations knew what "EZ" was really selling. It wasn't about the box or a pancake at all; it was about selling his product. He was using these bizarre auctions to showcase his unbelievable talent and creativity, and funneling lookers to his eBay store where hopefully they'd be convinced to "get some" for themselves!

"EZ" does not hog his talent to himself. That was never the plan. For a reasonable (seriously reasonable) price, you can own a piece of his brainstorming for your own auctions, your store, your Web site, even for your brick-and-mortar business! The eBay store name says it all: "EZ" wants to help you PIMP YOUR STUFF! And his Web site redirect, **www.PIMPINisEZ.com**, will send you to his store in a flash.

The empty box and the pancake auctions both zoomed to the "eBay Pulse's" main page in the same week. Imagine that; sellers wrack their brains trying to figure out what combination of words and photos will get them noticed, and here this punk from New Jersey does it twice in one week. The nerve of him!

While "EZ" may have his share of jealous competitors, he also has his very own cheering section. And it's about time.

So what does "EZ" hope to accomplish in the future? With plenty of fresh ideas up his sleeve, he's recently launched a new "social networking site for auctioneers," as he describes it, **www.myAuctionNetwork.com**. There's more to come in the future, both on that site and several others planned.

As for eBay, Brian says "I would like to continuously build a fan base and bring fresh new ideas [to eBay]." Is that all? Actually, he'd also like to "become a recognized expert in marketing on eBay and revolutionize the way people market their product or service on eBay." Oh, is that all? Somehow, it's not hard to imagine all that happening.

After all, if a guy with only 100 auctions behind him (but with a 100 percent feedback rating) can sell a pancake for $78.77, an empty box for $255, and an empty M&M's wrapper for $2,815.43, he can do darn near anything he wants!

The Chicken... or the Egg?

When considering an online business, one of the first decisions people make is where to sell. Get a Web site first, or sell on eBay first? Web site... eBay? Web site... eBay? It's like trying to figure out which came first: the chicken or the egg. For small businesses that don't already have a retail presence, eBay presents the perfect opportunity for the new business owner. However, the right Web site at the right time can also be a good way to start.

For those who choose to start with eBay first, they often hope their business will expand and they'll eventually have to rent a retail space. Maybe they hope that they will someday have their own Web site, in order to expand their reach to sellers. Steven (eBay user "celebglasses"), an eBay seller in the Seattle area, did things in the reverse order. He began his online business by selling his products through his own Web site and decided that, to expand his business, he'd add eBay to his market as well.

Steven had some distinct advantages, of course, such as already having many of the items and processes in place that many new eBay sellers need. Because he already had an e-commerce site where he sells his designer-inspired sunglasses, eyewear accessories, biker glasses, and other complementary items, he also had a business structure in place. He already had a product stream, thanks in part to his brother who directed him to some wholesale contacts he'd established for his own business. Prior work experience with some local companies had given Steven the knowledge to build his own Web site.

So why would someone with his own Web site even need to sell on eBay? Steven explains, "I decided to sell on eBay to assist and increase my sales and help promote my e-commerce site as well as getting rid of old stock on hand. With eBay's huge traffic and exposure, it was just a win-win situation."

Even though Steven has been an eBay member since October 2002, he'd previously sold his unused household and personal items, much like any run-of-the-mill hobby buyer and seller. When he decided to expand his sunglasses business into eBay in December 2004, he did have to learn a bit about the differences of selling this way as opposed to through his own Web site.

"One of the things I had to do is get a system down that isn't as prevalent on my Web site," he says. "I had to make time for listing items, leaving feedback, studying competitors' auctions and pricing, and learning what the most effective strategy is for the number of items you list via auction and items listed via store inventory."

Steven's store, Celebrity Glasses, showcases a large variety of sunglasses and accessories categorized in numerous ways for the browser who wants to consider many different styles. His personal e-commerce site, **www.celebrityglasses.com**, helps build brand recognition for him as well. These two selling outlets keep him busy — and crowded. Believe it or not, he manages both of these businesses out of his one-bedroom apartment. The lack of space would make some people ornery, but Steven takes it with a grain of salt. "I store my own inventory, package my own items, and ship everything from home," he notes. "Needless to say, I am hurting for room since my apartment looks like a small warehouse."

He also manages both sites and all aspects of the business entirely on his own, something that he admits "can get a bit overwhelming."

Managing two businesses simultaneously would be just that for most people, but Steven has managed so far and will continue to do so. He's pleased with how his business has grown. He's also managed to achieve some goals in quick order. In just six months, he rose to PowerSeller status with over 99 percent positive feedback. His current goals include maintaining that level of sales and customer satisfaction as well as moving up the PowerSeller ladder. In addition to becoming a PowerSeller, Steven was pleased when he hit the 500 mark in his feedback score.

Maintaining a high level of sales isn't always a "given," and Steven knows it. Especially when he wants to keep both of his business avenues profitable, he realizes that having a creative angle and high-quality products are two things that will set him apart from other sellers with similar or even identical merchandise. In addition to high-quality products, Steven tries to keep his product lines fresh and current with the trends.

Another important aspect of customer service is making sure the item arrives safely. He uses a special bubble wrap and crush-proof boxes in which to ship.

While he has things pretty well under control, Steven does admit to having tripped up a few times here and there. One mistake, he notes, is that he used to list items on eBay that he had not actually yet received in stock. A late shipment from a supplier or a damaged shipment that had to be replaced could wreak havoc for his eBay business when members bid and paid but didn't receive the item. To make sure that doesn't happen anymore, he only lists items and quantities that he has in his possession.

For some sellers, finding the right auction-creation software isn't as easy as downloading Turbo Lister. Steven tried Turbo Lister, but it just didn't meet his needs. He has been reviewing several other available products and currently is using Auctiva tools. For keeping his financial records straight, he uses spreadsheets that he created in Microsoft Excel, but he hopes to move to a specific accounting software in the near future. Inventory can be tracked right in his eBay store.

You could say that eBay has been a good move for Steven, who notes, "Unlike other sellers, I profit from every pair [of sunglasses] I sell, even when you factor in the fees eBay charges as well as my merchant account." This doesn't happen by magic, however, and he also notes that in order to make a profit, new sellers would be wise to "research and find a product that gives you the ability to mark up substantially, is easy to ship, and of course [you] have easy access to, yet is hard for your competitors to access."

That's a rather large order for someone who's considering delving into the world of online selling. But Steven has shown that with persistence, creativity, and hard work, it can be done!

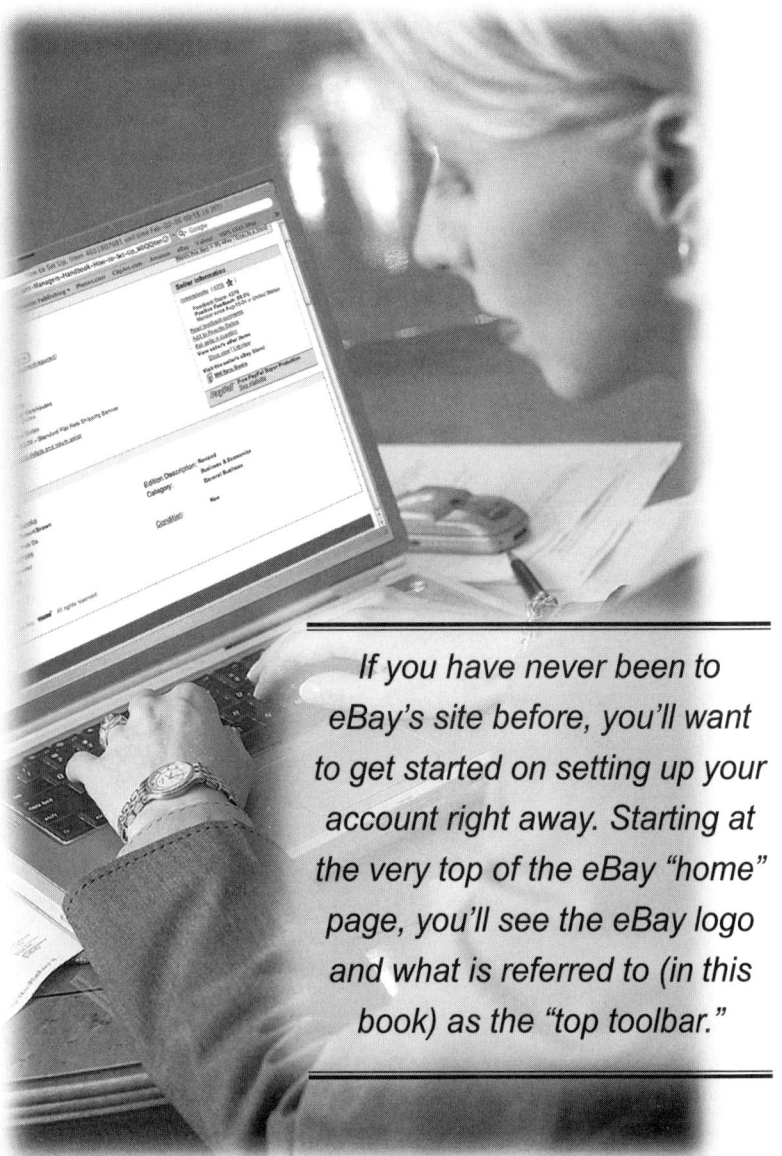

If you have never been to eBay's site before, you'll want to get started on setting up your account right away. Starting at the very top of the eBay "home" page, you'll see the eBay logo and what is referred to (in this book) as the "top toolbar."

Becoming an eBay Member & Basic Site Navigation

If you don't know how to get to eBay's site, you can easily find it through any Internet search engine, but the site's name is very easy to remember: **www.ebay.com**.

If you have never been to eBay's site before, you'll want to get started on setting up your account right away. Starting at the very top of the eBay "home" page, you'll see the eBay logo and what is referred to (in this book) as the "top toolbar." This is the white bar with these words in the individual boxes: Buy / Sell / My eBay / Community / Help. Above this toolbar are the links (blue underlined words) for home / pay / register / site map. To the right of these items are the search features. First, there's a box for a standard search. When you click in this box, the words "Start a new search" disappear and you can type in your search terms. Just below this box there is yet another link to the "Advanced" search feature.

These items are "static" on eBay's site. That means that no matter where you go on eBay, these items will always be at the top of every page. So you never have to worry about "getting lost" on this site! You can always go back to the home page, or to your own "My eBay" page (which you'll become very familiar with) with just one mouse-click.

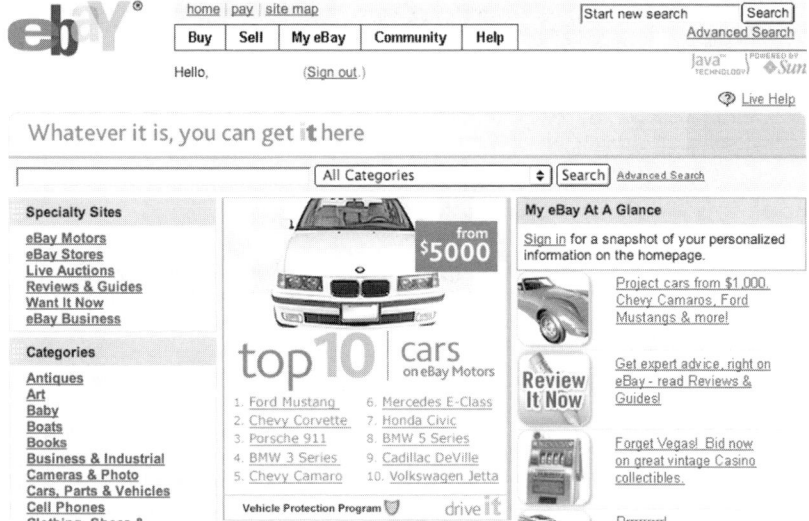

Just below the top toolbar, notice that it says: "Hello! Sign in or register." Once you have created an account, eBay will recognize you and welcome you by your username. This doesn't mean you'll never have to sign in, as security precautions will still require that from time to time.

To begin the registration process, click on the "register" link. The first step will ask you to enter the following information:

- First name

- Last name

- Street address

- City

- State/Province

- Zip/Postal code

- Country

- Primary telephone

- Secondary telephone (optional)

- Date of birth

- E-mail address (entered twice for accuracy)

You then have an opportunity to review the eBay User Agreement and Privacy Policy and are required to check a box agreeing to accept the policy and receive communications from eBay. As is standard with licensing agreements, if you don't accept, you cannot continue with the registration process.

EBay uses Secure Sockets Layer (SSL) formatting, which encrypts your personal data before it is sent over the Internet. This makes your information unreadable to anyone who does not have the decoding key. For added security, especially from a public or shared computer, it is recommended that you sign out of eBay when you are done with your session.

When you are done inputting your information, click the "Continue" box. On this page, you will choose your username and password. Your username needs to be between 2 and 20 characters long. Based on the information you entered on the first screen, eBay will suggest three possible usernames for you. If none of those are suitable, create your own.

You may use letters, numbers, and some symbols including underscores (_) and hyphens (-). You are not allowed to include profanity or Web site addresses, e-mail addresses, or phone numbers in your username.

With 135 million registered users, you may not be able to get your first choice of names. Try making a list of several names and variations of them before you actually begin the process. Each time you enter a username, eBay will tell you if it is available or not.

Usernames do not display with capital letters, so even if you enter it that way, it will not display that way on eBay's site. Consider using symbols (such as * or ~) in between words, so that you don't create a confusing run-on username.

Next, set up a password that is at least six characters long. Here are some tips about passwords:

- If you switch users too often, or sign on and off many times in a row, eBay may ask you to enter a series of four numbers shown on the screen, in addition to your user ID and password. This verifies that you are not a computer program mechanically hacking into someone's account.

- EBay recognizes Microsoft Passport for sign-in purposes. If you prefer to use this convenience, look for the "Microsoft Passport users click here" link toward the bottom of the sign-in page.

You will also be provided with a security question option. Some of the questions you can choose from (pick one that won't be easily guessed by a mere acquaintance) include:

- What street did you grow up on?

- What is your mother's maiden name?

- What is the name of your first school?

- What is your pet's name?

- What is your father's middle name?

- What is your school mascot?

If you forget your password, you can utilize this system to retrieve it by answering your question correctly. Note that it must be answered exactly the same way, so don't get too fancy in your answer.

Click the "Continue" box to move to the next page, where you will enter either your credit card information or a secondary e-mail that is tied to a company, school, organization, or mainstream Internet provider such as AOL or EarthLink. After submitting the information, you are then directed to check your e-mail. An e-mail titled "Complete Your eBay Registration" arrives quickly and includes a button that conveniently links you back to eBay.

It also includes a confirmation code and a link in the rare case that the button doesn't work. This e-mail is legitimate, and you will notice it does not solicit any additional information from you. When you follow the button or link, a new browser window is launched and you receive a congratulatory welcome to eBay message. Again, no further information is required. Now you are ready to start navigating through eBay.

Since it will be necessary for you to have a seller's account in order to launch your new business venture, the first time you log in to your account you should click the "Sell" box on the top toolbar. This will take you to a page where you'll set up your seller's account.

If you entered a secondary e-mail instead of your credit card information, you must either enter a credit card or establish a pre-paid account to use the selling features of eBay. The first time you try to create an auction, if you have not already entered your credit card information, you will be required to upgrade your registration by entering either your credit or debit card or checking account information.

EBay requires all users to enter credit card information, whether or not you ever make a purchase. The collection of this data allows eBay to verify that you are who you say you are, particularly that you are over the age of 18.

Chapter 7 discussed becoming ID Verified, which is a process that lets you circumvent the credit card information. Even if you enter credit card information, it's a good thing to become ID Verified. It will give your buyers one more reason to trust you.

What to Do If Your Security Is Compromised

While eBay does all they can to protect the information that you give them, they cannot protect information that you give to others. Obviously, you should safeguard your eBay password. More importantly, you should realize that eBay will never ask you to confirm your membership by providing sign-on, password, credit card, or other personal information via e-mail. Go back and review the information in Chapter 1 about e-mail scams.

If you suspect that your password has been obtained by someone who should not have it, the first thing you should do is change your password. You can do this on the eBay "Sign In" page by entering your user ID and then clicking on the "Forgot password" link. After your password is changed, you should then report the problem to eBay's Security Center by clicking on the link at the bottom of any eBay page.

Navigating eBay

Navigating through eBay is very simple. Recall that the top toolbar and items near it will always remain there. Use the links in this area to quickly go back and forth to the main sections of the site.

- Home—Takes you back to the eBay home page.

- Pay—You will go straight to a page that lists the items you've bought and still need to pay for.

- Register—Unless you are changing your username or adding an additional username, you will probably never use this link.

- Sign in—Even if eBay's site recognizes you and lists your username on the page, you may have to sign in to perform certain functions. To save you this hassle, you may wish to make a habit of signing in right away when you enter the site.

- Sign out—Be sure to sign out every time you leave your computer. Even if you have a computer dedicated to eBay (which is highly recommended), a family member or visitor might inadvertently create chaos. It is absolutely crucial that you click this link if you are using a computer that is used by other persons, especially in a public place (library, Internet café, etc.).

- Services—This links to a menu of helpful information about General Services, Bidding and Buying Services, and Selling Services.

- Site map—This leads to over 300 links organized by subject.

The top toolbar (also referred to by eBay as "tabs") underneath the links also takes you to a specific place when clicked.

- "Buy" leads you directly to a page aptly titled "Buy." This page has a search box and links to the "Advanced Search" feature, as well as a link to search in eBay stores only.

- "Sell" takes you to the page where you will start every auction (when you enter them the traditional way, not using any software such as Turbo Lister).

- "My eBay" is a place that you'll frequent often. It summarizes all of your watching, bidding, selling, and sold activities. Each categorized section is fully customizable to make it as user friendly as you'd like it to be. More about this is covered in Chapter 7.

- "Community" will send you to a page where you can read up on the latest news and announcements, see a calendar of events, join a discussion board, or post a question for other users to answer.

- "Help" takes you to a page where you can enter a term into a search box that will scour eBay's pages for matching items.

Other Things to Notice

There are a number of links at the bottom of the page that may change from time to time. They are mostly self-explanatory; that is, the link titled "Feedback Forum" will take you to a page that gives you an overview of the feedback system. Some of the links provide valuable information to the new user, so take a few moments to click on each one and at least be familiar with where to find this information if you go looking for it in the future.

The quickest way to reference an eBay policy that you just can't recall but want to brush up on is to click the "Policies" link at the bottom of the page. This will take you to a review that has links to all the specifics from the User Agreement to all the policies for sellers and buyers alike.

Another place to note is the "Shortcuts To" section that falls at the bottom of your pages. Use the drop-down menus provided to take you to places you visit often such as your favorite seller's page, your favorite searches page, and your favorite categories used.

The best way to learn about eBay is just to spend some time (okay, a lot of time) clicking and reading. Since there's no way you can get lost, go right ahead and wander!

While you're out wandering, however, one of the first places you should wander to is the "Learning Center," found at **http://pages.ebay.com /education/index.html**, or you can find it by clicking "Help" on the top toolbar then click on the link for the "Learning Center" in the left-hand box.

Hypertext mark-up language, (HTML) is a system of coding information to control how items are displayed on the computer screen.

Tools for Advanced Users

Hypertext Mark-Up Language

Hypertext mark-up language, otherwise known as HTML, can sound very scary and complicated to people with very little background or education in computers. But relax, it's really not that complicated. It's really just a system of coding information to control how items are displayed on the computer screen.

You've probably used HTML without ever knowing it. Have you ever used a word-processing software, such as Microsoft Word? If you've used the various drop-down menus and icons (buttons you click on) to make your text bold, italic, or highlighted, you were using HTML to do that. The only difference is that Microsoft has kindly done all the coding for you and allowed you to utilize that coding with the simple click of your mouse.

However, in some instances it may be nice to know the various codes yourself. When you become more proficient at auctions, you'll notice that you want more. After a while, you'll be wanting to have slicker auctions like you'll find your competitors use. Those things can be achieved through a combination of HTML and using Auction Creation Software, which we'll discuss shortly.

If you've already read Chapter 9, you'll recall that Suzy used an HTML string from her online photo hosting site to insert extra photos of her listing for no extra charge from eBay. Doing just one string of HTML to start with is a good way to feel comfortable with this "language."

When you're ready to learn more, there are a host of Web sites devoted to HTML. Find one that's free, easy to understand, and hopefully even has other members who are willing to help teach you.

Using the chart below, write up some HTML strings of your own. To see if you're doing it correctly, go to **www.practiceboard.com** and type them in. This is a good way to see your work in action. It's exciting to see that you can actually learn to work with this language and, using this knowledge, you are one step closer to a slick and professional-looking listing page.

Basic HTML formatting looks like this:
I want to make my <html tag>text<html tag> really stand out!

In this example, only the sixth word, "text" is between the bracketed "tags." This means that only that word will have the special formatting applied to it (depending on the tag used from the chart below).

In most cases there is a beginning tag and an ending tag for every particular formatting feature. These indicate the starting and stopping point for the formatting. The tags can be typed in upper or lower case letters; case is irrelevant for HTML coding. The table on the next page provides common HTML tags and their functions. Notice that the ending tags are often a repeat of the beginning tags but with a slash (/) in them.

Tag	Function	Example
<p>	Paragraph return, blank line between para-graphs	This is my opening paragraph. <p> This is my second paragraph.
 	Line break, differs from the paragraph	My first line is here, but I don't want a new paragraph, just a new line. So my second line starts here.

Tag	Function	Example
<p align=center> and </p>	Centers text	<p align=center>Title Centered on Page</p> **Result:** The tagged item will be centered.
<blockquote> and </blockquote>	Indents a block of text approximately ½ an inch	<blockquote>Use this feature to set an entire paragraph apart in a lengthy description</blockquote> **Result:** Text will be centered on page with ½ inch more indent than the rest of the text
<b> and </b>	Bold formatting	<b>Gone With The Wind</b> **Result: Gone With The Wind**
<i> and </i>	Italics formatting	I do <i>not</i> accept personal checks. **Result:** I do *not* accept personal checks.
<u> and </u>	Underline formatting	<u>Contact Seller with Questions.</u> **Result:** <u>Contact Seller with Questions.</u>
<ul> and </ul> <li> and </li>	Indicates a list Specifies individual items in a list section	I sell: <p> <ul> <li>Books</li> <li>DVDs</li> <li>Videos</li> </ul> </p> **Result:** I sell: • Books • DVDs • Videos

Tag	Function	Example
<table border=#> and </table> <tr> <td>	Inserts a table New row Cell data	<table border=2> <tr> <td>row 1 column 1</td> <td>row 1 column 2</td> </tr> <tr> <td>row 2 column 1</td> <td> row 2 column 2</td> </tr> </table>
<font size=#> and </font>	Changes size of font from 0 to 7	<font size=7>Free Shipping</font> **Result:** Free Shipping
<font color=colorname> and </font>	Changes color of text to any standard color named	<font color=red>Free Shipping</font> **Result:** Free Shipping
Font combinations	Combine font attributes into one tag	<font size=7 color=red>Free Shipping</font> **Result:** Free Shipping
<font color= #hexadecimal> and </font>	Use hexadecimal color codes to specify colors	<font color=#2573FF>Free Shipping</font> Search for "HTML color chart" on the Internet to find a list of code choices
&#3digitcode	Special characters such as cent signs or trademarks	™ enters the ™ sign ¢ enters the ¢ sign £ enters the £ sign © enters the © sign ® enters the ® sign
	Enters extra spaces between words	three spaces **Result:** three spaces
<a HREF=url> and </a>	Adds a link to another Web page	<a HREF= http://stores.ebay. com/Cosas-Muy-Bonitas-Texican-Store_W0QQsspagename ZFAVQ3aFQ3aSLLRQQtZkm> Link to my eBay store </a>

Tag	Function	Example
target=new_window	Opens a link in another browser window	\<a HREF= http://stores.ebay.com/Cosas-Muy-Bonitas-Texican-Store_W0QQsspagenam eZFAVQ3aFQ3aSLLRQQtZkm target=new_window> Link to my eBay store \</a>
\<IMG SRC=url>	Embeds an image by specifying a url where the image is located	\<IMG SRC= http://www.alibaba.com/photo/50082268/Multi_Functional_Food_Blender.jpg>
\<eBayUserID>	Inserts your user ID from eBay	I'm happy to answer any additional questions. Please contact me via my \<eBayUserID>.
\<eBayFeedback>	Shows your feedback as posted on eBay	Feel free to view my eBay feedback \<eBayFeedback>
\<eBayItemList>	Shows other items you are selling on eBay	If you like this beanie baby, I have more for sale: \<eBayItemList>

For long HTML strings that you are likely to use repeatedly, you might want to create a separate text file for them. For example, the string that commands a link to your store with a particular font and color size might appear as:

> \\<font size=5 color= blue>Link to my eBay \<a HREF= http://stores.ebay.com/Cosas-Muy-Bonitas-Texican-Store_W0QQsspage-nameZFAVQ3aFQ3aSLLRQQtZkm > store \</a>\</font>\

Instead of having to type this long string of information often, save this string as a file on your computer. Then, merely copy/paste the string into your auction text where desired.

 **Shortcuts Makes HTML Easier**

Having frequently used strings saved for copying/pasting is helpful to avoid innocent mistakes that are easy to make in HTML. It's easy to forget the "/" in the closing command or to get the closing commands out of order. In the example above, bold is opened, font is opened, then the link is opened. The commands must be closed in the reverse order. In other words, bold was first to be opened and is last to be closed.

Using **Auction Creation Software** and other template Web sites, many advanced users can take the speedy route with pre-existing backgrounds and borders. However, using HTML allows you to be truly unique, individual, and creative. If you want to express your uniqueness but still fear HTML, you can use a Web page creator such as FrontPage or Dreamweaver, which can be purchased at any software dealer or online. The Netscape suite includes a free version of Netscape Composer.

With many software packages, you can use those icons and other shortcuts that you're familiar with to create your page and let the software convert your creation to HTML. As noted in Chapter 9, eBay's description pages on the SYI form also do this for you, although their color choices and font sizes are more limited than what you can get when you do the HTML entirely yourself.

When you use software designed for Web sites, such as FrontPage, once you've got the page created and adjusted as you like, click on the HTML tab at the bottom of the FrontPage application and highlight all the HTML between the <body> tags then copy/paste it into the eBay text box for the eBay page you are creating. A similar step would be taken in the other applications as well.

EBay offers help with HTML as well, proof that they are okay with your using it to create your auction pages. Their help section can be found by selecting the "Help" tab at the top of the eBay screen. You'll need to click the "more..." links under "Selling," then under the "Listing Your Item" and again under the "Writing a Title & Description" sections to find the link to eBay's HTML page. On their page they explain how to use HTML to insert pre-formatted headings and lines, numbered lists, and more.

Some cautions about using HTML include going overboard. Lookers don't want every other paragraph to be in a different font color or every other word to be bolded. Don't make your HTML design so busy that it detracts from the item you're trying to sell.

 **Turbo Lister**

Turbo Lister is free and 100 percent compatible with eBay, as it is eBay software. Numerous PowerSellers use Turbo Lister with great results.

A number of auction creation software packets are available, each with its own pros and cons and costs. One of the most-used ones is Turbo Lister, which is an eBay software, so it's 100 percent compatible with eBay. And the best part is that it's free! When you have enough auctions under your belt that the SYI forms are becoming second nature, then you're ready to take on Turbo Lister.

The format is very different; you fill in all the auction details from one simple page, using drop-down menus and filling information into pop-up boxes. You can create templates and save them. This is very efficient if you sell the same merchandise repeatedly. You can also create listings without even being on the Internet (for those of us who are still living in the world of dial-up Internet) and then connect to the Internet and upload all your listings at one time!

The features built into this software are amazing for the price (did I mention it is free?). When you're ready, you can learn about Turbo Lister right on eBay at **http://pages.ebay.com/turbo%5Flister/**.

Additionally, you can combine Turbo Lister with any number of Web-based applications that offer hundreds of beautiful backgrounds, templates, and other slick features. Spend some time browsing auction listings. If you see one you particularly like, scroll down to the bottom and see if it lists the Web site used to create it. Unless the seller created the HTML entirely by his or herself, you'll find a site listed. Just a couple names that I've recently noted on the bottoms of some very nice listings were Auction Boutique and The Seller Sourcebook. A simple Internet search will provide you with plenty of different companies from which to choose. Be sure that you're not overpaying in fees, and make sure that, if you use Turbo Lister, the site is compatible.

Software is also available to advanced users who wish to do selective **market research**. Because the market is rather saturated with eBay software spinoffs, it's important to take time before buying any software to analyze your needs and research which product will best meet those needs.

Market-research software analyzes previously completed auctions and provides you with statistics regarding timing, auction enhancements that are worth the investment, and completed sales rates. This information helps you decide the best times and methods to use when selling specific items. It can even help you identify what items are good sellers. It is useful if you are considering venturing into a new market or product or wondering why your existing market or product is not producing the results you would like.

Administrative Support software automates auction tasks that are done on a repetitive basis. These include tasks such as creating auction listings, managing payments, tracking shipping, and keeping up with feedback. EBay offers some software packets that are very well integrated into their basic setup. One of these, Selling Manager, comes standard with an eBay store fee. You can always upgrade to other levels as well as you find more and more use for this software. An online search will also yield other sites and software that automate a lot of simple tasks for you. Make sure you thoroughly investigate any company you are considering doing business with. Make certain that they are compatible with eBay and that their servers are secure and safe.

Auction Research software does for you what "term paper sites" do for college students: they do the work for you (only it's acceptable for you while it isn't for college students). One of the most highly recommended auction analyzing services is ándale, **www.andale.com**. Of course, there are many other products and services available, found easily by searching the Internet for "eBay auction research."

You may want to research the research software. There is a Web site that will do this for you too: **www.auctionsoftwarereview.com** provides reviews on over a dozen analysis software packages, in addition to a variety of other eBay software tools. For a fee, you can have unlimited access to all the reviews on the site.

Many online Web sites that offer these services to eBay sellers will offer a 30-day free trial. Be sure to utilize these before signing up; you may not be so thrilled with the service after 15 days' use. Obviously, doing extreme market research isn't really going to be useful to a new seller, but keep this in mind for when your business really takes off!

State-by-State List of Sites for Starting a Small Business

Note: Web addresses do change occasionally, so if you find an error, follow the suggestions for searching online on page 18.

A

Alabama: **www.alabama.gov/business/startbusiness.php**

Alaska: **www.commerce.state.ak.us/dca/smallbus/starting.htm**

Arizona: **www.azcommerce.com/Webapps/SmallBusVR/intro .asp**

Arkansas: **www.soskids.arkansas.gov/starting-a-business.html**

C

California: **www.ss.ca.gov/business/resources.htm**

Colorado: **www.colorado.gov/ colorado-doing-business /start-business.html**

Connecticut: **www.sots.ct.gov/business/BusMainPage /StartABiz.htm**

D

Delaware: **www.delaware.gov/EGOV/Portal.nsf/ CategoryPages /Business – Start-Up**

F

Florida: **www.dos.state.fl.us/startbus**

G

Georgia: **www.georgia.gov/00/channel_title
/ 0,2094,4802_5033,00.html**

H

Hawaii: **www.ehawaiigov.org/working/html/starting.html**

I

Idaho: **business.idaho.gov/ICL/alias__business.idaho/ tabID
__4947/DesktopDefault.aspx**

Illinois: **business.illinois.gov/step_by_step_guides.cfm**

Indiana: **www.in.gov/idfa/businessresources**

Iowa: **www.iowa.gov/state/main/business_portal**

K

Kansas: **www.accesskansas.org/businesscenter**

Kentucky: **kentucky.gov/Portal/Category/bus_start - 28k**

L

Louisiana: **www.lded.state.la.us/businessresources**

M

Maine: **www.maine.gov/portal/business/starting.html**

Maryland: **www.choosemaryland.org/business/starting/index .asp**

Massachusetts: **www.mass.gov/portal/index.jsp**

Michigan: **www.michigan.gov/businessstartup**

Minnesota: **www.deed.state.mn.us/bizdev/start.html**

Mississippi: **www.mississippi.org/doing_busn/ busn_dev /how_to_start_busn.htm**

Missouri: **www.sos.mo.gov/business/links.asp**

Montana: **http://sos.state.mt.us/css/BSB/New_Business.asp**

N

Nebraska: **www.nlc.state.ne.us/nsf/Faq/businessinfo.html**

Nevada: **dbi.state.nv.us/**

New Hampshire: **www.nheconomy.com/nheconomy/ obid/main /index.php?ch_table=link3**

New Jersey: **www.nj.gov/Business.html**

New Mexico: **www.smallbusinessnotes.com/ stategovernment /newmexico.html**

New York: **www.gorr.state.ny.us/gorr/Startbus.html**

North Carolina: **www.nccommerce.com/servicenter/blio**

North Dakota: **www.nd.gov/businessreg**

O

Ohio: **business.ohio.gov**

Oklahoma: **www.okcommerce.gov**

Oregon: **www.sos.state.or.us**

P

Pennsylvania: **www.paopen4business.state.pa.us**

R

Rhode Island: **www2.sec.state.ri.us/faststart**

S

South Carolina: **www.myscgov.com/SCSGPortal/static /business_tem1.html**

South Dakota: **www.sdgreatprofits.com/DBISD/startup**

T

Tennessee: **www.state.tn.us/ecd/minority.htm**

Texas: **www.tded.state.tx.us/guide**

U

Utah: **business.utah.gov**

V

Vermont: **www.vermont.gov/doing_business/start_business. html**

Virginia: **www.yesvirginia.org/Virginia_ Advantage /SmallBusiness.aspx**

W

Washington State: **http://access.wa.gov/business/start.aspx**

Washington, D.C.: **brc.dc.gov/index.asp**

West Virginia: **www.wvsos.com/common/startbusiness.htm**

Wisconsin: **www.commerce.state.wi.us/BD/BD-COM-2600.html**

Wyoming: **www.wyomingbusiness.org/brc/service /starting_business.cfm**

EBay Terminology

A

ABOUT ME A page created to let other users know about you and your business.

ABSENTEE BID A bid placed by users before the start of the auction.

ACCOUNT GUARD A tool that shows users of a potentially fraudulent Web site.

ADMINISTRATIVE CANCELLATION When the ebay administration cancels a bid or auction.

ANNOUNCEMENT BOARDS Similar to a message board, the ebay announcement boards provide information on updates and current events.

ANSWER CENTER A page designed for users to ask questions and get help from other members.

ASKING PRICE The price asked by the seller.

AUCTION CURRENCY The type of currency for a specific auction decided by the seller.

AUCTION-STYLE LISTING The most widely used way to sell an item by placing an item for sale and selling it to the highest bidder.

B

BID CANCELLATION When a buyer or seller cancels a bid.

BID INCREMENT The amount a bid is raised before the current bid is outbid.

BID RETRACTION Cancellation of a bid.

BIDDER REGISTRATION REQUIREMENTS The requirements that must be met before a user is allowed to bid.

BIDDER SEARCH A search for the items that a member has placed bids on.

BIDDING To place a bid on an item.

BLOCK BIDDERS A way to prevent certain users from bidding on your items.

BUY IT NOW A listing that allows a buyer to purchase an item for the seller's set price without waiting for the auction to end.

BUYER'S PREMIUM Amount a buyer pays an auction house for all purchases in a live auction.

C

CATEGORY LISTING A category that an item goes under when listed for organization.

CHANGED USER ID ICON An icon that notifies viewers that member has changed his or her user ID in the past 30 days.

COMPLETED LISTINGS SEARCH Search for items that have ended within the last 15 days.

CYBERCRIME A technology crime related to a computer and the Internet.

D

DIGERATI Digital world-fluent people.

DISCUSSION BOARDS Web site where members post information and news.

DISUPTE CONSOLE The area on eBay where buyers and sellers dispute problems related to their auctions.

DUTCH AUCTION A listing with many similar items for sale.

E

EBAY An auction service on the Internet.

EBAY SHOP A shop that sells eBay collectibles.

EBAY STORE A Web site that offers all items being sold by an individual seller.

EBAY TIME The official eBay time correlated with the time of day in San Jose, California.

EBAY TOOLBAR A toolbar that can be downloaded and used in your Web browser.

E-MAIL Electronic mail.

EMOTICON A series of characters used to indicate emotion.

ESCROW A protection for the buyer where a third party holds a payment until the item is received from the seller.

EXPERT CONTACT Usually the seller; the expert contact provides all the information on upcoming auctions.

F

FAIR WARNING A warning from the seller that the auction will be closed.

FEATURED LISTING A marketing service where sellers can have their item placed at the top of the listing page in the "Featured" section.

FEEDBACK A rating that a buyer and seller receive after a transaction is completed.

FEEDBACK SCORE The number of feedbacks the seller or buyer has received.

FEEDBACK STAR A star that varies in color based on the amount of feedback received.

FINAL VALUE The final value that a listing sells for.

FINAL VALUE FEE A fee charged by eBay at the end of the auction.

FIXED PRICE FORMAT A format mostly used for Buy It Now listings where the price is unchanging.

FLAME An angry feedback or criticism.

G

GENTLY USED An item that has been used but does not show a lot of wear.

GIFT SERVICES A service offered by a seller that allows the buyer to purchase gift wrapping and shipment directly to the gift recipient; a gift box icon indicates the item would make a great gift.

H

HOT ITEM A hot item is an item that has received more than 30 bids.

I

ID VERIFIED Shows other users that a seller has a confirmed identity.

INDEFINITE SUSPENSION Suspension of a user with no reinstatement date.

INSERTION FEE A fee to sell an item.

INTERNET MERCHANT ACCOUNT An account where a seller can accept credit cards online.

ITEM LOOKUP A way of searching for an item by item number.

L

LIVE AUCTIONS Real-time auctions online.

LOT The item in an auction.

M

MARKUP The price that an item is increased to reach retail price.

MAXIMUM BID The maximum amount a buyer will pay for an item.

MEMBER PROFILE A page that informs buyers about the seller's feedback and customer comments.

MERGE Combining several eBay user IDs.

MERGE ACCOUNTS To combine more than one eBay account.

MINIMUM BID The lowest price that can be used to bid on an item.

MY EBAY The place on eBay where the user manages all aspects of their eBay activities.

N

NEW LISTING ICON Indication that an item has been placed within the last 24 hours.

NEW MEMBER ICON An icon that represents a member that has been registered for 30 days or less.

O

OPENING VALUE Starting price.

OUTBID When a second bidder places a higher bid on an item.

P

PASSWORD A secret word or group of words and numbers used to gain access to an account or information.

PAYMENT GATEWAY Used to process and authorize payments.

PAYPAL A free account that is used to pay for items online.

PAYPAL BUYER PROTECTION A protection of up to $1,000 for buyers who pay with PayPal.

PICTURE ICON Tells buyers that the listing includes a picture of the item.

PIRACY Illegally copying of copyrighted material.

POWERSELLER A user who has a 98% positive feedback and has a high volume of items listed.

PRIVATE AUCTION LISTING A listing where the bidders' user IDs are hidden.

PROCESSOR A credit card processor.

PROXY BIDDING A form of bidding where a user enters his or her maximum bid and eBay automatically bids when another user places a bid.

R

REAL ESTATE ADVERTISEMENT FORMAT A form of listing where a seller lists real estate without holding an auction listing.

REAL-TIME BIDDING Bidding during the live auction.

REGISTERED USER A user who has registered with eBay by providing contact information.

RE-LISTING To resell an item if it did not sell on the first auction.

RESERVE PRICE A secret price that the seller must receive to sell the item.

S

SECOND-CHANCE OFFER An offer to the second highest bidder when the winning bidder fails to pay.

SECURE SERVER A special server used to process credit card and other sensitive information.

SELL SIMILAR ITEM A feature that allows sellers to sell a similar item without inputting all the previous information.

SELLER SEARCH To search for a seller.

SELLER'S ASSISTANT A selling tool that helps with buying, listing, and selling on eBay.

SELLER'S RETURN POLICY The return policy stated by the seller on the listing.

SHILL BIDDING Placing bids artificially to raise the price of an auction; this action is not permitted on eBay.

SNAIL MAIL Delivery via the U.S. Postal Service.

SNIPING Placing a bid in the final seconds of an auction.

SPAM Unsolicited e-mail.

STARTING PRICE The price at which the seller opens the auction.

STORE INVENTORY FORMAT A way to list an item where the item is listed at a fixed price from the user's store.

T

TITLE SEARCH A search method of looking for an item by entering a keyword.

TRADEMARK A logo that is protected against others' use.

TURBO LISTER A program that is designed to allow users to quickly and easily create listings for auctions.

U

UNPAID ITEM PROCESS A process used when the seller does not receive payment for an item.

USER AGREEMENT Terms and conditions eBay users accept before they become members.

USER ID EBay username under which a buyer or seller operates.

V

VENDOR A supplier of products or services.

VERIFIED USER A user that has verified contact information.

VIEWING Watching the auction in real time while online or offline.

W

WANT IT NOW An area of eBay where buyers post what they want and sellers contact them if they have the item.

Good luck setting up your eBay business!

INDEX

Dedication

In memory of Ella Mae Drury Leibforth,
great-grandmother, poet, writer

To Mike Pratley, English teacher, and
Sarah Kay, my first born

– Cheryl L. Russell

About the Author

Cheryl L. Russell holds Bachelor of Arts and Bachelor of Science degrees from Winona State University in Minnesota. She first began using eBay as a casual buyer and began selling while at home raising her two youngest children. In addition to occasionally selling on eBay and being a full-time mother, Cheryl puts her education to work by freelance writing. She enjoys reading, designing custom dresses for her daughters, and other creative pursuits. Cheryl and husband Fred Miller live in southwest Wisconsin with their three daughters, six pet birds, and a pair of chinchillas.

DID YOU BORROW THIS COPY?

Have you been borrowing a copy of *eBay Income: How ANYONE of Any Age, Location, and/or Background Can Build a Highly Profitable Online Business with eBay* from a friend, colleague, or library? Wouldn't you like your own copy for quick and easy reference? To order, photocopy the form below and send to:

Atlantic Publishing Company
1210 SW 23rd Place • Ocala, FL 34474-7014